PUBLIC POLICYMAKING

An Introduction

PUBLIC POLICYMAKING

An Introduction

JAMES E. ANDERSON

Texas A&M University

HOUGHTON MIFFLIN COMPANY ▪ BOSTON

Dallas   Geneva, Illinois   Princeton, New Jersey   Palo Alto

Portions of this book were published previously in *Public Policy-Making*, Third Edition, by James Anderson (New York: Holt, Rinehart and Winston, 1984).

Photo Credits
Page 1: UPI/Bettmann Newsphotos. *Page 41:* AP/Wide World Photos. *Page 77:* UPI/Bettmann Newsphotos. *Page 109:* Jose R. Lopez/NYT Pictures. *Page 149:* UPI/Bettmann Newsphotos. *Page 171:* AP/Wide World Photos. *Page 221:* Allan Tannenbaum/Sygma. *Page 261:* UPI/Bettmann Newsphotos.

Printed in the U.S.A.

Library of Congress Catalog Card Number: 89-080908

ISBN: 0-395-46623-7

ABCDEFGHIJ-

CONTENTS

7 ▪ POLICY IMPACT, EVALUATION, AND CHANGE

221

EPILOGUE

261

PREFACE

Public Policymaking: An Introduction is a concise yet thorough overview of the policymaking process, from policy formation to impact, evaluation, and revision. The text also introduces major approaches to the study of public policy, describes the essential environment of policymaking, and considers the practical aspects of policy debate. In this new edition, I have made many changes to reflect new developments in the policymaking process itself, the expansion of the political science literature on public policy, and my own professional development. Some of the changes include making budgeting a separate chapter, the addition of new case studies to illustrate concepts, and the inclusion of new or expanded material on such topics as rational-choice theory, the role of research in policymaking organizations, presidential policymaking, political subsystems, agenda setting, cost-benefit analysis, and policy termination.

Chapters 1 and 2 outline the categories of public policy, the most common approaches to policy study, and the policy "environment," including official and nonofficial participants. Chapter 3 on policy formation includes two case studies of agenda setting, coal mine safety and environmental pollution control, and two narrative examples of how policy is formed through the legislative process, The Economic Recovery Act of 1981 and the Social Security Reform Act of 1986. Chapter 5 on the budget not only describes the complicated process of how the budget is drawn, but also discusses the impact of the budget on public policymaking in general. Key to this discussion is an examination of the Gramm-Rudman-Hollings Deficit Reduction Act. Chapter 6 discusses administrative policymaking and the issues surrounding policy implementation. Chapter 7 looks at impact and evaluation and includes a case study on the Head Start Program that illustrates the politics involved in these processes.

Although this edition contains more material on the content of public policies, its primary focus remains the policymaking process. A comprehensive treatment of the policy process is presented, beginning with the recognition of problems and the development of demands for action and continuing through the possibility (and reality) of policy termination. In no sense, though, does the book provide "everything anyone ever needs to know" on public policymaking. Rather, as its title indicates, it is a beginning point for the study of public policy. An updated and expanded annotated bibliography is provided to assist readers to delve more deeply into the policy process.

I have tried to be evenhanded and impartial in my treatment of the subject matter of the book even though such topics as abortion rights, budget deficits, and cost-benefit analyses produce sharp controversies in society. I do have my own values, preferences, and biases, and these will undoubtedly be detected by some readers. Let us say, then, that the intention of neutrality, whatever its success, has guided my efforts. Analysis rather than advocacy is my goal.

In my discussion of the policymaking process I undoubtedly have included information that some would view as ordinary knowledge, as knowledge not requiring the skills of political or social scientists to develop. It is, however, difficult to draw the line between ordinary knowledge and scientific knowledge. Indeed, knowledge produced by scientific research may in time become ordinary, as in the germ theory of disease and the rejection of the old belief that judges merely find or discover law. Consequently, I have not hesitated to include information that may seem obvious or commonplace when it adds meaning and clarity to the discussion of policymaking.

I wish to acknowledge the assistance of a number of people in the preparation of this edition. Several persons reviewed drafts of the manuscript. They include:

Phyllis Glick, Northeastern University
Malcolm Goggin, University of Houston
Richard Kearney, University of South Carolina
Gary Klass, Illinois State University
Michael Kraft, University of Wisconsin, Green Bay
Neale Pearson, Texas Tech University
John Schwarz, University of Arizona
Joseph Stewart, Jr., West Virginia University

Although I did not agree with or act on all of their comments and recommendations, collectively they helped to make this a better book. In addition, Tammy Zgabay typed much of the manuscript with good humor and efficiency. Judy Hogg also lent a helping hand on the typing. Various colleagues also supplied needed information, often without being aware of the purpose of my requests. And finally, Alberta (Mrs. Anderson) served once again in her capacity as a sounding board for some of my ideas and many of my complaints, and as a provider of encouragement.

                                                                    J.E.A.

PUBLIC POLICYMAKING
An Introduction

1

THE STUDY OF PUBLIC POLICY

Public Iran-Contra hearings in the Senate caucus room: Members of Congress examine the procedures and consequences of public policy made in secret.

Until the Great Depression of the 1930s, unemployment had been regarded as a personal problem, as something that was unfortunate for those affected perhaps, but not as a matter warranting governmental action. The Depression, however, which produced continuing high rates of unemployment, helped to change this attitude as unemployment came to be regarded as a public problem that government properly was expected to prevent or ameliorate. New Deal responses to this unemployment included unemployment compensation, aid in finding jobs, and public-works programs to create jobs, including the often-maligned Works Progress Administration (WPA). Since then, government in the United States has been committed to combating unemployment through a variety of policies and programs.

A major addition to the arsenal of unemployment programs in the 1960s was job training. Intended especially to help the chronically unemployed and underemployed, a number of job-training programs—skill training, on-the-job training, and work experience—were established.[1] Also, a bit later, a program providing funding for temporary, full-time public-service jobs for the unemployed with state and local agencies was enacted. Most of these job training and public employment measures were brought together in 1973 under the Comprehensive Employment and Training Act (CETA). Administrative responsibility for them was shifted from the national to the state and local governments, but much of the financing continued to be federal. Most programs were actually administered by local governments.

For a decade CETA was the mainstay of government unemployment policy. Spending on CETA programs ran as high as $10 billion annually in the late 1970s before being cut back by the Reagan administration. However, CETA had become sharply controversial soon after its enactment. Complaints about the complexity of the act and waste, inefficiency, and incompetence in the conduct of its programs were common. Public service employment was often derided as a "make-work, dead-end jobs" program. Politically, CETA suffered from a weak constituency (the disadvantaged) and a poor public image.

One of Ronald Reagan's first actions after becoming president in 1981 was to propose the elimination of most job-training and public-employment programs. A conservative, he viewed them as ineffective and beyond the proper province of government. The public-employment program, which was in trouble before Reagan took office, was quickly eliminated. Congress balked, however, at doing away with the job-training programs, of which the Democrats were especially supportive.

Within the year, however, President Reagan changed his position on job training. His administration's restrictive economic policies, which brought down the high inflation that had been afflicting the country, also created a growing unemployment rate. In the fall of 1982 it exceeded 10 percent, which was the highest rate of unemployment that the nation had experienced since the Great Depression. The President now endorsed job training, not because of a change of heart but rather because political realities, and the approaching 1982 congressional elections, made it politic to call for action on unemployment.

Following the 1982 elections, in which the Republicans fared poorly, both parties became committed to the formation of a new job-training policy. Much of the work in developing the new legislation was handled by those most interested in employment and job training programs, notably the House and Senate labor committees; various labor, community, and client groups; and the Department of Labor. For the first time business groups also became deeply involved. The primary bill in the Senate was sponsored by Senator Dan Quayle (R, Indiana) and Senator Ted Kennedy (D, Massachusetts), which was emblematic of the bipartisan support for job training legislation.

Enacted into law in early 1983, the Job Training Partnership Act (JTPA) continued many of the CETA training programs. Some important changes were made, however, to reflect compromises between the Democrats and Republicans in Congress and the Reagan administration. The state, rather than the local governments, as had been the case under CETA, were given primary responsibility for JTPA. Private industry councils (PICs) would manage the local training programs and give business the dominant voice in their operations. These programs were to be targeted at youth, welfare recipients, and high-school dropouts. The Job Corps program for disadvantaged youth was continued, as was the summer youth employment program. However, only limited payment of subsistence allowances to trainees was permitted, and public-service employment of trainees was prohibited. In all, the administration got much of what it wanted, and the President signed JTPA into law, while chiding the Democrats for not acting more quickly on the problem.

In the late 1980s federal expenditures in support of JTPA were around $4 billion annually and were going to more than five hundred local programs. More participants were receiving on-the-job training and were being placed in jobs, at lower cost, than under CETA. On the other hand, the General Accounting Office, which evaluates many programs for the Congress, contended that JTPA did a poor job of targeting those most in need of job training. Moreover, funding was available to provide training to only 5 percent of the eligible population.[2]

JTPA was a new program, but was it a better program? The conclusion reached by political scientists Donald C. Baumer and Carl E. Van Horn seems apt: "The passage of JTPA did nothing to 'solve' the fundamental problem faced by employment and training professionals: how can the low-income, long-term unemployed be helped to become self-sufficient, productive members of the labor force?"[3] Although employers were given an important role in the program, no major new tools for dealing with chronic unemployment were added. JTPA, in short, was a limited response to the problem of chronic unemployment, which continues to plague the nation.

As the JTPA example illustrates, public-policy making involves a complex web of participants who are influenced by many considerations. Numerous questions about policy making can be drawn from this example, including: How does the government decide to act on a problem? Who makes the decisions? What determines whether a policy will succeed or fail? This book will help you answer such questions and gain a better understanding of the policy process. As with any complex matter, we must begin with some basic definitions, including one for public policy itself, which is a slippery task. Other topics covered in this chapter include public-policy typologies, reasons for studying public policy, and some approaches to policy study. In all, this chapter should provide the reader with a general understanding of the nature and scope of public policy and how it can be studied.

WHAT IS PUBLIC POLICY?

In general usage, the term *policy* designates the behavior of some actor or set of actors, such as an official, a governmental agency, or a legislature, in a given area of activity, such as public transportation or consumer protection. *Public* policy may be viewed as whatever governments choose to do or not to do, although such definitions may be adequate in ordinary discourse. However, because this book is concerned with the systematic analysis of public policy, a more precise definition or concept of public policy is needed to structure our thinking and to facilitate more effective communication with one another.

The literature of political science contains many definitions of public policy. Sooner or later, it seems that almost everyone who writes about public policy yields to the urge to offer a definition, and does so with greater or lesser success in the eyes of critics. I will note a few such definitions here and remark upon their utility for analysis. To be really useful and to facilitate communication and understanding, an operational definition or concept (I am using these two words somewhat interchangeably) should indicate the essential characteristics or feature of the matter being defined or conceptualized.

One definition holds that public policy, "broadly defined," is "the relationship of a governmental unit to its environment."[4] Such a definition is so broad as to leave most students uncertain of its meaning; it could encompass almost anything. Another states that "public policy is whatever governments choose to do or not to do."[5] There is a rough accuracy to this definition, but it does not adequately recognize that there may be a divergence between what governments decide to do and what they actually do. Moreover, it could be taken to include such actions as routine personnel appointments or grants of drivers' licenses, which are usually not thought of as policy matters. Professor Richard Rose has suggested that policy be considered "a long series of more-or-less related activities" and their consequences for those concerned, rather than as a discrete decision.[6] Although somewhat ambiguous, his definition nonetheless embodies the useful notion that policy is a course or pattern of activity and not simply a decision to do something. Finally, political scientist Carl J. Friedrich regards policy as

> a proposed course of action of a person, group, or government within a given environment providing obstacles and opportunities which the policy was proposed to utilize and overcome in an effort to reach a goal or realize an objective or a purpose.[7]

To the notion of policy as a course of action, Friedrich adds the requirement that policy is directed toward the accomplishment of some purpose or goal. Although the purpose or goal of governmental actions may not always be easy to discern, the idea that policy involves purposive behavior seems a necessary part of its definition. Policy, however, should designate what is actually done rather than what is merely proposed in the way of action on some matter.

Taking into account the problems raised by these definitions, we offer the following as a useful concept of policy: *A purposive course of action followed by an actor or set of actors in dealing with a problem or matter of concern.* This concept focuses attention on what is actually done instead of what is only proposed or intended, and it differentiates a policy from a decision, which is a choice among competing alternatives.

Public policies are those policies developed by governmental bodies and officials. (Nongovernmental actors and factors may of course influence policy development.) The special characteristics of public policies stem from the fact that they are formulated by what political scientist David Easton has called the "authorities" in a political system, namely, "elders, paramount chiefs, executives, legislators, judges, administrators, councilors, monarchs, and the like." These are, he says, the persons who "engage in the daily affairs of a political system," are "recognized by most members of the system as having responsibility for these matters," and take actions that are "accepted as binding most of the time by most of the members so long as they act within the limits of their roles."[8]

It would be helpful now to consider some of the implications of my concept of public policy. First, the definition links policy to purposive or goal-oriented action rather than to random behavior or chance occurrences. Public policies in modern political systems do not, by and large, just happen. They are instead intended to accomplish specified goals or produce certain results, although these are not always achieved. Proposed policies may be usefully thought of as hypotheses that suggest that certain actions should be taken to achieve particular goals. Thus, for example, to increase farm income, the national government utilizes various income subsidies and production controls. These programs have enhanced the incomes of many but not all farmers.

In actuality, the goals of a policy may be somewhat loosely stated and cloudy in content, thus providing a general direction rather than precise targets for its implementation. Those wanting action on a problem may have had differing notions as to what should be done and how it should be done, respecting the problem. Ambiguity in language becomes a means for reducing conflict. Compromise to secure agreement and build support may then yield general phrasing and a lack of clarity in the statement of policy goals.

Second, policies consist of courses or patterns of action taken over time by governmental officials rather than their separate, discrete decisions. It is difficult to think of such actions as a presidential decision to honor Frank Sinatra or a Social Security Administration decision to award disability benefits to Joe Doaks as public policies. A policy includes not only the decision to adopt a law or make a rule on some topic but also the subsequent series of decisions that are intended to enforce or implement the law or rule. Industrial health and safety policy, for example, is shaped not only by the Occupational Safety and Health Act of 1970 but also by a stream of administrative and judicial decisions interpreting, elaborating, and applying (or not applying) the act to particular situations.

Third, public policies emerge in response to *policy demands*, or those claims for action or inaction on some public issue made by other actors— private citizens, group representatives, or other public officials—upon government officials and agencies. Such demands may range from a general insistence that a municipal government "do something" about traffic congestion to a specific call for the national government to prohibit the stealing of pet dogs and cats for sale to medical and scientific research organizations. In short, in some instances demands simply call for action, in others the nature of the action desired is specified.

In response to policy demands, public officials make *policy decisions* that give content and direction to public policy. Included here are decisions to enact statutes, issue executive orders or edicts, promulgate administrative rules, or make judicial interpretations of laws. Thus the decision by Congress to enact the Sherman Antitrust Act in 1890 was a policy decision, as was the 1911 Supreme Court ruling that the act prohibited only unreasonable restraints of trade rather than all restraints of trade. Each was of major importance in shaping that course of action called antitrust policy. Such decisions may be contrasted with the large numbers of relatively routine decisions made by officials in the day-to-day application of public policy. The Department of Veterans Affairs, for example, makes hundreds of thousands of decisions every year on veterans' benefits; most, however, fall within the bounds of settled policy and can be categorized as routine.

Policy statements in turn are the formal expressions or articulations of public policy. Included are legislative statutes, executive orders and decrees, administrative rules and regulations, and court opinions, as well as statements and speeches by public officials indicating the intentions and goals of government and what will be done to realize them. Policy statements are sometimes ambiguous. Witness the conflicts that arise over the meaning of statutory provisions or judicial holdings, or the time and effort expended analyzing and trying to divine the meaning of policy statements made by national political leaders, such as the president of the United States or the rulers of the Soviet Union. Different levels, branches, or units of government may also issue conflicting policy statements, as occurs on environmental pollution controls or consumer product liability.

Fourth, policy involves what governments actually do, not what they intend to do or what they say they are going to do. If a legislature enacts a law requiring employers to pay no less than a stated minimum wage but nothing is done to enforce the law, and consequently little if any change occurs in economic behavior, it seems reasonable to contend that public policy in this instance is really one of the nonregulation of wages.

It is useful here to mention the concept of *policy outputs*, or the actions actually taken in pursuance of policy decisions and statements. This concept focuses attention on such matters as taxes collected, highways built, welfare benefits paid, restraints of trade eliminated, traffic fines collected, and foreign-aid projects undertaken. An examination of policy outputs may indicate that a policy is actually somewhat or even greatly different from what policy statements indicate it should be.

Fifth, public policy may be either positive or negative. It may involve some form of overt governmental action to deal with a problem on which action was demanded (positive), or it may involve a decision by governmental officials to do nothing on some matter on which government involvement was sought (negative). In other words, governments can follow a policy of *laissez faire*, or hands off, either generally or on some aspects of economic activity. Such inaction may have major consequences for a society or some of its groups, as when the national government decided to cease regulating commercial airline rates and routes.

It should be stressed that inaction becomes a public policy when it follows from officials declining to act on some problem or, to put it another way, when they decide an issue negatively. This should be differentiated from nonaction on some matter that has not become a public issue and has not been brought to official attention. To use a slightly ludicrous example, there is no governmental action on the taking of earthworms—no seasons, no bag limits, or the like. Is this a public policy? The answer is no, because no issue existed and no decisions were made.

Lastly, public policy, at least in it positive form, is based on law and is authoritative. Members of a society usually accept as legitimate the facts that taxes must be paid, import controls must be obeyed, and highway speed limits must be complied with, unless one wants to run the risk of fines, jail sentences, or other legally imposed sanctions or disabilities. Thus public policy has an authoritative, legally coercive quality that the policies of private organizations do not have. Indeed, a monopoly of the legitimate use of coercion is a major characteristic distinguishing government from private organizations. Governments can legally incarcerate people; private organizations cannot.

Even though they are authoritative, some public policies may be widely violated, as with national prohibition in the 1920s and the 55-mile-per-hour speed limit existing today in some states. Moreover, enforcement may be limited or piecemeal. Are these still public policies? The answer is yes, because they either were or are currently on the statute books and enforcement existed. Whether such policies are effective or wise is another matter. Authoritativeness is a necessary but not a sufficient condition for effective public policy.

CATEGORIES OF PUBLIC POLICIES

Governments at all levels in the United States—national, state, and local—have been increasingly active in the development of public policies. Every year a large volume of laws and ordinances flows from the nation's national, state, and local legislative bodies. Their volume in turn is greatly exceeded by the quantity of rules and regulations produced by administrative agencies acting on the basis of legislative authorizations. This proliferation of public policies has occurred in such traditional areas of governmental action as foreign policy, transportation, education, welfare, law enforcement, business and labor regulation, and international trade. In addition, there has been much activity in areas that did not receive much if any attention until the last two or three decades—economic stability, environmental protection, equality of opportunity, medical care, nuclear energy, and consumer protection.

In 1988 Congress adopted over two hundred public laws. Some of the major statutes enacted, as measured by such loose criteria as the estimated

TABLE 1.1 Major Congressional Legislation, 1988

Agricultural Credit Act

Housing and Community Development Act

Civil Rights Restoration Act (strengthened the ban on sex discrimination)

Assistance to Central America (provided "nonlethal" aid for the Nicaraguan Contras)

Child Abuse Prevention, Adoption, and Family Services Act

Elementary and Secondary School Improvement Amendments

Veterans Benefits and Services Act

Medicare Catastrophic Coverage Act

Civil Liberties Act (authorized compensation for Japanese-Americans interned during World War II)

Disaster Assistance Act (provided financial aid for farmers)

Price-Anderson Amendments (established liability for nuclear accidents)

Fair Housing Act Amendments (strengthened enforcement of the act)

Omnibus Trade and Competitiveness Act

United States–Canada Free-Trade Implementation Act

Family Support Act (instituted welfare reform)

Department of Veterans Affairs Act (created the department)

Lead Contamination Control Act

Health Omnibus Programs Extension (renewed various health programs)

Technical and Miscellaneous Revenue Act (included 470 pages of "corrections" and changes in the Tax Reform Act of 1986)

Source: United States Statutes at Large (1988).

number of people affected and likely impact on society and economy are listed in Table 1.1. The table conveys a notion of the variety of matters with which Congress deals. Some, such as those called amendments, represent changes in or additions to existing policies; others are new additions to the collection of public policies. All of the policies contain biases that favor some groups and disadvantage others in varying degrees, which is indeed an intrinsic characteristic of public policies.

Given the scope, complexity, diversity, and vast number of public policies in the United States, the task of trying to make sense out of them is enormous. I will try to simplify this task in two ways. First, this book will focus mostly on national policy making and domestic public policies. Second, in this section a number of general typologies that political scientists and others have developed for categorizing public policies will be presented. These typologies will prove much more useful in distinguishing among and generalizing about policies than some of the more traditional and widely used categorization schemes, such as by *issue area* (e.g., labor, welfare, civil rights, and foreign affairs), *institution* (e.g., legislative policies, judicial policies, and departmental policies), and *time period* (e.g., New Deal era, post–World War II, and late nineteenth century). Although the latter are convenient for designating various sets of policies and organizing discussions about them, they are not helpful in developing generalizations, because they do not reflect the basic characteristics and contents of policies.

Substantive and Procedural Policies

First, policies may be classified as either substantive or procedural. *Substantive policies* involve *what* government is going to do, such as construction of highways, payment of welfare benefits, acquisition of bombers, or prohibition of the retail sale of liquor. Substantive policies directly distribute advantages and disadvantages, benefits and costs, to people. *Procedural policies*, in contrast, pertain to *how* something is going to be done or *who* is going to take action. So defined, procedural policies include organizational matters, such as which agencies are responsible for illegal drug enforcement.

A procedural policy of great importance is the federal Administrative Procedure Act of 1946. This statute, which represents a response to the expansion of administrative discretion in the twentieth century, prescribes procedures to be used by agencies in rule-making. For example, the act requires notice of the proposed rule-making, opportunity for interested persons to participate in the proceeding through oral or written submissions, publication of a proposed rule at least thirty days before it becomes effective, and opportunity for interested persons to petition for issuance, amendment, or repeal of a rule. The act's requirements for adjudication are much more detailed. Another example of a procedural policy is the environmental impact statement requirement imposed on agencies proposing major actions affecting the environment by the National Environmental Policy Act. It is intended to cause agencies to give consideration to environmental effects before making their decisions. In itself it adds nothing to the substance of policy.

Procedural policies may have important substantive *effects*. That is, how something is done or who takes the action may help determine what is actually done. A number of propositions concerning the possible impact of organizational decisions on substantive policy are presented in Chapter 6. Frequently, efforts are made to use procedural issues to delay or prevent the adoption of substantive decisions and policies. An agency action may be challenged on the ground that improper procedures were followed, when it is really the substance of the action that is being resisted. Some Washington lawyers have become highly skilled in manipulating procedural rules to delay agency action. Thus because of procedural delays and complications (most of which were produced by the maneuverings of the defendant company), it took the Federal Trade Commission thirteen years to complete a case compelling the manufacturer to remove the word "liver" from a product named "Carter's Little Liver Pills." (The product has no impact on one's liver.)

Distributive, Regulatory, Self-Regulatory, and Redistributive Policies

This typology differentiates policies on the basis of the nature of their impact on society and the relationships among those involved in policy formation.[9]

Distributive policies involve the distribution of services or benefits to particular segments of the population—individuals, groups, corporations, and communities. Some distributive policies may provide benefits to only one or a few beneficiaries, as in the cases of the Chrysler loan guarantee of the late 1970s, which kept the company from bankruptcy, and the subsidies for the construction and operation of merchant ships. Others may provide benefits for vast numbers of persons, as is true for agricultural price support programs, tax deductions for home mortgage payments, and provisions for free public school education.

Distributive policies typically involve the use of public funds to assist particular groups, communities, or industries. Those who seek benefits usually do not compete directly with one another, although in some instances they do, as in the case of site selection for the Super-Conducting Super Collider, where there could be only one winner. Nor do their benefits represent a direct cost to any specific group; rather the costs are assessed to the public treasury, which is to say all taxpayers. Given this, distributive policies appear to create only winners and no specific losers, although obviously someone does pay for their financial costs.

A standard example of distributive policy involves the rivers and harbors improvement and flood control legislation, customarily referred to as "pork-barrel" legislation, carried out by the Army Corps of Engineers. In 1986 Congress authorized the construction of 262 projects for such purposes as port development, flood control, water supply, and beach erosion control. Approximately three-quarters of the estimated costs of $16.3 billion was assigned to the national government, with the remainder to be paid by local governments and project users.[10]

These projects are scattered all around the country and have little relationship to one another, which supports Professor Theodore J. Lowi's contention that distributive policies "are virtually not policies at all but are highly individualized decisions that only by accumulation can be called a policy."[11] Each locality and its supporters seek authorization and funding for their own project without challenging the right of others to do likewise. Most projects consequently have some friends and no enemies in Congress, and presidents usually leave them alone. President Jimmy Carter upset the applecart in 1977, when he successfully eliminated some water projects on the ground that they were unnecessary. Many members of Congress were antagonized by this action, and a few of the projects were restored.

Regulatory policies involve the imposition of restrictions or limitations on the behavior of individuals and groups. Or, to put it differently, they reduce the freedom or discretion to act of those who are regulated, whether bankers, utility companies, meat packers, or whomever. In this sense they clearly differ from distributive policies, which operate to increase the freedom or discretion of the affected persons or groups.

When we think of regulatory policies our attention usually focuses on business regulatory policies, such as those pertaining to pollution control or the regulation of transportation industries. These, among other things, have been the focus of the movement for deregulation. The most extensive variety of regulatory policies, however, is that which deals with criminal behavior against persons and property. Many civil rights policies are also regulatory in nature.

The formation of regulatory policy usually involves conflict between two groups or coalitions of groups, with one side seeking to impose some sort of control on the other side, which customarily resists, arguing either that control is unnecessary or that the wrong kind of control is being proposed. Given this situation, regulatory decisions involve clear winners and losers, although the winners usually get less than they initially sought. This is not to deny, however, that it is often difficult to identify all of the purposes and consequences of regulatory policies. It is worthwhile at this point to indicate some of the variety in regulatory policies.

Some regulatory policies set forth general rules of behavior, directing that certain actions be taken or commanding that others not be taken. The Sherman Act in effect tells businesses, "Thou shalt not monopolize or attempt to monopolize or act to restrain trade." These prohibitions are enfored by actions brought in the federal courts against particular violators. In contrast, public utility regulation handled by the state governments involves the detailed control of entry into the business, standards of service, financial practices, and rates of charge of electric, telephone, and other utility companies. Comparatively, antitrust regulation entails much less restriction of business discretion than does the public utility regulation.

Consumer protection policies illustrate other variations in regulatory policies. Some statutes, such as the Pure Food and Drug Act of 1960 and the Drug Amendments of 1962, set quality standards that must be met by drug manufacturers. Thus, before new drugs can be put on the market, they must be shown to meet the standards of *safety* in use and *efficacy* for the purposes intended. Other consumer legislation—for example, the Consumer Credit Protection Act of 1968, requires creditors to provide borrowers with accurate information on interest and other financing costs for credit purchases. The first sort of policy is intended to prevent products not meeting designated standards from entering the marketplace; the second sort seeks to provide consumers with adequate information to make informed decisions.

Some regulatory policies, for instance those that restrict entry into a business such as television broadcasting or electric power distribution, are implemented by decisions that confer benefits on some and deny them to others. There may be several applicants for a television broadcast license for a particular city before the Federal Communication Commission. Only one applicant can be propitiated. Here, as Lowi states, "regulatory policies are distinguishable from distributive in that in the short run the regulatory decision involves a direct choice as to who will be indulged and who deprived."[12] Decisions are also made by the application of some kind of general rule to particular institutions.

Self-regulatory policies are similar to regulatory policies in that they involve the restriction or control of some matter or group. Unlike regulatory policies, however, self-regulatory policies are usually sought and supported by the regulated group as a means of protecting or promoting the interests of its members. In 1988, more than eight hundred professions and occupations, ranging from tree surgeons and auctioneers to lawyers and physicians, were licensed in one or more states, and about sixty were licensed in a majority of states. Commonly licensed health professionals included chiropractors, dentists, dental hygienists, emergency medical technologists, optometrists, pharmacists, physicians, podiatrists, practical and registered nurses, psychologists, sanitarians, and social workers.[13]

The usual pattern here is for a professional or occupational group acting on its own to seek licensing legislation from the state legislature. Outside the ranks of the interested group little interest in the matter usually exists. The result is the enactment of a licensing law, whose implementation is delegated to a board dominated by members from the licensed group. Over time, entry into the licensed occupation or profession may be restricted and the prices charged for its specialized services may increase. It is unclear to what extent licensing improves the quality of services available to the public.[14]

Supervised self-regulation may also occur. For example, under the Agricultural Marketing Agreement Act of 1937, the producers and handlers of fruits, vegetables, and specialty crops such as almonds sold on the fresh market collectively act to obtain marketing orders from the Agricultural Marketing Service (AMS). Put into effect with the approval of two-thirds of the producers of a commodity, these orders, which are binding on all producers, may authorize research and promotional programs, the setting of quality standards, and the control of the movement of products to market so as to ensure "orderly marketing." Marketing orders, which are managed by producer-dominated administrative committees and are subject to AMS supervision, are intended to improve the economic situation of producers.

Redistributive policies involve deliberate efforts by the government to shift the allocation of wealth, income, property, or rights among broad classes or groups of the population, for example, haves and have-nots, proletariat and bourgeoisie. "The aim involved is not use of property but property itself, not equal treatment but equal possession, not behavior but being."[15] In American societies redistributive policies ultimately involve disagreements between liberals (pro) and conservatives (con) and tend to be highly productive of conflict.

The usual pattern in redistributive policy is the shifting of resources from the haves to the have-nots. It is possible, however, for the flow to be in the opposite direction. Farm subsidy payments under the agricultural price support programs go mostly to large commercial farmers; small-scale farmers derive few benefits, yet everyone who pays taxes contributes to the financing of the programs. Such instances, however, are typically not debated in terms of redistribution,[16] perhaps because of a reluctance to acknowledge that sometimes the haves benefit at the expense of the have-nots.

Redistribution policies are difficult to secure because they involve the reallocation of money, rights, or power. Those who possess money or power rarely yield them willingly, regardless of how much some may discourse upon the "burdens" and heavy responsibility attending their possession. Since money and power are good coinage in the political realms, those who possess them have ample means to resist their diminution.

Policies that have (or have had) some redistributive impact include the graduated income tax, Medicare and Medicaid, War on Poverty, the Voting Rights Act, and legislative reapportionment. The Johnson administration's war on poverty represented an effort to shift wealth and other resources to blacks and poor people. Encountering much resistance from conservatives and lacking strong presidential support, it was gradually dispersed and dismantled. Although most of the individual antipoverty programs (such as Head Start and the community action or service programs) still exist, they have lost much of their redistributive quality. The Voting Rights Act, which on the whole has been enforced with considerable strength by the Justice Department, has helped to produce a substantial increase in black voter registration, voting, and state and local office holding in the South.

The graduated income tax, which is based on the principle of ability to pay (i.e., those who have more income can fairly be expected to pay at progressively higher rates) has now lost much of its redistributive potential. The top rate once was as high as 91 percent. In the early 1980s the rates ranged from 14 to 50 percent over a dozen income brackets, which still held out the possibility of considerable redistribution. The Tax Reform Act of 1986, enacted by Congress with the strong support of President Reagan, who believed that high marginal tax rates both infringed on individual liberties and discouraged economic growth, provided for two tax brackets of 15 and 28 percent (some will pay 33 percent). Whether rates will stay at these levels will depend partly upon the government's future revenue needs.[17] However, low marginal tax rates do have much political appeal.

Redistributive policies are not only difficult to obtain, they are also hard to retain, as the discussion of the income tax indicates. Equality of result or condition (that is, equality in incomes or standards of living) is not overly appealing to most Americans, whatever their thought on equality of opportunity.

Material and Symbolic Policies

Public policies may also be described as either material or symbolic, depending upon the kind of benefits they allocate.[18] *Material policies* actually either provide tangible resources or substantive power to their beneficiaries, or impose real disadvantages on those who are adversely affected. Legislation requiring employers to pay a prescribed minimum wage, appropriating money for a public housing program, or providing income support payments to farmers is material in content and impact.

Symbolic policies, in contrast, have little real material impact on people. They do not deliver what they appear to deliver; no tangible advantages and disadvantages are allocated by them. Rather, they appeal to the cherished values of people, such as peace, patriotism, and social justice. A prime example of a symbolic policy is the Kellogg-Briand Pact of 1928, by which the United States and fourteen other countries agreed to outlaw war. The Humphrey-Hawkins Act, adopted by Congress in 1978 after much debate and political struggle, set the goals of reaching a 3 percent annual unemployment rate and a 3 percent annual inflation rate within five years; in ten years the inflation rate was to be zero. The act did not prescribe any actions to meet these goals, however. Consequently it has been only symbolic and without substantive impact on macroeconomic policies, as an examination of unemployment and inflation rates will indicate.

Occasionally, a policy that appears symbolic may turn out to have important consequences. The Endangered Species Act of 1973, for example, which is intended to help ensure the survival of rare animals and plants, initially appeared to be a statement of good intentions with few if any costs. Little opposition attended its enactment. However, as implemented the act has had important effects, sometimes being used to block construction projects, timber cutting, and other activities that would threaten or destroy the habitats of endangered species.

Most policies are neither entirely symbolic nor wholly material. The symbolic and material categories should instead be viewed as the poles of a continuum, with most policies being ranged along the continuum depending upon the extent in practice to which they are more or less symbolic or material. The Sherman Act, as an instrument for "trust busting," for breaking up large monopolistic companies, has long been symbolic. No trusts have been broken up since the Progressive Era. On the other hand, on occasions it has been applied with some vigor against collusive behavior—such as price fixing, bid rigging, and market allocation, most notably during the Carter and Reagan administrations. Here it has had substantial material impact.

Policies that are ostensibly material in nature on the basis of legislative language, may be rendered essentially symbolic by administrative action or by the failure of the legislature to provide adequate funds for their implementation. The public housing goals of the Housing Act of 1949 and later laws, for example, were made substantially symbolic by the subsequent failure of Congress to provide funds for housing construction.[19] On the other hand, policies may move from the more symbolic to the more material category. Professor Bruce I. Oppenheimer argues that oil pollution control policy was largely symbolic during the 1947–1966 period. Legislation existed but it had little enforcement impact. After 1966 oil pollution control became more material as a consequence of growing public concern about pollution, increased enforcement, activity, and additional congressional action.[20]

The material-symbolic typology is especially useful to keep in mind when analyzing policy impacts as it directs our attention beyond formal policy statements. It also alerts us to the important role that symbols play in political behavior.

Policies Involving Collective Goods
or Private Goods

Public policies may also involve the provision of either collective (indivisible) goods or private (divisible) goods.[21] The nature of *collective goods* is such that if they are provided for one person, they must be provided for all. A standard example is national defense: There is no effective way to provide it for some citizens and to deny it to others, nor to calculate that some citizens benefit more from it than others. Given this, an economically rational person would never voluntarily pay for national defense. Hence it must be provided, if we want it, by government and financed through taxation. Other examples of collective goods include clean air, public safety, traffic control, and mosquito abatement.

Private goods, in contrast, may be broken into units and charged for on an individual user or beneficiary basis, and are available in the marketplace. Various social goods provided by government (garbage collection, postal service, medical care, museums, public housing, and national parks) have some of the characteristics of private goods. Charges are sometimes but not always levied on users. Whether such goods, which conceivably could be provided by the market economy, are provided by the government as a function of political decisions influenced by tradition, notions of the proper functions of government, or the desire of users or beneficiaries to shift their costs to others, and the like, is dependent upon public policy.

Some might still argue that only collective goods should be the subjects of public policies. The tendency has been, however, to more and more convert private goods into social goods through government action. Ill health, unemployment, environmental pollution, industrial accidents and disease, and misrepresentation in the marketplace are viewed by many as collective rather than individual problems, as matters affecting the entire population, and hence as involving public goods for which the entire society should pay. Generally, the more something is seen as having the qualities of a public good, the more likely it is that its provision by government will be accepted. If it seems clear that some benefit more directly than others, there may also be a desire to levy charges, fees, or taxes on the direct beneficiaries to cover part of the costs. Thus we encounter user fees at national parks, tuition at public colleges, rent in public housing projects, and tolls for some bridges and highways.

The *privatization* movement, which was encouraged by the Reagan administration, represented a counterforce to the long-run tendency to expand the scope of social goods. Based on free-market economic theory, privatization supports transferring many government assets or programs to the private sector and contracting with private companies for the handling of many public services, whether the collection of garbage or the operation of prisons. "The private sector, it is argued, will perform these functions more efficiently and economically than the public sector."[22]

The results of the privatization movement at the national level are mixed. A successful example is the sale of Conrail, which operated several railroads in the northeast and midwest, to a private corporation. Nothing, however, came out of proposals from the Reagan administration and others to sell public lands in the western states to private buyers. Even western ranchers and other supporters of the "sagebrush rebellion," which promoted transferring ownership of public lands to state and local governments, were not much interested in privatization. Their access to low-cost public grazing lands would have been jeopardized by privatization. Congress was also quite skeptical towards the sale of public lands.

Liberal and Conservative Policies

Finally, discussions of public policies are frequently conducted in terms of liberals versus conservatives. These terms, however, are rather slippery and difficult to define. Just what distinguishes "liberal" from "conservative"? Lowi argues that in the latter part of the nineteenth century and the early years of the twentieth century, it was possible to make a fairly precise distinction.[23] Generally, *liberals* favored the use of government to bring about social change, usually in the direction of greater equality. *Conservatives*, in turn, were opposed to the use of government for such purposes, if not always to the purposes themselves. Liberals spoke of the need for public policies to correct injustices and shortcomings in the existing social order. Conservatives either found the existing order satisfactory, or contended that change should occur slowly and gradually through "natural" social processes. By and large, those who advocated economic regulatory programs were liberals. Conservatives supplied the opposition. Later, when welfare programs became an issue, support for them came from liberals, resistance from conservatives.

It is Lowi's contention, however, that the old distinction between liberals and conservatives has broken down. "The old dialogue has passed into the graveyard of consensus. Yet it persists. Old habits die hard. Its persistence despite its irrelevance means that the liberal-conservative debate has become almost purely ritualistic."[24] The nineteenth-century notion of a minimal government that would "do only those things people could not do better for themselves" (and not many things were put in this category) has been replaced by positive government, by government with extensive responsibilities for meeting human needs and problems. The old criteria thus no longer distinguish liberals and conservatives.

The disappearance of the liberal-conservative distinction is illustrated by Table 1.2. Government ("liberal") policies are located above the center line, while private ("conservative") policies are located below it. Policies that are likely to produce change ("liberal") are located toward the left side of the table, while those that tend to maintain existing practices ("conservative") are located toward the right side. Were the old criteria involving attitudes toward the use of government and the promotion of change still determinative, liberal policies would be concentrated in the upper left-hand corner of the table and conservative policies would be nested in the lower right-hand corner. This is not what one sees, however, for both public and private policies range from left to right across the table; both may be

TABLE 1.2 Selected Public and Private Policies Arranged According to Probable Effect on Society

Social Security programs based on graduated income tax Civil rights package Low tariffs	Luxury taxes Real antitrust "Yardstick" regulation (TVA)	Growth fiscal policies Graduated income tax (United States)	Countercyclical fiscal policies Sales taxes Aids to small business	Social Security programs based on insurance principles (U.S.) Direct regulation (e.g., FCC, ICC, CAB, etc.) Antitrust by consent decree	Existing farm programs Restraint of competition (NRA, fair trade, antiprice discrimination) Tax on colored margarine	High tariffs Import quotas Utilities Group representation on boards Strict gold standard with no bank money
Competition in agriculture New interest groups	Competitive business Corporate philanthropy Merit hiring and promotion	Oligopoly with research competition	Oligopoly without competition (steel, cigarettes) Brand names Ethnic appeals of political campaigns	Trade associations Pools Basing points Price leadership Fair trade policies Union unemployment and automation policies		Monopoly Old interest groups (NAM, AFL-CIO, TWU, etc.)

Above the line: Public policies ("liberal")
Below the line: Private policies or practices ("conservative")
Toward the left: Policies likely to produce change ("liberal")
Toward the right: Policies likely to maintain existing practices ("conservative")
Source: Theodore J. Lowi, *The End of Liberalism*, 2d ed. (New York: Norton, 1979), p. 45.

used either to promote or to restrict change. To put it differently, government is variously used for both "liberal" and "conservative" purposes, that is, both to promote and restrict change. The same is true for private policies or action. Because of this, Lowi concludes that the old distinction between liberals and conservatives no longer is valid.

Admittedly, Table 1.2 is somewhat impressionistic. However, a couple of conclusions about public policies can be derived from it. Public policies can be either productive of change or designed to help maintain the existing order. Vigorous equal employment opportunity programs are designed to do the former, protective tariffs the latter. Public policies can also derive their support from either liberal or conservative officials and groups. For example, even in the nineteenth century conservatives were not opposed to all uses of government for economic purposes. Protective tariffs and governmental action to restrain labor unions drew their support mostly from conservatives, who in other instances might claim laissez faire as the best policy. There has always been an element of pragmatism in the actions of both conservatives and liberals when they are advancing the interests of groups that they favor.

This leads to another of Lowi's contentions: *The most important difference between liberals and conservatives, Republicans and Democrats—however they define themselves—is to be found in the interest groups they identify with.*[25] Whether one identifies with interests of business or labor, well-to-do or poor, the "establishment" or ethnic minorities, is what really matters. Support for one or another of them can be based on principle, whether this involves a desire for greater equality, the need to ameliorate social conflict, or a wish to maintain the status quo. Principles, to be legitimate, do not need to be accepted as proper or appropriate by all, nor must they be adhered to in any and every case. Relatively few of us are constant, consistent ideologues, whether our ideology is described as conservative, neoconservative, liberal, radical, or socialist. In short, if we can say something like "conservatives tend to support policies, public or private, that advance the interests of business, while liberals tend to favor policies that protect the interests of consumers and minorities," we have said something meaningful.

Given the great changes that have occurred in our society and economy during the past century and especially since the 1930s, it is not surprising that the liberal-conservative conflict has shifted away from the issue of whether there should be governmental intervention and toward the issues of when intervention should occur, in what form, and on whose behalf. As sociologist Robert McIver states,

> Wherever technology advances, wherever private business extends its range, wherever the cultural life becomes more complex, new tasks are imposed upon government. This happens apart from, or in spite of, the particular philosophies that governments cherish. . . . In the longer run the

tasks undertaken by the governments are dictated by changing conditions, and governments on the whole are more responsive than creative in fulfilling them.[26]

The Reagan administration took office in 1981 with the goal of substantially reducing the role of the national government in the domestic life of the nation. While the administration had some initial success in securing the adoption of its economic program, resistance grew with time, especially in the Democratic-controlled House. Although President Reagan was overwhelmingly reelected in 1984, the Republicans lost control of the Senate in 1986.

During its eight years in office, the Reagan administration was most successful in altering national tax policies. (It also had success, especially early on, in increasing defense spending.) Mostly the administration was able to make only limited or marginal changes in domestic policies. Most of the major economic deregulatory legislation (as for airlines and railroads) was enacted during the Carter years. Sweeping changes in domestic public policies and governmental intervention in the economy, such as occurred in the 1930s during the New Deal, usually require major changes in the distribution of political power in society. This did not occur in the 1980s. As a consequence, McIver's viewpoint still seems valid.

WHY STUDY PUBLIC POLICY?

Political scientists, in their teaching and research, have customarily been most concerned with political institutions, such as legislatures or international organizations; with political processes, such as the electoral and judicial processes; and with elements of the political system, such as public opinion and interest groups. This is not to say, however, that they have been totally unconcerned with public policies. Foreign policy and civil rights and liberties policies have traditionally been viewed as appropriate for their attention. So too has what Professor Robert H. Salisbury calls "constitutional policy," or the "decisional rules by which subsequent policy actions are to be determined."[27] Among the procedural and structural "givens" that make up constitutional policy are legislative apportionment, the city manager form of government, and federalism. Each helps to shape decisions and public policies. Some political scientists with a normative bent are also concerned with what governments *should* do, with the nature of "correct" or "proper" public policies. Their value-oriented approach, however, places them outside the mainstream of political science, which as a "science," is supposed to be rigorous, objective, and value-neutral.

In the last couple of decades, however, political scientists have been giving more attention to the study of public policy and specifically to the description, analysis, and explanation of its causes and effects. Professor Thomas Dye has aptly summarized the various objectives of policy study:

> This involves a description of the content of public policy; an assessment of the impact of environmental forces on the content of public policy; an analysis of the effect of various institutional arrangements and political processes on public policy; an inquiry into the consequences of various public policies for the political system; and an evaluation of the impact of public policies on society, both in terms of expected and unexpected consequences.[28]

Students of public policy consequently seek answers to such questions as the following: What effect do urbanization and industrialization have on welfare policies? How does the organization of Congress help shape agricultural or welfare policies? What role do interest groups play in environmental policy formation? What is the actual content of antitrust policy? Who benefits and who does not from current tax policies? What are the problems in implementing hazardous waste disposal programs? Although such questions are often difficult to answer, especially with precision, they direct our attention to the actual operation of the policy process and its societal consequences.

We now come to the question posed in the heading of this section: Why study public policy? One response is to say that it is important, that we are all affected in many ways by public policies, and thus we should know something about them. This is certainly the case. However, a more systematic response is needed, and this can be framed in terms of the scientific, professional, and political reasons for studying public policies.[29]

Scientific Reasons

Public policies can be studied in order to gain greater understanding of their origins, the processes by which they are developed and implemented, and their consequences for society. This in turn will increase our understanding of the political processes and political behavior. Policy may be regarded as either a dependent or an independent variable for this sort of analysis. When it is viewed as a *dependent* variable, as the product of various political factors, attention is focused on the environmental and political factors contributing to its adoption and content. For instance, how is policy affected by the distribution of power among the various levels of government? Were pressure groups or public opinion important in the adoption of a policy? If public policy is viewed as an *independent variable*, our focus shifts to the impact of policy on the nature and operation of the political process and its environment. One may then seek answers to such questions as these: How does policy affect support for the political system? What effect does policy have on social well-being? Do policy-making processes vary depending upon the kind of policy involved?

I will use the term *policy studies* to designate the study of public policy undertaken to gain greater basic understanding of political behavior and the governmental process.

Professional Reasons

Don K. Price draws a distinction between the "scientific estate," which seeks only to discover knowledge, and the "professional estate," which strives to apply scientific knowledge to the solution of practical social problems.[30] Here we encounter those practitioners of "policy analysis" whose numbers both inside and outside the government have multiplied greatly in recent years. Policy analysis has an applied orientation and is concerned with determining the most efficient (or best) alternative (i.e., the one that will yield the largest net social benefits) for dealing with a current problem, such as the reduction of air pollution or the collection of household garbage.[31] A variant of policy analysis is evaluation research, which assesses the societal effects of particular public policies. The policy evaluator wants to know, for instance, whether a job-training program increases the employment prospects and earnings of its enrollees, and, if so, by how much.

Policy analysis relies heavily upon economic theory and statistical and mathematical techniques of analysis. Cost-benefit analysis, for example, is widely used in determining the efficiency of proposed alternatives or actual policies. In appraising the efficiency of government actions, the policy analyst is concerned with their impact on society generally, on whether society as a whole gains or loses, rather than with their distributional consequences. Which particular groups receive the benefits and which pay the costs of a policy are not of real concern. In sum professional policy analysis tries to identify and adopt good public policies, as measured by the efficiency criterion. Achieving a basic understanding of political and other human behavior is at best a secondary consideration.

Political Reasons

As noted, some political scientists do not believe that political scientists should strive to be neutral or impartial in the study of public policy. (This view is shared by some members of other social science disciplines.) Rather, they contend that the study of public policy should be directed toward helping to ensure that governments adopt favored public policies to attain the "right" goals. They reject the notion that policy analysts should strive to be value-free, contending rather that political science should not be silent or impotent on how best to deal with current political and social problems. In short, they engage in *policy advocacy* and are undeterred by the substantial disagreement in society over what constitute "correct" policies or the "right" goals of policy. Research engaged in by policy advocates is often skewed by the desire to develop "evidence" to support their cause. Policy study, in contrast, is motivated by the intent to be impartial.

This book will use the *scientific policy studies* approach to develop a basic understanding of the policymaking process, which is here viewed as an inherently political process involving conflict and struggle among people (public officials and private citizens) with conflicting interests, values, and desires on policy issues. In describing and analyzing the policymaking process, the scientific policy studies approach has three basic concerns.[32] First, its primary goal is to explain policy rather than to identify or prescribe "good" or proper policy. Analysis rather than advocacy is its style. Second, it rigorously searches for the causes and consequences of public policies by applying social scientific methodology, which is not restricted to the use of quantitative data and methodology. Third, this approach aims to develop reliable theories concerning public policies and their politics. Given these, policy studies can thus be both theoretical and of some relevance to the more practical aspects of policymaking. As has been said, there is nothing as practical as a good theory.

APPROACHES TO POLICY STUDY

Political and social scientists have developed many models, theories, approaches, concepts, and schemes for the analysis of policymaking and its related component, decision making. Indeed, political scientists have often displayed more facility and verve for theorizing about public policymaking than for actually studying policy and the policymaking process. Nonetheless, theories and concepts are needed to guide the study of public policy, to facilitate communication, and to suggest possible explanations for policy actions. When one sets out to study policy some guidelines and criteria of relevance are needed to focus effort and to prevent aimless meandering through the fields of political data. What we find when we engage in research depends partly upon what we are looking for; policy concepts, models, and theories give direction and structure to our inquiry.

In this section I will survey a number of theoretical approaches to the study of public policy. Before turning to this task, however, it is essential to distinguish between policymaking and decision making, which is not always done with clarity, if at all, by students of public policy. Decision making, which will be treated in Chapter 4, involves choosing from among two or more alternatives, such as whether or not to read further in this book. Theories of decision making are concerned with the criteria and processes used in making such choices. A policy, to repeat my earlier definition, is "a purposive course of action followed by an actor or set of actors in dealing with a problem or matter of concern." Policymaking thus typically encompasses a pattern of action that extends over time and includes many decisions, some routine and some not so routine. Rarely will a policy be synonymous with a single decision. To use a mundane illustration, it would not be accurate for a person to state that it was his policy to bathe on Saturday nights, if in fact he did so only infrequently, however elegant and thoughtful the decision-making process that led to his doing so on a rare Saturday. It is the course of action, the pattern or regularity, that defines policy, not an isolated event. In the example, the policy is best thought of as going dirty.

The theoretical approaches discussed here include political systems theory, group theory, elite theory, institutionalism, and rational choice theory. Although most of these approaches were not developed specifically for the analysis of policy formation, they can readily be bent to that purpose. They are useful to the extent that they direct our attention to important political phenomena, help clarify and structure our thinking, and suggest explanations for political activity or, in our case, public policies. Certain of their limitations and criticisms will be noted as the discussion proceeds.

Political Systems Theory

Public policy may be viewed as a political system's response to demands arising from its environment. The *political system*, as defined by Easton, comprises those identifiable and interrelated institutions and activities (what we usually think of as governmental institutions and political processes) in a society that make authoritative allocations of values (decisions) that are binding on society. The environment consists of all those phenomena—the social system, the economic system, the biological setting—that are external to the boundaries of the political system. Thus at least analytically one can separate the political system from all the other components of a society.[33]

Inputs into the political system from the environment consist of demands and supports. *Demands* are the claims for action made by individuals and groups to satisfy their interests and values. *Support* is rendered when groups and individuals abide by election results, pay taxes, obey

FIGURE 1.1   The Agenda-Setting Process

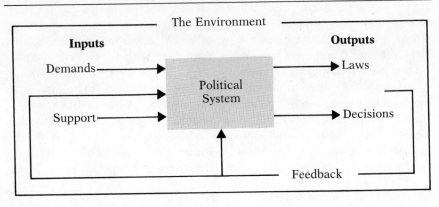

laws, and otherwise accept the decisions and actions taken by the political system in response to demands. The support for a political system indicates the extent to which it is regarded as *legitimate*, or as authoritative and binding on citizens.

Outputs of the political system include laws, rules, judicial decisions, and the like. Regarded as the authoritative allocations of values, they constitute public policy. The concept of *feedback* indicates that public policies (or outputs) made at a given time may subsequently alter the environment and the demands arising therefrom, as well as the character of the political system itself. Policy outputs may produce new demands, which lead to further outputs, and so on in a never-ending flow of public policy (see Figure 1.1).

The usefulness of systems theory for the study of public policy is limited by its highly general and abstract nature. It does not, moreover, say much about the procedures and processes by which decisions are made and policy is developed within the "black box" called the political system. Indeed, systems theory sees government as simply responding to demands made upon it. Nonetheless, this approach can be helpful in organizing inquiry into policy formation. It also alerts us to some important facets of the political process, such as the following: How do inputs from the environment affect the content of public policy and the operation of the political system? How in turn does public policy affect the environment and subsequent demands for policy action? How well is the political system able to convert demands into public policy and preserve itself over time?

Group Theory

According to the group theory of politics, public policy is the product of the group struggle. As one writer states, "What may be called public policy is the equilibrium reached in this [group] struggle at any given moment, and it represents a balance which the contending factions or groups constantly strive to weight in their favor."[34] Many public policies do reflect the activities of groups. Examples include the AFL-CIO and minimum-wage legislation, farm groups and agricultural subsidies, shipping companies and maritime subsidies, and the National Education Association and the creation of the Department of Education.

Group theory rests on the contention that interaction and struggle among groups are the central facts of political life. A group is a collection of individuals that may, on the basis of shared attitudes or interests, make claims upon other groups in society. It becomes a political interest group "when it makes a claim through or upon any of the institutions of government."[35] And many groups do just that. The individual is significant in politics only as a participant in or a representative of groups. It is through groups that individuals seek to secure their political preferences.

A central concept in group theory is access. To have influence to be able to help shape governmental decisions, a group must have access, or the opportunity to express its viewpoints to decision makers.[36] Obviously, if a group is unable to communicate with decision-makers, if no one in government will listen to it, the chances that it will be able to affect policymaking are slim. Access may result from the fact that the group is organized, that it has status, good leadership, or resources such as money for campaign contributions. Social lobbying, the wining, dining, and entertaining of legislators and other public officials, can be understood as an effort to create access by engendering a feeling of obligation to the groups involved. Then, when a group wishes to discuss policy matters with an official, it will have an opportunity to present its case.

In the nature of things, some groups will have more access than others. Public policy, at any given time, will reflect the interests of those that are dominant. As groups gain and lose power and influence, public policy will be altered in favor of the interests of those gaining influence against the interests of those losing influence.

The role of government ("official groups") in policy formation has been described in the following manner by one proponent of group theory:

> The legislature referees the group struggle, ratifies the victories of the successful coalitions, and records the terms of the surrenders, compromises, and conquests in the form of statutes. Every statute tends to represent

compromises because the process of accommodating conflicts of group interests is one of deliberation and consent. The legislative vote on any issue tends to represent the composition of strength, i.e., the balance of power, among the contending groups at the moment of voting. . . . Administrative agencies of the regulatory kind are established to carry out the terms of the treaties that the legislators have negotiated and ratified. . . . The judiciary, like the civilian bureaucracy, is one of the instrumentalities for the administration of the agreed rules.[37]

Group theory, while focusing attention on one of the major dynamic elements in policy formation, especially in pluralist societies such as the United States, seems both to overstate the importance of groups and to understate the independent and creative role that public officials play in the policy process. Indeed, many groups have been generated by public policy. The American Farm Bureau Federation, which developed around the agricultural extension program, is a notable example, as is the National Welfare Rights Organization. Public officials also may acquire a stake in particular programs and act as an interest group in support of their continuance. In the United States some welfare agency employees, including social workers, prefer current programs, with their emphasis on supervision and services (as well as benefits), to a guaranteed annual income, which would probably eliminate some of their jobs. In the Soviet Union the bureaucracy has even been depicted as a "new class" that benefits from and supports the current system of state planning and controls.

Another shortcoming of group theory is that many people (e.g., the poor and disadvantaged) and interests (e.g., such diffuse interests as natural beauty and social justice) are either not represented or only poorly represented in the group struggle. As Professor E. E. Schattschneider has remarked concerning the underorganization of the poor: "The flaw in the pluralist heaven is that the heavenly chorus sings with a strong upper-class accent."[38] Those who are not represented will have little voice in policy making and thus their interests will likely be slighted therein.

Finally, from a methodological perspective, it is misleading and inefficient to try to explain politics and policymaking solely in terms of the group struggle. This leads to the neglect of many other factors, such as ideas and institutions, that abound and that independently affect policy development. The reductionism or unicausal explanation that results when all political phenomena are crammed into the group concept should therefore be avoided.

Elite Theory

Approached from the perspective of elite theory, public policy can be regarded as reflecting the values and preferences of a governing elite. The essential argument of elite theory is that public policy is not determined by the demands and actions of the people or the "masses" but rather by a ruling elite whose preferences are carried into effect by public officials and agencies.

Professors Thomas Dye and Harmon Zeigler have provided a summary of elite theory:

1. Society is divided into the few who have power and the many who do not. Only a small number of persons allocate values for society; the masses do not decide public policy.
2. The few who govern are not typical of the masses who are governed. Elites are drawn disproportionately from the upper socioeconomic strata of society.
3. The movement of non-elites to elite positions must be slow and continuous to maintain stability and avoid revolution. Only non-elites who have accepted the basic elite consensus can be admitted to governing circles.
4. Elites share a consensus on the basic values of the social system and the preservation of the system. [In the United States, the elite consensus includes private enterprise, private property, limited government, and individual liberty.]
5. Public policy does not reflect demands of the masses but rather the prevailing values of the elite. Changes in public policy will be incremental rather than revolutionary. [Incremental changes permit responses to events that threaten a social system with a minimum of alteration or dislocation of the system.]
6. Active elites are subject to relatively little direct influence from apathetic masses. Elites influence masses more than masses influence elites.[39]

So stated elite theory is a provocative theory of policy formation. Policy is the product of elites, reflecting their values and serving their ends, one of which may be a desire to provide for the welfare of the masses. Dye has argued that development of civil rights policies in the United States during the 1960s can be suitably explained through the use of elite theory. These policies were "a response of a national elite to conditions affecting a small minority of Americans rather than a response of national leaders to majority sentiments." Thus, for example, the "elimination of legal discrimination and the guarantee of equality of opportunity in the Civil Rights Act of 1964 was achieved largely through the dramatic appeals of middle-class black leaders to the conscience of white elites."[40] Dye's interpretation presents a narrow perspective on both who is affected by or interested in civil rights policies and the explanation for the Civil Rights Act of 1964. Certainly leadership in Congress and the executive branch were very important, but so were civil rights protests and marches, public opinion, and support from an array of nonblack organizations. The civil rights movement of the 1960s was far more than an effort by black leaders to appeal to the conscience of white elites.

Elite theory does focus our attention on the role of leadership in policy formation and on the fact that, in any political system, a few govern the many. Whether the elites rule and determine policy, with little influence by the masses is a difficult proposition to handle. It cannot be proved merely by assertions that the "establishment runs things," which has been a familiar plaint in recent years. Political scientist Robert Dahl argues that to defend the proposition successfully one must identify "a controlling group, less than a majority in size, that is not a pure artifact of democratic rules; . . . a minority of individuals whose preferences regularly prevail in cases of differences of preferences on key political issues."[41] It may be that elite theory has more utility for the analysis and explanation of policy formation in some political systems, such as developing or Eastern European countries, than in others, such as the pluralist democracies of the United States and Canada.

Institutionalism

The study of government institutions is one of the oldest concerns of political science. This is not surprising, since political life generally revolves around governmental institutions such as legislatures, executives, courts, and political parties; public policy, moreover, is initially authoritatively determined and implemented by these institutions.

Traditionally, the institutional approach concentrated on describing the more formal and legal aspects of governmental institutions: their formal organization, legal powers, procedural rules, and functions or activities. Formal relationships with other institutions might also be considered. Usually little was done to explain how institutions actually operated as opposed to how they were supposed to operate, to analyze public policies produced by the institutions, or to discover the relationships between institutional structure and public policies.

Subsequently, political scientists turned their attention in teaching and research to the political processes within governmental or political institutions, concentrating on the behavior of participants in the process and on political realities rather than formalism. To use the legislature as an example, concern shifted from simply describing the legislature as an institution to analyzing and explaining its operation over time, from its static to its dynamic aspects. In the academic curriculum the course on the legislature often became one on the legislative process.

Institutionalism, with its emphasis on the formal or structural aspects of institutions, can nonetheless be usefully employed in policy analysis. An *institution* is a set of regularized patterns of human behavior that persist over time. It is their differing sets of behavior patterns that really distinguish courts from legislatures, from administrative agencies, and so on. These regularized patterns of behavior, which we often call rules or structures, and the like, can affect decision-making and the content of public policy. Rules and structural arrangements are usually not neutral in their impact; rather, they tend to favor some interests in society over others and some policy results over others. For example, it is contended that some of the rules (and traditions, which often have the effect of rules) of the Senate, such as those relating to unlimited debate and action by unanimous consent, favor the interests of minorities over majorities.

In the American federal system, which allocates governmental power among the national and state governments, several different arenas of action are created. Some groups may have more influence if policy is made at the national level, whereas others may benefit more from state policy making. Civil rights groups, for example, have received a better response in Washington, D.C., than in the capitals of the southern states. Groups advocating the adoption of English as the nation's official language, however, have fared better at the state level. Between 1983 and 1989, seventeen state legislatures enacted such laws, while the Congress has been unsympathetic. Indeed, the Voting Rights Act provides that ballots must be printed in foreign languages in some states.

In summary, institutional structures, arrangements, and procedures often have important consequences for the adoption and content of public policies. They provide part of the context for policymaking, which must be considered along with the more dynamic aspects of politics, such as political parties, groups, and public opinion, in policy study. By itself, however, institutional theory can provide only partial explanations of policy.

Rational-Choice Theory

The rational-choice theory, which is sometimes called social-choice, public-choice, or formal theory, originated with economists and involves the application of the principles of microeconomic theory to the analysis and explanation of political behavior (or nonmarket decision making). It has now gained quite a few adherents among political scientists.

Perhaps the earliest use of rational-choice theory to study the political process is Anthony Downs's *Economic Theory of Democracy*.[42] In this influential book, Downs assumes that voters and political parties act as rational decision makers who seek to maximize attainment of their preferences. Parties formulated whatever policies would win them the most votes, while voters sought to maximize that portion of their preferences that could be realized through government action. In attempting to win elections political parties moved toward the center of the ideological spectrum in order to appeal to the greatest number of voters and maximize their voting support. Thus rather than providing voters with "meaningful alternatives," parties will become as much alike as possible, thereby providing an "echo rather than a choice."

Let us now look more closely at the major components of rational-choice theory. One of its basic axioms is that political actors, like economic actors, act rationally in pursuit of their own self-interest. Thus economist James Buchanan, a leading proponent of rational-choice theory, contends that politicians are guided by their self-interest rather than an altruistic commitment to such goals as statesmanship or the national interest. "This should be no surprise," says Buchanan, "because governments are made up of individuals, and individuals operate from self-interest when they are engaged in a system of exchange, whether this is in the market economy or in politics."[43] Individuals who are engaged in decision-making exchanges or transactions, such as voting, also have preferences that vary from person to person. Being rational, individuals are able to comprehend and rank their preferences from most to least desired. In making decisions (whether economic or political), they are guided by these preferences and will seek to maximize the benefits they gain. In short, people are self-interested utility maximizers, not the uninformed, confused, or irrational choice makers often depicted in analyses of political behavior.

A second basic axiom of rational-choice theory involves methodological individualism. The individual decision maker is the primary unit of analysis and theory. The individual's preferences or values are assumed to be more important than other values—collective, organizational, or social. Conversely, rational-choice theorists argue that the actions of organizations and groups can be satisfactorily explained in terms of the behavior of a model individual. Nothing substantial in explaining the behavior of all persons will be lost by so doing.

For example, a rational-choice explanation of why Congress delegates discretionary power to administrative agencies begins with the assumption that the first preference of members of Congress is to get reelected.[44] To this end, legislators delegate power to agencies knowing that in exercising that power the agencies will create problems for their constituents. Legislators will then be called on by their constituents to assist them with their bureaucratic problems and, in return for assistance, the grateful constituents will vote for the reelection of the legislators. The pursuit of self-interest by the members of Congress thus explains the delegation of power and the growth of bureaucracy.

Rational-choice studies of political behavior are often characterized by rigid and narrow assumptions, mathematical equations, abstractions, and remoteness from reality. Even William C. Mitchell, an early enlistee in the rational-choice movement, has remarked that as it appears in textbooks, rational-choice theory "hardly involves government, politicians, bureaucrats, and interest groups. Little of the exposition . . . has anything to do with the fiscal or regulatory lives of the community or state."[45] A more positive view holds that "in its pure form it is one, but only one, useful, partial explanation of politics."[46]

Rational-choice theory both alerts us to the importance of self-interest as a motivating force in politics and policy making, and provides a better understanding of decision-making processes. Surely, however, politics is not as devoid of altruism and concern for the public interest as the rational-choice theorists assume. The adoption of "good public policy," for example, is frequently a goal of members of Congress.[47]

Commentary

Although individual political scientists often manifest strong preferences for one or another of these theoretical approaches (or others, such as incrementalism which is presented as a decision-making theory in Chapter 4), I cannot authoritatively state which is the "best" or the most satisfactory. Each focuses attention on different aspects of policy making and politics, and thus seems more useful for understanding some situations or events than others.

Group theory and elite theory are mutually exclusive explanations of how the policy process operates and, most importantly, of who controls or dominates and benefits from the process. Or, to put it succinctly, who rules? Sharp intellectual struggles have been waged between group (or pluralist) theorists and elite theorists as to who controls decision-making on public policy in American communities. Much heat if not light was generated by this controversy, which has quieted down without the issue having been resolved.

Systems theory and institutionalism both focus on the process of policy making, albeit in different ways, and are not incompatible. Institutionalism can be used to help explain what goes on within the "black box" (the political system) which is neglected by systems theory. Since neither theory confronts the question of who rules, either group or elite theory could be combined with them to some degree. Rational-choice theory, given the narrowness of its focus, must stand pretty much by itself. Institutions appear as the individual writ large; little attention is given to the policy environment or how issues are brought to the attention of government. However, like institutionalism, rational choice theory does show some concern with how rules and structures help determine the outcomes of decision making. Rational choice scholars often are concerned with how the manipulation of rules can produce intended decisions.

On the question of who rules, rational-choice theory asserts that democratically elected officials will promote their own interest rather than the people's. This leads to the normative (and conservative) conclusion that less government is better government. In the view of group theorists, the interest of dominant groups (however determined) prevail, while for elite theorists the few (a ruling class) govern in their interests.

The various theories thus raise some controversial questions about politics and the policymaking process. They also tend to skew research findings. For example, pluralists find groups in control, elite theorists see the dominance of an elite, and rational choice theorists find that self-interest predominates. These theories are therefore not simply neutral alternatives for guiding analysis. What one finds in policy research depends in important part on what one is looking for, just as those who go about town "looking for trouble" are more apt to find it than are more peacefully oriented citizens.

To conclude on a conciliatory note, it is wise not to be bound too dogmatically or rigidly to a single model or approach. A good rule is to be eclectic and flexible, and to draw from those theories or concepts that seem most useful for the satisfactory and fair-minded description and explanation of particular political events and policies. It is the explanation of political behavior rather than the validation of one's preferred theoretical approach that should be the goal of political inquiry. Each of the theories discussed, if drawn upon skillfully and selectively, can contribute to an understanding of policymaking.

THE PLAN OF THIS BOOK

The central concern of this book is the policy process, which is a shorthand way of designating the various processes by which public policy is actually formed. There is, it should be stressed, no one single process by which policy is made. Variations in the subject of a given policy will produce variations in the nature and techniques of policymaking. Foreign policy, taxation, railroad regulation, aid to private schools, professional licensing, and reform of local government are each characterized by distinguishable policy process. Policymaking may vary depending on whether its primary institutional location is the legislature, executive, judiciary, or administrative agencies. And certainly the process of forming tax policy, for instance, differs in the United States, the Soviet Union, and, say, Ethiopia.

This does not mean, however, that each policymaking situation is

unique and that it is impossible to develop generalizations on policy formation. Given the complexity and diversity in policy processes, it is not now
possible to develop a "grand theory" of policy formation. But a useful start
can be made toward what political scientists call "theory building" by
seeking to generalize on such matters as who is involved in policy formation
and on what kinds of issues, under what conditions, in what ways, and to
what effect. Nor should we neglect the question of how policy problems
develop. Such questions are really not as simple as they may first appear.

To provide a conceptual framework to guide our discussion, the policy
process will be viewed as a sequential pattern of action involving the following functional categories (or stages) of activity that can readily be
distinguished analytically but may be more difficult to separate empirically
(see also Table 1.3).

1. *Problem identification and agenda formation:* What is a policy problem?
   What makes it a public problem? How does it get on the agenda of
   government? Why do some problems not achieve agenda status?
2. *Formulation:* How are alternatives for dealing with the problem developed? Who participates in policy formulation?
3. *Adoption:* How is a policy alternative adopted or enacted? What requirements must be met? Who adopts policy? What processes are used?
   What is the content of the adopted policy?
4. *Implementation:* Who is involved? What is done, if anything, to carry a
   policy into effect? What impact does this have on policy content?
5. *Evaluation:* How is the effectiveness or impact of a policy measured?
   Who evaluates policy? What are the consequences of policy evaluation?
   Are there demands for change or repeal?

Within this framework, policy formation and implementation are perceived as political in that they involve conflict and struggle among individuals and groups having conflicting interests and desires on public policy
issues. Policymaking is "political," it involves "politics," and there is no
reason to resist or disparage this conclusion, or to imitate those who dis-
miss policies they do not like with such phrases as, "It's nothing but politics."

This approach has a number of advantages. First, policymaking often
does follow the stages described. The sequential approach thus helps capture the flow of action in the policy process. But not always. Policy formulation and adoption may be smudged together, as when proposed legislation
is modified during its consideration to secure the votes needed for its passage. Again, administrative agencies may help shape policy as they are
implementing it (see Chapter 6). Even in such instances, however, with the
sequential approach one can analytically distinguish among the different
activities involved.

Second, the sequential process is open to change and elaboration.[48]

TABLE 1.3   The Policy Process

Policy Terminology	Stage 1: Policy Agenda	Stage 2: Policy Formulation	Stage 3: Policy Adoption	Stage 4: Policy Implementation	Stage 5: Policy Evaluation
Definition	Those problems, among many, that receive the serious attention of public officials	Development of pertinent and acceptable proposed courses of action for dealing with a public problem	Development of support for a specific proposal so that a policy can be legitimized or authorized	Application of the policy by the government's administrative machinery	Efforts by the government to determine whether the policy was effective and why or why not
Common sense	Getting the government to consider action on the problem	What is proposed to be done about the problem	Getting the government to accept a particular solution to the problem	Applying the government's policy to the problem	Did the policy work?

Source: Adapted from James E. Anderson, David W. Brady, and Charles Bullock, III, *Public Policy and Politics in the United States,* 2d ed. (Monterey, Calif.: Brooks/Cole, 1984).

Additional steps can be introduced if experience indicates that they are needed to improve description and analysis. Various forms of data collection and analysis—whether quantitative, historical, legal, or normative—are compatible with it. Third, it yields a dynamic and developmental rather than a cross-sectional or static view of the policy process. Moreover, it helps emphasize the relationships among political phenomena rather than simply listing factors or developing classification schemes. Such items as political parties, interest groups, legislative procedures, and presidential commitments become important and are tied together as they help to explain the development of public policy. Fourth, the sequential approach is not "culture bound" and can be readily utilized to study policy making in foreign political systems. It also lends itself to manageable comparisons, such as how problems are placed on the policy agendas or how policies are adopted in various countries. A few such comparisons will be noted in this book.

In Chapter 2, the environment or context of policy making and the official and unofficial participants in the policy process will be surveyed. Chapter 3 focuses on the nature of policy problems and agendas, agenda-setting processes, and the formulation of policy proposals. In Chapter 4 the adoption of policies is treated. A case study on natural gas traces the rise, elaboration, and decline of a policy. Chapter 5 discusses the budgetary process, especially as it relates to policy implementation. The concern of Chapter 6 is the implementation of policies by administrative agencies. Policy evaluation is handled in Chapter 7, along with policy impacts, which precede evaluation, and policy termination, which may follow evaluation. In Chapter 8, I set forth some general conclusions and comments on the American policy process.

Notes

1. This account is based on Donald C. Baumer and Carl E. Van Horn, *The Politics of Unemployment* (Washington, D.C.: CQ Press, 1985), esp. chaps. 1 and 6.
2. Macon Morehouse, "Job-Training Act, Under Attack, to Shift Focus to Neediest," *Congressional Quarterly Weekly Report*, Vol. 47 (April 8, 1989), pp. 747–750.
3. Baumer and Van Horn, *op. cit.*, p. 186.
4. Robert Eyestone, *The Threads of Public Policy: A Study in Policy Leadership* (Indianapolis: Bobbs-Merrill, 1971), p. 18.
5. Thomas R. Dye, *Understanding Public Policy*, 5th ed. (Englewood Cliffs, N.J.: Prentice-Hall, 1984), p. 1.
6. Richard Rose (ed.), *Policy Making in Great Britain* (London: Macmillan, 1969), p. x.

7. Carl J. Friedrich, *Man and His Government* (New York: McGraw-Hill, 1963), p. 79.
8. David Easton, *A Systems Analysis of Political Life* (New York: Wiley, 1965), p. 212.
9. The basic typology is from Theodore J. Lowi, "American Business, Public Policy Case Studies, and Political Theory," *World Politics*, XVI (July, 1964), pp. 677–715. The self-regulatory category is from Robert H. Salisbury, "The Analysis of Public Policy: A Search for Theories and Roles," in Austin Ranney (ed.), *Political Science and Public Policy* (Chicago: Markham, 1968), pp. 151–175.
10. *Congressional Quarterly Weekly Report*, Vol. 44 (October 18, 1986), p. 2625.
11. Lowi, *op. cit.*, p. 690.
12. *Ibid.*, pp. 690–691.
13. *The Book of the States, 1988–1989* (Lexington, Ky.: Council of State Governments, 1988), pp. 382–387.
14. For a thorough discussion of licensing, see Kenneth J. Meier, *Regulation: Politics, Bureaucracy, and Economics* (New York: St. Martin's, 1985), chap. 7.
15. Lowi, *op. cit.*, p. 691. On redistributive policies, see Randall B. Ripley and Grace A. Franklin, *Congress, the Bureaucracy, and Public Policy* (Homewood, Ill.: Dorsey, 1976), chap. 6.
16. Randall B. Ripley, *Policy Analysis in Political Science* (Chicago: Nelson-Hall, 1985), pp. 68–69.
17. Paul E. Peterson and Mark Rom, "Lower Taxes, More Spending, and Budget Deficits," in Charles O. Jones (ed.), *The Reagan Legacy: Promise and Performance* (Chatham, N.J.: Chatham House, 1988), pp. 218–221.
18. On the symbolic aspects of policies, see Murray Edelmann, *The Symbolic Uses of Politics* (Urbana: University of Illinois Press, 1964), chap. 2; and Charles D. Elder and Roger W. Cobb, *The Political Uses of Symbols* (New York: Longman, 1983).
19. Richard O. Davis, *Housing Reform During the Truman Administration* (Columbia: University of Missouri Press, 1966), chap. 10.
20. Bruce I. Oppenheimer, *Oil and the Congressional Process* (Lexington, Mass.: Heath, 1974), pp. 130–145.
21. Cf. L. L. Wade and R. L. Curry, Jr., *A Logic of Public Policy* (Belmont, Calif.: Wadsworth, 1970), chap. 5.
22. Ronald C. Moe, "Exploring the Limits of Privatization," *Public Administration Review*, XLVII (November–December, 1987), p. 453.
23. This discussion draws on Theodore J. Lowi, *The End of Liberalism*, 2d ed. (New York: Norton, 1979), chap. 3.
24. *Ibid.*, p. 57.
25. *Ibid.*, p. 72. His emphasis.
26. Robert McIver, *The Web of Government* (New York: Macmillan, 1947), pp. 314–315.
27. Robert H. Salisbury, "The Analysis of Public Policy: A Search for Theories and Roles," in Austin Ranney (ed.), *Political Science and Public Policy* (Chicago: Markham, 1968), pp. 13–18.
28. Dye, *op. cit.*, pp. 5–7.

29. Austin Ranney, "The Study of Policy Content: A Framework for Choice," in Ranney (ed.), *Political Science and Public Policy* (Chicago: Markham, 1968), p. 159.
30. Don K. Price, *The Scientific Estate* (Cambridge, Mass.: Harvard University Press, 1965), pp. 122–135.
31. This discussion of policy analysis is informed by Robert D. Behn, "Policy Analysis and Policy Politics," *Policy Analysis*, VII (Spring, 1981), pp. 199–226.
32. Dye, *op. cit.*, p. 7.
33. David Easton, "An Approach to the Analysis of Political Systems," *World Politics*, IX (April, 1957), pp. 383–400. Cf. Easton, *A Framework for Political Analysis* (Englewood Cliffs, N.J.: Prentice-Hall, 1965); and *A Systems Analysis of Political Life* (New York: Wiley, 1965). Those wishing to explore systems theory in depth should consult these works.
34. Earl Latham, *The Group Basis of Politics* (New York: Octagon Books, 1965), p. 36.
35. David Truman, *The Governmental Process* (New York: Knopf, 1951), p. 37.
36. Alan C. Isaak, *Scope and Methods of Political Science* (Chicago: Dorsey Press, 1988), pp. 269–270.
37. Latham, *op. cit.*, pp. 35–36, 38–39.
38. E. E. Schattschneider, *The Semisovereign People* (New York: Holt, Rinehart and Winston, 1960), p. 35.
39. Thomas R. Dye and L. Harmon Zeigler, *The Irony of Democracy*, 8th ed. (Monterey, Calif.: Brooks/Cole, 1990), p. 7.
40. Dye, *op. cit.*, pp. 59–63.
41. Robert A. Dahl, "A Critique of the Ruling Elite Model," *American Political Science Review*, LII (June, 1958), p. 464.
42. Anthony Downs, *An Economic Theory of Democracy* (New York: Harper & Row, 1957).
43. Roger Lewin, "Self-Interest in Politics Earns a Nobel Prize," *Science*, CCXXXIV (November 21, 1986), p. 941.
44. Morris P. Fiorina, *Congress: Keystone of the Washington Establishment* (New Haven: Yale University Press, 1977).
45. William C. Mitchell, "Textbook Public Choice: A Review Essay," *Public Choice*, XXVIII (1982), p. 99.
46. Louis F. Weschler, "*Methodological Individualism in Politics.*" *Public Administration Review*, XLII (May–June, 1982), p. 294.
47. See Richard J. Fenno, Jr., *Congressmen in Committees* (Boston: Little Brown, 1973). Fenno indicates the members of Congress are variously influenced by the desires to be reelected, to help enact good public policy, and to acquire influence in the House.
48. See, generally, Richard Rose, "Concepts for Comparison," *Policy Studies Journal*, I (Spring, 1973), pp. 122–127.

2

THE POLICY MAKERS
AND THEIR
ENVIRONMENT

Policy makers—official and unofficial—spend much of their time negotiating policy differences. Here, Majority Whip William Gray and House Speaker Tom Foley work on the federal budget.

In the American political system, political power is fragmented and dispersed by constitutional prescription and political practice. Many points of official decision making exist, and many officials share in the exercise of political power and the formation of public policy.

At the national level, the Framers of the Constitution provided for the separation of power among the legislative, executive, and judicial branches. Thus, Article I provides that "all legislative Powers herein granted shall be vested in a Congress of the United States. . ." Article II states that "The executive Power shall be vested in a President of the United States of America." In turn, Article III ordains that "The judicial Power of the United States, shall be vested in one supreme court and such inferior Courts as the Congress may from time to time ordain and establish." This separation was reinforced by the provision of different selection processes for each branch. Thus, the House of Representatives was to be chosen by the voters, the Senate by the state legislatures (changed to the voters by the Sixteenth Amendment), the president by the Electoral College, and the judges by the president with the consent of the Senate.

The separation of powers was not rigidly imposed, however. By the corollary principle of checks and balances, the Framers gave each branch some means to interfere with—to check—the exercise of power by the other two branches. Thus Congress was given primary responsibility for the enactment legislation, but the President was authorized to recommend matters for its attention and to veto laws, although the veto could be overcome by a two-thirds vote of both houses. Many presidential appointments, including those to the federal courts, require Senate approval. The Supreme Court can declare actions of the other branches unconstitutional, but Congress can regulate the jurisdiction of the courts and the kinds of cases they may hear. What the Framers really created was a set of separated institutions sharing power.

The Framers' intent was to use the principles of separation of powers and checks and balances to prevent the abuse of power and the intrusion of government on individual liberty. Whatever their impact in these respects, these principles have had other consequences that should be noted. One is the decentralization of power. Another was the creation of the need for cooperation and deference among the branches for the government to act effectively. Indeed, if each branch were to insist on the fullest exercise of its prerogatives, the government would likely be gridlocked. A third was to help make American government inefficient in its operation. Much time and effort is often required to make policy decisions.

Power in the American political system is further dispersed by the principle of federalism, which created separate national and state governments, each deriving its power from the Constitution. Essentially, the Constitution assigned delegated and implied ("necessary and proper") powers to the national government, and reserved powers to the state governments. As summarized in the Tenth Amendment, "The powers not delegated to the United States by the Constitution, nor prohibited by it to the States, are reserved to the States respectively, or to the people." As now interpreted, the Constitution does not reserve any specific policy areas for state action.

Since the adoption of the Constitution, there has been continual growth in the power of the national government. It is today vastly more powerful than it was in 1800, 1900, or even 1950, and acts in many areas earlier regarded as the domain of the states. The state governments (and their local subdivisions), however, are still very important in many policy areas, including law enforcement, public education (both lower and higher), land-use controls, highway and street construction and maintenance, occupational licensing, mental health, and public sanitation services. There are no policy areas—even foreign policy and national defense—in which the states do not have some involvement or impact. However, there is much cooperation, and sometimes conflict, among the national, state, and local governments in the development and implementation of public policies.

Even though the Constitution does not require the states to follow the principle of separation of power, all do. Although the state governments are *unitary* in that they formally possess all constitutionally permissible power, they have created large numbers of local governments (some 83,000 separate units in 1987) to handle state functions and provide for local self-government. In practice, local governments often enjoy substantial independence from state government supervision and control. They, along with the states, thus become additional arenas for policy making and implementation.

To describe and analyze policymaking in all three arenas—national, state, and local—would be a task too enormous for a single book. Hence I will focus on national governmental action on domestic matters, but not to the complete exclusion of other political systems or foreign policy. In this chapter, official and unofficial participants in the policy-making process will be surveyed. Before turning to that task, however, the policy environment in which they operate will be discussed. The environment or context in which government acts helps to shape its actions, which is something that tends to be ignored by rational-choice theory.

THE POLICY ENVIRONMENT

Policymaking cannot adequately be studied apart from the environment or context in which it occurs. According to systems theory, demands for policy actions stem from problems and conflicts in the environment and are transmitted by groups, officials, and others to the political system. At the same time, the environment both places limits on and gives direction to what policy makers can effectively do. The environment, broadly viewed, includes geographical characteristics such as climate, natural resources, and topography; demographical variables such as population size, age distribution, and spatial location; political culture; social structure, or the class system; and the economic system. Other nations also become an important part of the environment when foreign and defense policies are involved. The discussion here will focus on a pair of these environmental factors that have received much attention from political scientists (although not always from a policy studies perspective): political culture and socioeconomic conditions.

Political Culture

Every society has a culture that differentiates the values and lifestyles of its members from those of other societies. The anthropologist Clyde Kluckhohn has defined culture as "the total life way of a people, the social legacy the individual acquires from his group. Or culture can be regarded as that part of the environment that is the creation of man."[1] Most social scientists seem to agree that culture shapes or influences social action but does not fully determine it. Culture is only one of many factors that may affect human behavior.

What is of interest here is that portion of the general culture of a society that can be designated as political culture—widely held values, beliefs, and attitudes concerning what governments should try to do and how they should operate, and the relationship between the citizen and government.[2] Political culture is transmitted from one generation to another by a socialization process in which the individual, through many experiences with parents, friends, teachers, political leaders, and others, learns politically relevant values, beliefs, and attitudes. Political culture, then, is acquired by the individual, becomes a part of his or her psychological makeup, and is manifested in his or her behavior. Within a given society, variations among regions and groups may result in distinctive subcultures. In the United States there are noticeable variations in political culture (subcultures) between North and South, black and white, and young and old.

Political scientist Daniel J. Elazar contends there are three identifiable political cultures—individualistic, moralistic, and traditionalistic—and mutations thereof scattered throughout the United States.[3] The *individualistic* political culture emphasizes private concerns and views government as a utilitarian device to do what the people want. Politicians are interested in office as a means of controlling the favors or rewards of government. The *moralistic* political culture views government as a mechanism for advancing the public interest. Government service is considered public service. More governmental intervention in the economy is accepted, and there is much concern about policy issues. Moralistic political culture is strong in states like Minnesota and Wisconsin, while individualistic political culture is dominant in Illinois and New York. The *traditionalistic* political culture takes a paternalistic and elitist view of government, and favors its use to maintain the existing social order. Real political power centers in a small segment of the population, while most citizens are expected to be relatively inactive in politics. Moralistic political culture has been strong in some of the southern states. Where such variations in political culture exist, they clearly compound the tasks of description and analysis.

No attempt will be made here to provide a full statement of the political culture of the United States or any other society. Rather, discussion will be confined to indicating and illustrating some of the implications and significance of political culture for policy formation.

The sociologist Robin M. Williams has identified a number of "major-value orientations" in American society, including individual freedom, equality, progress, efficiency, and practicality.[4] Values such as these—and others, such as democracy, individualism, and humanitarianism—clearly have significance for policy making. For example, the general approach of Americans to the regulation of economic activity has been practical or pragmatic, emphasizing particular solutions to present problems rather than long-range planning or ideological consistency. Moreover, concern with individual freedom has created a general presumption against restriction of private activity and in favor of the broadest scope possible for private action. Stress on individualism and private property finds expression in the notion (often departed from in practice) that a person should generally be free to use his or her property as he or she sees fit.

Differences in public policy and policymaking in various countries can be explained at least partially in terms of variations in political culture. Public medical care programs are of longer standing and are more numerous and extensive in Western European countries than in the United States, because there have been greater public expectation and acceptance of such programs in Europe. Again, most people in Great Britain approve of governmental ownership, whereas those in the United States disapprove of it.[5] It is thus not surprising to find considerably more governmental ownership of business and industry in Great Britain. Americans much prefer governmental regulation to ownership when control seems necessary.

Professor Karl W. Deutsch suggests that the time orientation of people—their view of the relative importance of the past, present, and future—has implications for policy formation. A political culture oriented more to the past than to the present or future may better encourage the preservation of monuments than the making of innovations, and may enact legislation on old-age pensions years before expanding public higher education. Great Britain, for example, passed an old-age pension law in 1908, but it did not significantly expand public higher education until after 1960. In contrast, Deutsch notes that the United States, with a more future-oriented culture, adopted legislation for land-grant colleges in 1862 and for Social Security in 1935.[6]

Gabriel A. Almond and Sidney Verba have differentiated between parochial, subject, and participant political cultures.[7] In a *parochial* political culture, citizens have little awareness of or orientation toward either the political system as a whole, the input process, the output process, or the citizen as a political participant. The parochials expect nothing from the system. It is suggested that some African chiefdoms, kingdoms, and tribal societies as well as modern-day Italy are illustrative of parochial political cultures. In a *subject* political culture, like that of Germany, the citizen is oriented toward the political system and the output process yet has little awareness of input processes or of the individual as a participant. He or she is aware of governmental authority and may like or dislike it, but is essentially passive. The person is, as the term implies, a subject. In a *participant* political culture, which Almond and Verba found the United States to be, citizens have a high level of political awareness and information along with explicit orientations toward the political system as a whole, its input and output processes, and meaningful citizen participation in politics. They also understand how individuals and groups can influence decision making.

Some of the implications of these differences in political culture for policy formation seem readily apparent. Obviously, citizen participation in policy formation in a parochial political culture is going to be essentially nonexistent, because government will be of little concern to most citizens. The individual in a subject political culture may believe that he or she can do little to influence public policy, whether he or she likes it or not. This may lead to passive acceptance of governmental action that may be rather authoritarian in style. In some instances, frustration and resentment may build until redress or change is sought through violence. In the participant political culture, individuals may organize into groups and otherwise seek to influence governmental action to rectify their grievances. Government and public policy are thus viewed as controllable by citizens. One can also assume that more demands will be made on government in a participant political culture than in either a parochial or a subject culture.

To return to an earlier point, political culture helps shape political behavior; it "is related to the *frequency* and *probability* of various kinds of behavior and not their rigid determination."[8] Common values, beliefs, and attitudes inform, guide, and constrain the actions of both decision makers and citizens. Political culture differences help ensure that public policy is more likely to favor economic competition in the United States, where individual opportunity is a widely held value, while it is more likely to tolerate industrial cartels in West Germany, where economic competition has not been highly valued. Some political scientists shy away from using political culture as an analytic tool because they see it as too imprecise and conjectural. Although this argument has some merit, political culture does have utility for the analysis and explanation of policy.

Socioeconomic Conditions

The term *socioeconomic conditions* is used here because it is often impossible to separate social and economic factors as they impinge on or influence political activity. The levels of educational attainment in a society, for instance, have both social and economic effects.

Public policies often arise out of conflicts among groups of people, private and official, with differing interests and desires.[9] This is especially true for regulatory and redistributive policies. One of the prime sources of conflict, particularly in modern industrial societies, is economic activity. Conflicts may develop between the interests of big business and small business, employers and employees, wholesalers and retailers, bankers and securities dealers, hospitals and medical insurance companies, farmers and agricultural importers, and consumers and manufacturers.

Groups that are underprivileged or dissatisfied with their existing relationships with other groups in the economy may seek governmental assistance to improve their situation. Thus it has been labor groups, dissatisfied with the wages sometimes resulting from bargaining with employers, that have sought minimum-wage legislation. Consumer groups, who feel disadvantaged in the marketplace have sought protection against unwholesome food and hazardous products. Customarily, in a private conflict it is the weaker or disadvantaged party, at least in a comparative sense, that seeks to expand the conflict by bringing government into the fray. The dominant group, which can achieve its goals satisfactorily by private action, has no incentive to bring government into the conflict and will usually seek to privatize it by contending that governmental action is unnecessary, improper, or unwise.

Satisfactory relationships between groups may be disrupted or altered by economic change or development. Those that feel adversely affected or threatened may then demand government action to protect their interests or establish a new equilibrium. Rapid industrialization and the growth of big business in the United States in the latter part of the nineteenth century, for example, produced new economic conditions. Farmers, small business operators, reform elements, and aggrieved others called for government action to control big business. The eventual results were the enactment by Congress of the Sherman Act in 1890 and the Clayton and

Federal Trade Commission acts in 1914. More recently, American manufacturing companies, economically threatened by an increasing volume of less costly imported products, have sought and sometimes obtained both voluntary and mandatory import quotas. The Omnibus Trade and Competitiveness Act of 1988, for example, authorizes retaliation against countries that discriminate against the sale of American products while benefiting from American market opportunities.

It is a truism to state that a society's level of economic development will impose limits on what government can do in providing public goods and services to its citizens. Nonetheless, this fact is occasionally overlooked by those who assume that the failure of governments to act on problems is invariably due to recalcitrance or unresponsiveness rather than limited resources. Clearly, one factor affecting what governments can provide in the way of welfare programs is the availability of economic resources. A scarcity of economics resources will of course be more limiting in many of the developing countries than in an affluent society such as the United States, although even American governments do not have the funds to do everything that everyone wants. National health insurance legislation, which seemed highly likely to be adopted in the 1970s, lost its appeal in our era of large budget deficits. So too has there been delay in the improvement and repair of highways, bridges, and other parts of the transportation infrastructure.

Within the United States, resources are very unequally distributed among state and local governments, which affects their capacity to deal with such social problems as public education, poverty, prison overcrowding, and traffic congestion. Consequently, substantial variations exist among the states on welfare spending and within the states among school districts on educational expenditures (as measured by expenditures per student). Cities, pressed for funds, devote most of their resources to police and fire protection and street maintenance while cutting back in "amenities" such as libraries, parks, and recreation programs.

Social change and conflict also stimulate demands for governmental action. The growing concern in the United States about women's rights and the increased use (and acceptance) of marijuana, especially by middle class people, has produced demands for alterations in public policies. In consequence, greater protection has been provided for women's rights, including the right to terminate pregnancies through abortion, equal employment opportunity, and in some states comparable pay for comparable work and parental leave programs. Reduced penalties have also been provided for the use and possession of small amounts of marijuana. Those with conflicting interests and values have strongly, sometimes vehemently, opposed such demands. Because such conflicts are difficult to resolve, public officials often find themselves hard-pressed to devise acceptable policy solutions.

The ways in which socioeconomic conditions influence or constrain public policies in the states have been subjected to considerable analysis by political scientists. Controversy has developed over the relative influence of both political and socioeconomic variables on policy. One of the most prominent examinations of this question has been Thomas R. Dye's study of policy outputs in the fifty states.[10] He contended that the level of economic development (as measured by such variables as per capita personal income, percent urban population, median level of education, and industrial employment) had a dominant influence on state policies on such matters as education, welfare, highways, taxation, and public regulation. He compared the impact of economic development with the impact of the political system and found that political variables (voter participation, interparty competition, political party strength, and legislative apportionment) had only a weak relationship to public policy. Dye summarized the findings of his sophisticated statistical analysis as follows:

> Much of the literature in state politics implies that the division of the two-party vote, the level of interparty competition, the level of voter participation, and the degree of malapportionment in legislative bodies all influence public policy. Moreover, at first glance the fact that there are obvious policy differences between states with different degrees of party competition, Democratic dominance, and voter participation lends some support to the notion that these system characteristics influence public policy. . . .
>
> However, partial correlation analysis reveals that these system characteristics have relatively little *independent* effect on policy outcomes in the states. Economic development shapes both political systems and policy outcomes, and most of the association that occurs between system characteristics and policy outcomes can be attributed to the influence of economic development. Differences in the policy choices of states with different types of political systems turn out to be largely a product of differing socioeconomic levels rather than a direct product of political variables. Levels of urbanization, industrialization, income, and education appear to be more influential in shaping policy outcomes than political system characteristics.[11]

It should be noted that Dye argued not that political variables do not have *any* impact on state policy, but rather that they are clearly subordinated to socioeconomic factors in explanation of differences in state public policies.

Richard Dawson and James Robinson also attempted to demonstrate that socioeconomic variables have a stronger impact on policy than political factors.[12] They analyzed the effect of interparty competition and certain economic variables on public welfare policy to determine whether party competition had a significant influence on welfare policy (especially expenditures). They concluded that environmental factors had a greater impact than party competition. "The level of public social welfare programs in the American states seems to be more a function of socioeconomic factors, especially per capita income."[13] The conclusions of these and similar studies were quickly accepted by some political scientists. One declared that such research provides "a devastating set of findings and cannot be dismissed as not meaning what it plainly says—that analysis of political systems will not explain policy decisions made by those systems."[14]

But is public policy really primarily an outcome of some kind of socioeconomic determinism? Are studies such as those cited really conclusive on this issue? Two scholars cautioned against a "simple acceptance" of such a conclusion.[15] While not discounting the importance of socioeconomic factors in influencing policy outputs, they indicated there are a number of problems and limitations in these studies.

First, there is a tendency to exaggerate the strength of the economy-policy relationship. Thus they state that "Dye reports 456 coefficients of simple correlations between policy measures and his four economic measures of income, urbanism, industrialization and education, but only 16 of them (4 percent) are strong enough to indicate that an economic measure explains at least one-half the interstate variation in policy."[16] This leaves quite a bit unexplained statistically. Second, the political variables used in such studies have been of limited scope, focusing only on a few aspects of the political process. Third, there is a tendency to overlook variations in the influence of economic factors on policy making. Officials of local governments appear more strongly influenced than state officials by economic factors. Further, local officials are not equally influenced by the character of the local economy:

> Where the locality has adopted reformed government structures there is less of an economy-policy linkage than where local government has an unreformed structure. The principal features of a reformed local government structure are a professional city manager, nonpartisan elections for local offices, and a council selected at-large rather than by wards. These features seem to depoliticize the social and economic cleavages within a community, permitting local officials to make their policy decisions with less concern for economics.[17]

Another limitation is that most of these studies are concerned with the statistical relationships between various political and socioeconomic variables and public policy. If, when condition A exists, policy B usually occurs with it, and the relationship is not caused by some third factor, then we can predict that when A exists, B will occur. Such a prediction, however, is not an explanation, and we are still left with the task of explaining *how* political decisions are actually made. If per capita income is directly related to the level of welfare spending, then we must try to explain the relationship. This is neither an insignificant task nor an easy one. Glib answers should be avoided but, obviously, decisions are made by individuals and not socioeconomic variables.

Two conclusions can be fairly drawn from this discussion. One is that to understand how policy decisions are made and why some decisions are made rather than others, we must consider social and economic as well as political factors. The second is that whether socioeconomic factors are more important than political factors in shaping public policy is still an open question. Most of the research along this line has been focused on the American states, and it is less than conclusive.

THE OFFICIAL POLICY MAKERS

Official policy makers are those who possess the legal authority to engage in the formation of public policy. (I recognize, of course, that some who have the legal authority to act may in fact be controlled by others, such as political party bosses or pressure groups.) These include legislators, executives, administrators, and judges. Each performs policy-making tasks at least somewhat different from the others.

It is useful to differentiate between primary and supplementary policy makers. *Primary policy makers* have direct constitutional authority to act; for example, Congress does not have to depend upon other government units for authorization to act. *Supplementary policy makers,* such as national administrative agencies, must gain their authority to act from others (primary policy makers) and hence are at least potentially dependent upon or controllable by them. Administrative agencies who derive their operating authority from congressional legislation will typically feel a need to be responsive to congressional interests and requests. Congress in turn has less need to be responsive to the agencies.

The conflict between the President and Congress during the second Nixon Administration over whether the President could refuse to spend appropriated funds and act on his own to terminate previously authorized programs illustrates the importance of the distinction between primary and supplementary policy makers. If the President lacked constitutional authority for impounding funds, as many in Congress contended, then Congress could ultimately control spending. This conflict over constitutional authority was essentially a conflict over whether the President could act as a primary policy maker, which would increase the independence and power of the executive vis-à-vis Congress. The issue was resolved in favor of Congress by several federal court decisions. Also, the Budget and Impoundment Control Act of 1974 provided that presidential decisions to impound (not spend) appropriated funds were subject to control by Congress (see Chapter 5). Given the different interests and constituencies of the two branches, who prevails on such matters can have profound policy implications.

The following survey of official policy makers is intended only to be suggestive, that is, to convey a notion of their general role in policy formation, not to catalogue all of their powers and activities.

Legislatures

The easy response to the question "What do legislatures do?" is to say that they legislate, that is, that they are concerned with the central political tasks of lawmaking and policy formation in a political system. It cannot be assumed, however, that a legislature, merely because it bears that formal designation, really has independent decision-making functions. This is a matter to be determined by empirical investigation rather than by definition.

Legislatures at all levels in the United States, in contrast to those in most other countries, do often legislate in an independent decisional sense. At the national level, policies on such matters as taxation, civil rights, social welfare, consumer protection, economic regulation, and environmental protection tend to be shaped in substantial part by Congress through the enactment of substantive and appropriations legislation. The committee and subcommittee system, and legislative norms (i.e., accepted rules of conduct) encouraging members to concentrate their attention on particular policy areas have provided Congress with its own policy specialists. Specialization in turn gives members more opportunity to influence policy in their areas of expertise, whether tax policy, welfare programs, or banking regulation.

The capacity of Congress to engage effectively in policy making has been much enhanced by the expansion of its staff assistance, which is of three types:

1. *Personal staff:* These serve individual members of Congress, either in Washington or in their home districts.
2. *Committee and subcommittee staffs:* Members of these staffs have increased greatly in number in the last two decades. Committee staff often have considerable influence on legislation—drafting bills, developing support, working out compromises on disputed provisions, and the like.
3. *Institutional staff:* Agencies which serve Congress include the Congressional Research Service (part of the Library of Congress), the Office of Technology Assessment, the Congressional Budget Office, and the General Accounting Office. These agencies variously provide Congress with research studies, policy evaluations, and budgetary data.

All of this staff assistance has the effect of making Congress less dependent upon others—the executive, administrative agencies, and interest groups—for information.

In enacting legislation, the members of Congress are concerned with the care of state and local interests as well as with broad national or public interests. Former Speaker of the House Thomas ("Tip") O'Neill was fond of saying that "all politics are local." Some critics would say that the members of Congress are much too concerned with local or parochial interests. Certainly legislators do receive a good deal of pressure from their constituents and narrowly based interests. However, they are also under pressure from the executive and congressional leaders to support more general and national interests. As a consequence, members are caught between conflicting concerns. As Professor Walter A. Rosenbaum remarks with respect to the energy policy area: "Thus, representatives and Senators must fashion a national energy policy within a vortex of competing political powers and pressures: national interest versus local interests, and commitments to party or congressional leaders versus loyalty to local power centers."[18] Members, of course have their own values and policy preferences that also affect their decisions.

In the states, the role of the legislature often varies with the nature of the issue. Many state legislatures, because of their limited sessions, rather "amateur" membership, and inadequate staff assistance, are often unable to act independently on complex, technical legislative matters. They may simply enact bills agreed upon elsewhere. For example, in a not atypical case, several years ago the Texas legislature passed a law on pooling (or unitization) for the common development of oil fields almost in the identical form in which it was introduced after having been agreed to and drafted by representatives of the major and independent petroleum producers' organizations; the legislature did not really have the capacity to do otherwise. On other issues, such as criminal legislation, the legislature clearly does "legislate." It does not require any special skills to determine, for example, what the penalty should be for embezzlement or automobile theft. Such questions do not admit of scientific or technical determination.

The British Parliament has been said merely to consent to laws that are originated by political parties and interest groups, drafted by civil servants, and steered through the House of Commons by the government (the prime minister and the cabinet). This, however, oversimplifies the situation. The government usually gets what it wants from Commons partly because it knows what Commons will accept and requests only measures that are acceptable. Conversely, what is recommended by the government helps make it acceptable to its members in Commons. In the course of approving legislation, Commons performs the vital functions of deliberating, scrutinizing, criticizing, and publicizing governmental policies and activities and their implications for the public.

In comparison, the Russian national legislature, the Supreme Soviet, often merely ratifies or confirms decisions made by high officials within the Communist Party. So too are many Latin American legislatures dominated by the executive and do little if anything in the way of independent decision making. For such political systems, the student of policy formation may be wasting time if too much attention is given to legislative organization and processes.

To conclude with a global generalization, legislatures are more important in policy formation in democratic than in authoritarian countries. Within the democratic category, legislatures generally tend to have a larger role in presidential systems (like the United States) than in parliamentary systems (like Great Britain). In some countries, such as Oman and Saudi Arabia, there is no legislature.

The Executive

We live in what has been called an "executive-centered era," in which the effectiveness of government depends substantially upon executive leadership and action in both policy formation and in policy execution. Consider the case of the president of the United States.

The president's authority to exercise legislative leadership is both clearly established by the Constitution and legislation, and accepted as a practical and political necessity. The fragmentation in Congress stemming from the committee system and the lack of strong party leadership renders that body incapable of developing a comprehensive legislative program. In the twentieth century Congress has come to expect the president to present it with proposals for legislation. This does not mean, however, that the Congress does whatever the president recommends. For example, less than 40 percent of President Nixon's policy proposals were adopted in some form by Congress, which was controlled by the Democratic Party throughout his term. President Jimmy Carter also had much difficulty in getting what he wanted from Congress, even though it was controlled by his own party. After getting much of what he wanted from Congress during his first year in office, Ronald Reagan also experienced many trying times with Congress. In 1987 and 1988, Congress supported the president on less than half the issues on which he took a clear position. This was the poorest presidential performance on this measure in over three decades.[19]

Although the presidency may be a lonely place, the president does not act alone on policy matters. The Executive Office of the President (EOP) comprises several staff agencies whose raison d'etre is advising and assisting the president in handling his responsibilities, including policy development and implementation. The White House Office includes many personal aides and advisors such as the chief of staff, the special assistant on national security affairs, the press secretary, and the counsel to the president. The Office of Management and Budget assists the president in preparation of the annual budget, the supervision of expenditures, and the management of the executive branch. Set up in 1947 to help the president coordinate foreign, military, and domestic policies relating to national security, the National Security Council has become a major player in the development and conduct of foreign policy. The Council of Economic Advisors, which is staffed by professional economists, provides the president with information and advice on micro- and macroeconomic policy issues. A domestic policy office helps develop policy proposals and coordinate action in the domestic sphere. These agencies, and other EOP units have emerged in response to the expansion of presidential duties and responsibilities in recent decades. Collectively, they have enhanced the capacity of the president to act, and to act effectively, as a policy maker.[20]

Congress often delegates significant policy-making authority to the president. Foreign trade legislation, for example, gives the president discretionary authority to raise or lower tariff rates on imported goods. Presidents have used this authority to lower rates significantly on most imports. The Taft-Hartley Act authorizes the president to intervene in labor-management disputes that threaten the national health and safety. Such presidential interventions have been infrequent, however, because they tend to be both controversial and unwelcome. Perhaps the most extensive delegation of power came with the Economic Stabilization Act of 1970, which gave the president virtually a blank check to impose wage and price controls to combat inflation. President Nixon said he did not want this authority and would not use it if it were granted. He subsequently changed his mind, however, and surprised the nation with a price-wage freeze in August 1971. This was followed by systems of mandatory and voluntary controls, until the whole effort was abandoned in 1974.

In the areas of foreign and military policy, which often merge, the president possesses greater constitutional authority and operating freedom than in domestic policy. U.S. foreign policy is largely a product of presidential leadership and action. American policy toward Vietnam, as we well know, was shaped by the presidents in office between 1950 and 1975. The decision to seek more open and friendly relations with the People's Republic of China in the early 1970s was President Nixon's, and the decision to invade Grenada in 1983 was President Reagan's. Foreign policy is to a great extent the domain of the executive, not only in the United States but elsewhere in the world.

In recent decades Congress has sought to expand its role in foreign policy, however. One manifestation of this was the War Powers Resolution of 1973, which was stimulated by the Vietnam War. Enacted over President Nixon's veto, the resolution requires the president to consult with Congress "in every possible instance" involving the use of American armed forces in hostile situations. The president must report to Congress within forty-eight hours after the use of the forces. Unless Congress provides otherwise, military action must be halted within sixty to ninety days. Presidents have been highly critical of the resolution as an improper intrusion in their constitutional domain, and their compliance with it has been spotty at best. Congress was also the source of much opposition to the Reagan administration's military and financial involvements in Central America. No longer can presidents count on bipartisan support for military and foreign policy actions as they could in the first decade or two after World War II. By no means is Congress simply a rubber stamp for presidential initiatives.

In developing countries such as Ghana, Iraq, and Thailand, the executive probably has even more influence in policy making than in more modern industrialized countries, as Yehezkel Dror explains:

> Because there are few policy issues, a larger proportion of them can reach the cabinet level in developing countries; because there is often no professional civil service, the executive plays a larger role in forming public policies about most issues; because power is more highly concentrated, the political executive is free to establish policies on many more issues without worrying as much about having to build coalitions.[21]

In short, in many developing countries, the policy-making structure is rather simple: executive policymaking prevails. In such countries, too, interest groups have little impact on policymaking because of their limited independence from existing political institutions.

Reflective of the important policymaking role of the American executive is that in evaluating an executive—whether the president, a governor, or some other chief executive—our focus is on policymaking rather than administrative activities. Presidents, for their part, are more interested in policy initiation than administration, because it enables them to build more visible records of accomplishment.

Administrative Agencies

Administrative systems throughout the world differ with respect to such characteristics as size, complexity, hierarchical organization, and degree of autonomy. Although it was once common doctrine in political science that administrative agencies only carried into effect, more or less automatically, policies determined by the "political" branches of government, it has now become axiomatic that politics and administration are blended, and that administrative agencies are often significantly involved in the development of public policy. This is particularly so given the concept of policy as what government actually does concerning particular matters. Administration can make or break a law or policy made elsewhere. For example, in the eighteenth century, Catherine II of Russia decreed the abolition of a large part of the institution of serfdom. However, the landowning aristocracy, which really controlled the administration of the government, was largely able to prevent the implementation of this decision. In the United States, the effectiveness of state pollution-control laws has often been blunted by heel-dragging and nonenforcement by the administering agencies.

Especially in complex industrial societies, the technicality and complexity of many policy matters, the need for continuing control, and the legislators' lack of time and information have led to the delegation of much discretionary authority, often formally recognized as rule-making power, to administrative agencies. Consequently, agencies make many decisions that have far-reaching political and policy consequences. Illustrations include the choice of weapons systems by the Department of Defense, the development of air-safety regulations by the Federal Aviation Agency, the location of highways by state highway departments, and the regulation (or nonregulation) of savings and loan institutions by the Federal Home Loan Bank Board (now defunct) in the 1980s. As Professor Norman C. Thomas comments, "It is doubtful that any modern industrial society could manage the daily operation of its public affairs without bureaucratic organizations in which officials play a major policymaking role."[22]

Agencies are also a major source of proposals for legislation in such political systems as the United States and Great Britain. Moreover, American agencies typically not only suggest needed legislation but also actively lobby and otherwise seek to exert pressure for its adoption. Thus the Department of Agriculture has been known to round up pressure-group support for its price-support proposals, thereby in effect lobbying the lobbyists. In all, there is much accuracy in the view that "policy is at the mercy of administrators."

The Courts

Nowhere do the courts play a greater role in policy formation than in the United States. The courts, notably national and state appellate courts, have often greatly affected the nature and content of public policy through exercise of the powers of judicial review and statutory interpretation in cases brought before them.

Basically, judicial review is the power of courts to determine the constitutionality of actions of the legislative and executive branches, and to declare them null and void if they are found to be in conflict with the Constitution. Clearly, the Supreme Court was making policy when, in various cases up to 1937, it held that no legislature, state or national, had constitutional authority to regulate minimum wages. After 1937, the Constitution was found (i.e., interpreted) to permit such legislation. Clearly, too, the Court has helped shape public policy by holding that segregated school systems, prayers in public schools, and malapportionment of state legislatures were unconstitutional. The thrust of policy is importantly affected by such decisions.

Although the Court has used its power of judicial review somewhat sparingly, the very fact it has such power may affect the policymaking activities of the other branches. Congress may hesitate to act on some matter if there is some expectation that its action would be found unconstitutional. State supreme courts also have the power of judicial review but frequently have less discretion in its exercise because of the detailed and specific nature of most state constitutions.

The courts are often called upon to interpret and decide the meaning of statutory provisions that are generally stated and open to conflicting interpretations. When a court accepts one interpretation rather than another, the consequence is to give effect to the policy preference of the winning party. In 1984 in the *Grove City* case, the meaning or intent of Title IX of the 1972 Education Act Amendments was at issue.[23] This provision prohibited sex discrimination by educational institutions receiving federal aid for any "program or activity." Did this ban on discrimination apply to the entire institution being aided, as many members of Congress and civil rights groups contended? Or did it apply only to the specific "program or activity" receiving funding, as the Reagan administration argued? The Supreme Court took the latter position, which much restricted the impact of the 1972 statute and three other civil rights laws containing similar provisions.

After this ruling, a legislative campaign was initiated to correct what many critics saw as an improper interpretation of the 1972 law. It culminated in the Civil Rights Restoration Act of 1988, enacted over President Reagan's veto.[24] The act overcame the Court's *Grove City* decision by specifying that if one part of an institution received federal funds then the ban on sex discrimination applied to the entire institution. This was the view of the 1972 law's scope that had prevailed prior to the Court's decision.

The judiciary has also played a major role in the formation of economic policy in the United States. Much of the law relating to such matters as property ownership, contracts, corporations, and employer-employee relationships has been developed and applied by the courts in the form of common law and equity. These are systems of judge-made law fashioned over the years on a case-to-case basis. They originated in England but have been adapted to American needs and conditions by American judges. Much of this law was developed by the state courts, and much of it is still applied by them.[25]

Today the courts are not only becoming more involved in policy formation, they are also playing a more positive role, specifying not only what government cannot do but also what it must do to meet legal or constitutional requirements. For instance, in *Roe* v. *Wade* (1973), the Supreme Court declared unconstitutional a Texas statute prohibiting abortion as a violation of the privacy protected by the First and Fourteenth Amendments.[26] The majority then went on to specify the standards future abortion laws would have to meet to comply with the Constitution. During the first trimester of pregnancy, abortion was left to the decision of a woman and her physician. During the second trimester, abortion could be regulated to protect the mother's health. During the third trimester, however, after the fetus gained viability, abortion could be prohibited, except when necessary to protect the mother's life or health. This ruling clearly possessed a legislative-like quality. It also touched off a major, continuing political controversy.

In 1989 the Court, which had become more conservative because of three Reagan appointees, partially overruled *Roe* v. *Wade.* In *Webster* v. *Reproductive Health Services,* the Court upheld a Missouri state law that prohibited the performance of abortions in public hospitals and clinics and the use of state funds for counseling women about abortion.[27] Also, testing before performing an abortion after twenty weeks was required to determine whether the fetus was viable outside the womb. This decision, by giving state legislatures more authority to regulate abortions, made the abortion issue even more contentious and thrust it into the legislative arena in the fifty states. The Supreme Court in 1989 also agreed to hear three more abortion cases, thereby ensuring that it will continue to be involved in the political controversy over abortion.

The growing impact of government on people's lives, the failure or refusal of the legislative branches to act on some problems, the dissatisfaction that often arises when they do act, the willingness of the courts to become involved, and the increasing litigiousness of at least some segments of the population seem to guarantee continued judicial involvement in policy formation. Americans have become quite adept at converting political issues into legal issues that the courts are then called on to decide.

Although courts in such other Western countries as Canada, Australia, and West Germany have some power of judicial review, they have had less impact on policy than American courts. In the developing countries, the courts appear to have no meaningful role. The American practice of settling many important policies issues, including such technical matters as clean air and industrial health and safety standards, remains unique.

UNOFFICIAL PARTICIPANTS

In addition to the official policy makers, many others, including interest groups, political parties, research organizations, the communications media, and individual citizens, may participate in the policy process. They are designated as unofficial participants because, however important or dominant they may be in various situations, they themselves do not usually possess legal authority to making binding policy decisions. They provide information, they exert pressure, they seek to persuade, but they do not decide.

Interest Groups

Interest groups appear to play an important role in policy making in practically all countries. Depending upon whether they are democratic or dictatorial, modern or developing, countries may differ with respect to how groups are constituted and how legitimate they are. Thus, groups appear to be more numerous and to operate much more openly and freely in the United States or Great Britain than they do in the Soviet Union. In all systems, however, groups perform an interest articulation function; that is, they express demands and present alternatives for policy action. They may also supply public officials with much information, often of a technical sort, concerning the nature and possible consequences of policy proposals. In doing so, they contribute to the rationality of policymaking.

Interest groups, such as those representing organized labor, business, and agriculture, are a major source of demands for public policy action in the United States. Given the pluralist nature of American society, it is not surprising that pressure groups are many in number and quite diverse in their interests, size, organization, and style of operation. This does not mean, however, that some societal interests may not be poorly represented, if at all, by groups. Migrant workers are a case in point. Typically, an interest group wants to influence policy in a specific subject area. Because several groups often have conflicting desires on a particular policy issue, public officials are confronted with the necessity of having to choose from among, or reconcile, conflicting demands. Groups that are well organized and active are likely to fare better than those whose potential membership is poorly organized and inarticulate. The group struggle is not a contest among equals.

In recent years, there has been an expansion in the number of "single-issue" interest groups, which focus their attention on a single issue or set of related issues such as gun control, milk prices, and abortion legislation. The proliferation of subcommittees in Congress with narrow jurisdictions has both stimulated the development of such groups and contributed to their importance by permitting concentration of their efforts. Among the single-issue groups of the past that had substantial effects on public policy were those advocating the abolition of slavery, women's suffrage, and nation-wide prohibition.

Public-interest groups also are important players in the policy process. Whereas most pressure groups represent interests of direct, material benefit to their members, public-interest groups usually represent interests that in their absense would go unrepresented, such as those of consumers, nature lovers, environmentalists, and "good government" proponents. Frequently these interests involve intangible matters such as honesty, beauty, and safety.[28] The members of public-interest groups usually do not benefit selectively from the interests they advocate and indeed may not benefit at all in any immediate sense. Members of groups advocating the abolition of the death penalty, for example, do not expect to be in personal jeopardy. Examples of public-interest groups include the Sierra Club and the National Wildlife Federation, which support environmental protection and wilderness programs; Common Cause, which advocates more open and accountable government; and the Pacific Legal Foundation, which engages in litigation in support of free enterprise and economic development. Not all public-interest groups are liberal in their policy inclinations, as is sometimes assumed.

At the national level, many associations of state and local governmental officials now routinely seek to influence the content of national policies. Three factors seem to have been especially significant in generating this "intergovernmental lobby."[29] One is the increasing professionalism of state and local governments. The second is the growth in federal grants-in-aid to state and local governments, which amounted to $105.9 billion in 1985, as a major source of their revenues. The third is the many regulations and requirements that these and other federal programs impose on the states and localities, and that are open to modification.

Some of these associations represent elected or appointed officials with executive and legislative duties, such as the National Conference of State Legislators, the U.S. Conference of Mayors, and the National Association of Counties. Others involve functional specialists in highways, education, recreation, and other matters, such as the American Association of State Highway and Transportation Officials, the Council of Chief State School Officers, and the National Association of County Park and Recreation Officials. They gain influence from their expertness and the support of state and local politicians. Many individual states, cities, countries, and public universities also have their own Washington lobbyists or representatives. As with other interest groups, the intergovernmental lobby is not a monolithic force. Its component groups will frequently disagree among themselves. Thus the highway officials want more funding for interurban highways, while city officials see a need for more spending on mass transit systems.

The influence of interest groups upon decisions depends on a number of factors, including (subject to the rule of *ceteris paribus*—other things being equal) the size of the membership, its monetary and other resources, its cohesiveness, the skill of its leadership, its social status, the presence or absence of competing organizations, the attitudes of public officials, and the site of decision making in the political system. (On this last item, recall the discussion of institutionalism in Chapter 1.) With other things again being equal, a large, well-regarded group (e.g., the American Legion) will have more influence than a smaller, less well-regarded group (e.g., Friends of the Earth), and a union with a large membership will have more influence than one with few members. Also, as a consequence of the factors enumerated here, a group may have a strong or controlling influence on decisions in one policy area and little if any influence in another. Whereas, the National Association of Manufacturers has much influence on some economic issues, it has little impact in the area of civil rights.

In a study of the strength of pressure groups generally in the American states, Harmon Zeigler and Hendrick van Dalen focused on the impact of three variables: strength of party competition, legislative cohesion (strength of parties in the legislature), and the socioeconomic variables of urban population per capita income and industrial employment.[30] Two patterns emerged from their analysis: Strong pressure groups (their particular purposes aside) seemed to be associated with weak parties, both electorally and legislatively, low urban population, low per capita income, and a higher rate of nonindustrial employment (argriculture, fishing, and forestry). Moderate or weak pressure groups seemed associated with strong, competitive parties and higher rates of urban population, per capita income, and industrial employment. Their study represents a systematic attempt to discover what affects group strength, although the findings should be viewed as suggestive rather than conclusive. Moreover, it should be kept in mind that they were not concerned with the strength of particular groups.

The relatively open and fluid pressure system in the United States is markedly different from the neocorporatist pattern of group relationships in some Western European countries, such as Austria, Norway, Sweden, and West Germany, that combine democratic politics with a formally structured group system. In the neocorporate scheme of things, access to policy makers is controlled by the government. Policies are adopted after close consultation, bargaining, and compromise between the government and groups that are the officially recognized representatives of farmers, labor unions, and employers. Groups can withdraw from this partnership with the government but may lose influence as a consequence. Some groups, such as those representing consumer and environmental interests, find it difficult to gain access to the government. Neocorporatism has found little support in the United States.

Political Parties

In the United States, political parties are concerned primarily with contesting elections in order to control the personnel of government. They are, in short, concerned more with power than with policy. This situation has often led to the complaint that the Republican and Democratic parties represent a choice between Tweedledee and Tweedledum, and that, so far as public policy is concerned, it makes little difference which party is in office. Although the parties are not highly policy oriented, such complaints ignore the meaningful impact that the parties do have on policy.

Clearly, the parties appeal to different segments of society. Thus the Democratic Party draws disproportionately from big city, labor, and minority and ethnic voters; the Republican Party draws disproportionately from rural, small town, and suburban areas, Protestants, and businesspeople and professionals. The parties often come into conflict on such issues as welfare programs, labor legislation, business regulation, public power projects, public housing, and agricultural price-support legislation. The reader should not have much difficulty in differentiating between the parties on these issues. Given such policy inclinations and the fact that party members in Congress often vote in accordance with party policy positions, which party controls Congress or the presidency has important policy implications.

In the American state legislatures, the importance of political parties varies significantly. In one-party states, it is obvious that parties do not exercise much discipline over legislative voting, and the party has little, if any, effect on policymaking, as in the Texas and Louisiana legislatures. In contrast, in such states as Connecticut and Michigan both parties are active and cohesive and have considerable impact on legislative decision-making. When conflict over policy occurs in such states, the function of parties is to provide alternatives. In many cities, an effort has been made to eliminate party influence on policy through the use of nonpartisan elections for city officials. Policy is supposed to be made "objectively." An unintended consequence of nonpartisanship, it might be noted, is a reduction of interest and participation in politics.

In modern societies generally, political parties often perform a function of "interest aggregation"; that is, they seek to convert the particular demands of interest groups into general policy alternatives. The way in which parties "aggregate" interests is affected by the number of parties. In predominantly two-party systems, such as the United States and Great Britain, the desire of the parties to gain widespread electoral support "will require both parties to include in their policy 'package' those demands which have very broad popular support and to attempt to avoid alienating the most prominent groups."[31] In multiparty systems, on the other hand, parties may do less aggregating and act as the representatives of fairly narrow sets of interests, as appears to be the case in France. Generally, though, parties have a broader range of policy concerns than do interest groups; hence, they will act more as brokers than as advocates of particular interests in policy formation. In some one-party systems, such as the Soviet Union, they are the predominant force in policymaking.

Research Organizations

Private research organizations, which are frequently and inelegantly referred to as "think tanks," are another set of important players in policy making. These organizations are staffed with full-time policy analysts and researchers, some of whom are ex-government officials. Their studies and reports provide basic information and data on policy issues, develop alternatives and proposals for handling problems, and evaluate the effectiveness and consequences of public policies. Some prominent research organizations are the Heritage Foundations, the Cato Institute, the American Enterprise Institute, the Brookings Institution, the Institute for International Economics, the Urban Institute, and the Council on Foreign Relations. Collectively, they add much substance to policy debates.

Many of these organizations have policy biases and distinct ideological leanings. The American Enterprise Institute and the Brookings Institution, for example, are widely regarded as conservative and liberal, respectively, in orientation. In addition to their policy-analysis activities, these organizations may also engage in policy advocacy. The Heritage Foundation, which is staunchly conservative, played an important role in launching the Reagan administration in 1981 and in shaping its policies on issues such as environmental protection, social welfare, and economic regulation.[32] For a time, its study *Mandate for Leadership* was a best seller in Washington. Other research organizations, taking their cue from the Heritage Foundations, developed "policy blueprints" to influence the Bush administration in 1988, none appeared to have much impact.

Universities also often have policy or research centers that produce policy studies and evaluations on national, state, and local issues. Several, for instance, house groups concerned with coastal and marine resource matters. Individual university researchers also occasionally produce studies of direct value to policy makers, sometimes doing this under contract.

Communications Media

The communications media—newspapers, news magazines, radio, and television—participate in policy making as the suppliers and transmitters of information and, whether intentionally or otherwise, the shapers of attitudes. For many people, the evening television news is their primary source of information on public affairs. Those seeking more in-depth coverage and information rely more heavily on newspapers and news magazines. Complaints about bias by the media in their coverage and reporting of public affairs are commonplace, as are allegations that public officials are managing or manipulating the news. Whatever their validity, such complaints attest to the importance the media are thought to have in politics and policy making.

With good reason, Washington officials are quite sensitive to what is reported by the national media, which means newspapers such as the *New York Times* and the *Washington Post* and the major television networks. A survey found that over 70 percent of senior federal officials believed that a positive press increased the likelihood they would attain their goals and that negative coverage would reduce their chances of doing so. Here the perceived power of the media does not involve changing policy but rather influences the capacity of officials to convert their ideas into policy. However, the substance of policy may also be affected.[33] Unfavorable coverage of the Reagan administration's attempts to tighten the eligibility requirements for Social Security disability benefits, for example, contributed to the eventual abandonment of the effort.

Officials of course are not simply acted upon by the media but also strive to use the press for their own purposes. Through interviews, press releases, and news "leaks," they seek to use the media to test and influence the attitudes of both the general public and other officials toward particular proposals or actions. Those who oppose a certain decision may "leak" premature or adverse information in an effort to kill it. This happened early in the Bush administration to a proposal to secure funds to bail out bankrupt savings and loans by taxing their depositors.

President Reagan was often called the "great communicator" because of his ability to use radio and television addresses to shape public opinion in support of his purposes. He used this ability, for instance, to build support for income-tax reform, which became a reality in 1986. Speaker of the House O'Neill, who was not personally inclined to support tax reform, felt the pressure generated by the president's speeches. "I have to have a bill, the Democratic party has to have a [tax] bill . . . ," he was quoted as saying. "If we don't we'll be clobbered over the head by the President of the United States."[34]

The Individual Citizen

In discussions of policy making, the individual citizen is often neglected in favor of legislatures, interest groups, and more prominent participants. This is unfortunate, however, as the individual often does seem to make a difference. Although the task of policymaking is generally assigned to public officials, in various instances citizens can still participate directly in decision making. In some of the American states (notably California) and some countries (such as Switzerland), citizens can and do still vote directly on legislation. Moreover, in most states, constitutional amendments are submitted to the voters for approval. In many local jurisdictions, bond issues and increases in tax rates must be authorized directly by the voters. In Texas the approval of voters in local governmental units is required for local sales taxes, the sale of liquor by the drink, and the operation of bingo games. A great many citizens, of course, do not avail themselves of these opportunities to shape policy directly because of inertia or indifference.

This leads to the frequently made comment that citizen participation in policymaking, even in democratic politics, is slight. Many people do not vote, engage in party activity, join pressure groups, or even display much interest in politics. Survey research indicates, moreover, that voters are influenced comparatively little by policy considerations when voting for candidates for public office. Granting this, however, it still does not hold that citizens have no impact on policy except in the limited situations mentioned in the preceding paragraph. Let us note some possibilities.

Even in authoritarian regimes, the interests or desires of common citizens are consequential for public policies.[35] The old-style dictator will pay some attention to what his people want to keep down unrest. As a Latin American dictator supposedly once said, "You can't shoot everyone." Modern totalitarian regimes, such as the Soviet Union, also seem concerned to meet many citizen wants even as they exclude citizens from more direct participation in policy formation. Thus in recent years the Soviet regime has increased production of consumer goods and has even indicated a desire to surpass the United States in the level of consumer benefits.

Elections in democratic countries may serve indirectly to reinforce official responsiveness to citizen interests, as Professor Charles E. Lindblom summarizes:

> The most conspicuous difference between authoritarianism and demo-cratic regimes is that in democratic regimes citizens choose their top policy makers in genuine elections. Some political scientists speculate that voting in genuine elections may be an important method of citizen influence on policy not so much because it actually permits citizens to choose their officials and to some degree instruct these officials on policy, but because the existence of genuine elections put[s] a stamp of approval on citizen participation. Indirectly, therefore, the fact of elections enforces on proxi-mate policy makers a rule that citizens' wishes count in policymaking.[36]

The "rule" Lindblom refers to is sometimes expressed in the aphorism that citizens have a right to be heard and that officials have a duty to listen. The effect of such considerations on policy makers is worth thinking about, al-though they are not amenable to rigorous measurement, given the present state of political science.

Some presidential elections in the United States have been classified as "critical" because they produce major realignments in voter coalitions and shifts in public policy. The presidential election of 1932 is a prime example. The Republican and Democratic candidates differed substantially on how they proposed to deal with the crisis of the Great Depression. The voters gave Franklin D. Roosevelt and the Democrats an overwhelming victory. The flood of New Deal legislation that followed produced major changes in government-economy relationships and in the role of government in Ameri-can society generally. In such instances, large numbers of newly elected officials, chosen because of their stand on the critical question, enact legis-lation consistent with their party's stand. The voters, through the electoral process, help to produce basic changes in public policy. Other critical elec-tions were those of 1860 and 1896.[37]

Initially some observers thought that the election of 1980, in which the Republican Party elected Reagan and gained control of the Senate, might have been a critical election. That turned out not to be the case. The Demo-cratic gains in the 1982 congressional elections indicated that no basic realignment in voter's allegiances had occurred. The Democratic Party re-mains the majority party among voters having a party preference. "Land-slide" elections are thus not necessarily critical elections.

Some citizens, through their intellectual and agitational activities, con-tribute new ideas and directions to policy process. Thus Rachel Carson, through *Silent Spring*, and Ralph Nader, through *Unsafe at Any Speed*, had a considerable impact on the policy of pesticide control and automobile safety, respectively. In an article published in *Foreign Affairs* in 1947, under the byline *X*, George Kennan outlined the policy of containment of the

Soviet Union. This became the basic approach of the United States in deal-ing with the Soviet Union in the international arena. Only in the last few years has the United States begun to develop new responses to the Soviets.

Others may substantially affect policy action through their political activism. Social Security legislation in the 1930s, for example, was cer-tainly affected by the activities of Dr. Francis Townsend, who advocated that every person over sixty should be paid a monthly pension of $200, and the large following he developed. In the 1960s, Reverend Martin Luther King, Jr. provided leadership for the civil rights movement and impetus for civil rights legislation. Fifteen years of effort by Howard A. Jarvis cul-minated in the adoption of Proposition 13 in California in 1977. Proposi-tion 13, adopted through the initiative process, provided for substantial re-duction in property taxes and touched off a "tax revolt" which produced similar actions in other states.

LEVELS OF POLITICS

Not all the participants in policymaking discussed above are involved in every policymaking or decision-making situation. Some matters arouse much attention and attract a wide range of participants. Others will be less visible or affect only a few people and will consequently stir little attention and participation. Professor Emmette S. Redford has identified three levels of policies based on the scope of participation normally characteristic of each and, to a lesser extent, the kind of issue involved: micropolitics, sub-system policies, and macropolitics.[38]

Micropolitics involves efforts by individuals, companies, and com-munities to secure favorable governmental action for themselves. Subsys-tem politics is focused on particular functional areas of activity, such as airline regulation or river and harbor improvements, and involves interre-lationships among congressional committees, administrative agencies (or bureaus), and interest groups. Macropolitics occurs when "the community at large and the leaders of government as a whole are brought into the discussion and determination of [public] policy."[39]

Micropolitics

Micropolitics often occurs when an individual seeks a favorable ruling from an administrative agency or a special bill offering an exemption from a requirement of the immigration laws, when a company seeks a favorable change in the tax code or a television broadcasting license, or when a community seeks a grant for the construction of an airport or opposes the location of a public housing project in its area. What is involved in each of these instances is the specific, differentiated, and intense interest of one or a few in a society of many individuals, companies, and communities. What is required or sought is a decision applicable to one or a few. Typically, only a few persons and officials will be involved in or even aware of such decision-making situations, however important they may be for those seeking action, and whatever the ultimate consequences of such decisions or a cluster of them may be.

In the short run at least, micropolitical decisions appear to be distributive and can be made without concern for limited resources. That is, such decisions appear to affect only those immediately concerned and can be made on the basis of mutual noninterference, with each seeking their own benefits (or subsidies) and not opposing or interfering with the efforts of others to do likewise. Benefits received by one individual or group do not appear to be at the expense of other individuals or groups.

The enactment of special tax provisions by Congress illustrates micropolitics. Almost every year Congress enacts a number of laws that make particular changes in the internal revenue code.[40] Their effect is to grant special treatment to particular groups or individuals and enable them not to pay taxes they otherwise would have to pay. A notorious example is the "Louis B. Mayer amendment," which was adopted in 1951 and saved the movie mogul about $2 million in income taxes by treating income he had received from his company at retirement as capital gains. Although written in the form of general legislation, its terms were such that it was assumed that the amendment covered only Mayer and one other person. Such legislation arouses little attention on its way through Congress and becomes law with most of the public completely unaware of its existence. Whether these special tax bills create "loopholes" or correct "inequities" depends upon one's perspective and whether one benefits from them.

As governmental programs become more numerous and extensive, as they provide more benefits for, or impose more requirements on, individuals, groups, and communities, both the opportunity and the incentive to engage in micropolitics increases. As this occurs, the likelihood of favoritism and unequal treatment for particular persons and groups increases.

Subsystem Politics

In what has become a frequently quoted passage, in 1939 political analyst Ernest S. Griffith called attention to the existence of political subsystems and the value of studying them:

> One cannot live in Washington for long without being conscious that it has whirlpools or centers of activity focusing on particular problems. . . . It is my opinion that ordinarily the relationship among these men—legislators, administrators, lobbyists, scholars—who are interested in a common problem is a much more real relationship than the relationship between congressmen generally or between administrators generally. In other words, he who would understand the prevailing pattern of our present governmental behavior, instead of studying the formal institutions or even generalizations of organs, important though all these things are, may possibly obtain a better picture of the way things really happen if he would study these "whirlpools" of special social interests and problems.[41]

Since Griffith wrote that, political scientists and others have devoted considerable attention to the examination of political subsystems (also variously called subgovernments, policy clusters, and policy coalitions).

For many years subsystems were usually described as iron triangles (or cozy little triangles, or triple alliances). An iron triangle involves a pattern of stable relationships among some congressional committees (or subcommittees), an administrative agency or two, and the relevant interest groups centered around a particular policy area.[42] All have a direct, material interest in the policy matters being treated. A classic iron triangle was focused on the area of rivers and harbors development activity. It comprised the Army Corps of Engineers (who still handle many civilian water projects), the congressional committees on public works, and the National Rivers and Harbors Congress, an interest group. This triangle, which was resistant to wider participation, dominated policy making on water projects. As with other triangles, the participants preferred policy to be made cooperatively and quietly.

The national government was often described as being heavily populated with iron triangles. Although these arrangements provided participants with continuing access and much influence on the content of policy, those who were excluded—policy experts (often within the academic community), groups adversely affected by their policies, and others—were very critical of them. They were charged with contributing to governmental fragmentation, causing a lack of policy coordination, and acting contrary to the public interest. Moreover, the governmental agencies involved were frequently alleged to have been captured by the dominant groups; for example, the Civil Aeronautics Board (now defunct) and the Interstate Commerce Commission were called the captives of the commercial airlines and railroads, respectively. Policy analysts had to be concerned with iron triangles because of their importance in the development of public policies, but analysts also tended to view them as a malign force.

The iron triangle concept recently came under attack by political scientist Hugh Heclo, who contended that it was "not so much wrong as it was disastrously incomplete."[43] The concept, he said, "suggests a stable set of participants coalesced to control fairly narrow public programs which are in the direct economic interest of each party to the alliances." Heclo's view was that other, larger sorts of arrangements also exist, which he referred to as "issue networks." He went on to explain that an issue network included a large number of participants who constantly moved into and out of the network, including public officials, interest-group representatives, political activists, and technical or policy experts from universities, research organizations, and elsewhere. Within these somewhat "cloud-like" or amorphous configurations, no one seemed to be in control of the policies and issues. So what does an issue network look like? I will let Heclo answer:

> It is difficult to say, precisely, for at any given time only one part of a network may be active, and through time the various connections may intensify or fade among the policy intermediaries and the executive and congressional bureaucracies. For example, there is no single health policy network but various sets of people knowledgeable and concerned about cost-control mechanisms, insurance techniques, nutritional programs, prepaid plans, and so on. At any one time these expert in designing a nationwide insurance system may seem to be operating in relative isolation, until it becomes clear that previous efforts to control costs have already created precedents that have to be accommodated in any new system, or that the issue of federal funding for abortions has laid land mines in the path of any workable plan.[44]

Many of those involved in a network will not have direct material interests at stake; rather, their ideas and beliefs concerning proper public policy will be the basis for their participation.

Political scientists have enthusiastically embraced the concept of issue networks, despite a dearth of empirical data on the actual presence and operation of networks. The political science literature is replete with references to networks and to how they have replaced iron triangles in the policy process. In reality, a lot of iron triangles probably survive, especially in the area of distributive policy.

It would seem, however, that there is no need to assume that only one kind of subsystem can exist at a time. (That was not Heclo's position.) Why not rather assume that subsystems take a variety of forms that can be arrayed along a continuum? At one pole we could put iron triangles, with their limited participation, resistance to external influences, and concern with material interests. At the other pole we could put the issue network with its amorphous nature, wide and changing participation, issue experts, and unclearness as to who is in control. Other forms of subsystems could be appropriately arrayed between the poles.[45]

What I call a *policy community* is more open and broader in participation than an iron triangle but less amorphous and more under identifiable control than an issue network. Thus the antitrust community includes primarily the Antitrust Division of the Department of Justice and the Federal Trade Commission, the House and Senate Judiciary committees (or their antitrust subcommittees), the relevant appropriations subcommittees, writers of books and journal articles on antitrust, the private antitrust bar, and the federal courts that rule on antitrust cases. This community has much impact on the nature and implementation of antitrust policy as long as important new legislation is not involved. Significant changes in antitrust policy can be achieved through variations in the interpretation and enforcement of existing laws by members of the antitrust community.

Subsystems, whatever their precise form and style, play an important role in policy development and implementation. It may be that issue networks are more important in emerging or unsettled areas of public policy, such as health care and the control of hazardous waste, while political communities or iron triangles are more common in more stable policy areas. The clear tendency has been for subsystems to become broader in scope. For example, the iron triangle focused on water projects has lost its dominance because of the movement of many environmental groups into the policy area. Life has become more complex for the Army Corps of Engineers.

Macropolitics

Some policy issues will attract enough attention or become sufficiently controversial as to be ripe for action in the macropolitical arena. Certain issues are "born" to be macropolitical, such as the escalation of the war in Vietnam, the 1981 air traffic controllers strike, President Reagan's proposal for a major reduction in personal income taxes, and aid to the Nicaraguan rebels. Because of their controversial nature and major consequences they attract wide interest and participation.

Many other issues may be moved from the subsystem to the macropolitical level by the action of public officials or other interested parties. Policy proposals developed within subsystems often require the approval of the larger political system. Then, because of their importance or magnitude, they attract extensive interest and participation. Such was the case with the Job Partnership Training Act and the 1988 legislation strengthening the Fair Housing Act. On the other hand, efforts by the Reagan administration to secure legislation from Congress that would have weakened some of the restrictions of the antitrust laws came to naught.

Some matters may begin their political lives at the micropolitical level and then escalate into macropolitical issues because of their symbolic, scandalous, or substantive characteristics. Consider the instance of the snail darter (a species of minnow), which was accorded protection under the Endangered Species Act [ESA] of 1973. Its designation as endangered by the U.S. Fish and Wildlife Service was a routine instance of policy implementation. What followed was not, as this summary reveals:

> The discovery of the snail darter in the Little Tennessee River in eastern Tennessee in August 1973, its subsequent listing as endangered in October 1975, and the designation of its critical habitat in April 1976 led to a major conflict with the Tennessee Valley Authority's Tellico project, a multipurpose water resource development project that was to provide economic development, hydroelectric, flood control, and recreation benefits. The conflict turned into litigation that went as high as the Supreme Court, resulting in front page headlines across the nation in mid-1978. The Supreme Court ruling that the ESA prohibited completion of the project led to amendments to the act that established an interagency panel to review projects for possible exemptions from the act's provisions. In January 1979, the panel ruled that the Tellico project should *not* be exempted because the project was "ill-conceived and uneconomic. . . ." However, by attaching a rider onto an omnibus public works appropriation bill, Tennessee congressmen were able to sneak through a provision that directed the TVA to complete the project. Citing political problems and the difficulty of vetoing a bill that would fund numerous other projects, President Carter signed the bill "with regret" in September 1979.[46]

Thus did the snail darter and the Endangered Species Act became the focus of a macropolitical struggle.

The central participants in macropolitics include the president, party and congressional leaders (who often overlap), and the executive departments. The communications media, who often drum up public attention on an issue, and a variety of group leaders are also usually deeply involved. This level of politics attracts the most attention in studies of policymaking because it is often quite visible and salient as well as sharply conflictual and sometimes sensational.

Decisions made in the macropolitical arena may differ considerably from what they would have been if made at one of the other levels. Among other things, when an issue moves, say, from the subsystem to the macropolitical arena, the conflict is expanded in scope. More players take part, and, as E. E. Schattschneider suggests, expanding the conflict often changes the nature of the settlement, that is, the policy decision.[47] Broad public interests are likely to receive fullest consideration at the macropolitical level.

A distinctive characteristic of macropolitics is presidential involvement. Whether the president more adequately represents national interests than does the Congress, as some contend, is open to debate. What is certainly true, however, is that those interests that are represented by the president enjoy an advantage in the macropolitical arena. Because of the centrality and visibility of his office, his capacity to formulate policy alternatives, and the resources he can draw upon in support of his proposals, the president can be the policy leader here if he so chooses. His actions will substantially affect the content and direction of public policies. Compare, for example, the differing impacts of the Johnson, Nixon, and Reagan administrations on antipoverty policy.

In the next chapter we will look at the emergence of public problems and the formation of policy proposals, especially as they involve the macropolitical arena.

Notes

1. Clyde Kluckhohn, *Mirror for Man* (Greenwich, Conn.: Fawcett, 1963), p. 24.
2. For an extended discussion of political culture, see Gabriel A. Almond and Sidney Verba, *The Civic Culture* (Boston: Little, Brown, 1965); and Donald J. Levine, *The Political Culture of the United States* (Boston: Little, Brown, 1972).
3. Daniel J. Elazar, *American Federalism: A View from the States* (New York: Harper & Row, 1984), chap. 4.
4. Robin M. Williams, Jr., *American Society*, 3d ed. (New York: Knopf, 1974), chap. 11.
5. Levine, *op. cit.*, pp. 210–211.
6. Karl W. Deutsch, *Politics and Government* (Boston: Houghton Mifflin, 1970), p. 207.
7. Almond and Verba, *op. cit.*, pp. 11–26.
8. Deutsch, *op. cit.*, p. 207.
9. Cf. E. E. Schattschneider, *The Semi-Sovereign People* (New York: Holt, Rinehart and Winston, 1960), chap. 1.
10. Thomas R. Dye, *Politics, Economics, and the Public Policy Outcomes in the Fifty States* (Chicago: Rand-McNally, 1966). Dye used the term "policy outcome" to designate what were described as policy outputs in Chapter 1.
11. *Ibid.*, p. 293.
12. Richard Dawson and James Robinson, "The Relation Between Public Policy and Some Structural and Environmental Variables in the American States," *Journal of Politics*, XXV (May, 1963), pp. 265–289.
13. *Ibid.*, p. 289.
14. Robert H. Salisbury, "The Analysis of Public Policy," in Austin Ranney (ed.), *Political Science and Public Policy* (Chicago: Markham, 1968), p. 164.
15. Ira Sharkansky and Richard I. Hofferbert, "Dimensions of State Policy," in Herbert Jacob and Kenneth N. Vines (eds.), *Politics in the American States*, 2d ed. (Boston: Little, Brown, 1972), esp. pp. 318–323.
16. *Ibid.*, p. 320.
17. *Ibid.*, p. 321. Cf. Robert L. Lineberry and Edmund P. Fowler, "Reformism

and Public Policies in American Cities," *American Political Science Review,* LXI (September, 1967), pp. 701–716.

18. Walter A. Rosenbaum, *Energy, Politics, and Public Policy,* 2d ed. (Washington, D.C.: CQ Press, 1987), p. 51.
19. *Congressional Quarterly Weekly Report,* Vol. 46 (November 19, 1988), p. 3327.
20. William M. Lunch, *The Nationalization of American Politics* (Berkeley: University of California Press, 1987), pp. 122–123.
21. Yehezkel Dror, *Public Policymaking Reexamined* (Scranton, Pa.: Chandler, 1968), p. 118.
22. Norman C. Thomas, *Rule 9: Politics, Administration, and Civil Rights* (New York: Random House, 1966), p. 6.
23. *Grove City College* v. *Bell,* 465 U.S. 555 (1984).
24. *Congressional Quarterly Weekly Report,* Vol. 46 (January 23, 1988), pp. 160–163; Vol. 46 (March 26, 1988), pp. 774–776.
25. Emmette S. Redford, *American Government and the Economy* (New York: Macmillan, 1965), pp. 53–54.
26. *Row* v. *Wade,* 410 U.S. 113 (1973).
27. *Webster* v. *Health Reproductive Services,* No. 88–605 (1989). Also *New York Times,* July 4, 1989, pp. A1, A8–A12.
28. This discussion is based on Kay Lehman Scholzman and John T. Tierney, *Organized Interests and American Democracy* (New York: Harper & Row, 1986), pp. 28–35.
29. Thomas J. Anton, *American Federalism and Public Policy* (New York: Random House, 1989), pp. 94–95: Schlozman and Tierney, *op. cit.,* pp. 55–57.
30. Harmon Zeigler and Hendrick van Dalen, "Interest Groups in the States," in Herbert Jacob and Kenneth N. Vines (eds.), *Politics in the American States,* 3d ed. (Boston: Little, Brown, 1976), pp. 94–95.
31. Gabriel A. Almond and G. Bingham Powell, Jr., *Comparative Politics: A Developmental Approach* (Boston: Little, Brown, 1966), p. 103.
32. Don Bonafede, "Issue Oriented Heritage Foundation Hitches Its Wagon to Reagan's Star," *National Journal,* Vol. 14 (March 20, 1982), pp. 502–507.
33. Martin Linsky, *Impact: How the Press Affects Federal Policymaking* (New York: Norton, 1986), pp. 114–115.
34. Steven B. Roberts, "A Most Important Man on Capitol Hill," *New York Times Magazine,* September 22, 1984, p. 48.
35. This discussion draws on Charles E. Lindblom, *The Policy-Making Process* (Englewood Cliffs, N.J.: Prentice Hall, 1968), p. 44.
36. *Ibid.,* p. 45.
37. For further discussion, see James R. Sundquist, *Dynamics of the Party System: Alignment and Realignment of Party Systems in the United States* (Washington: Brookings Institution, 1972); David W. Brady, "Critical Elections, Congressional Parties and Clusters of Policy Changes," *British Journal of Political Science,* VIII (January, 1978), pp. 79–99; and Warren E. Miller and J. Merrill Shanks, "Policy Directions and Presidential Leadership: Alternative Interpretations of the 1980 Presidential Election," *British Journal of Political Science,* XII (July, 1982), pp. 299–358.
38. Emmette S. Redford, *Democracy in Administrative State* (New York: Oxford University Press, 1969), p. 107.

39. *Ibid.*, p. 53.
40. Stanley S. Surrey, "The Congress and the Tax Lobbyist—How Special Tax Provisions Get Enacted," *Harvard Law Review*, LXX (May, 1957), pp. 1145–1182.
41. Ernest S. Griffith, *The Impasse of Democracy* (New York: Harrison-Hilton Books, 1938), p. 182.
42. The subsystem concept is discussed in J. Leiper Freeman, *The Political Process*, rev. ed. (New York: Random House, 1965).
43. Hugh Heclo, "Issue Networks and the Executive Establishment," in Anthony King (ed.), *The New American Political System* (Washington, D.C.: American Enterprise Institute, 1978), pp. 87–124.
44. *Ibid.*, p. 104.
45. For a similar, independently arrived at suggestion, see John Creighton Campbell with Mark A. Baskin, Frank R. Baumgartner, and Nina P. Halpern, "Afterword on Policy Communities: A Framework for Comparative Research," *Governance: An International Journal of Policy and Administration*, II (January, 1989), pp. 86–94.
46. Steven Lewis Yaffee, *Prohibitive Policy: Implementing the Federal Endangered Species Act* (Cambridge, Mass.: MIT Press, 1982), p. 165.
47. Schattschneider, *op. cit.*, chap. 4.

3

POLICY FORMATION

Helping to set the policy agenda: demonstrators against military spending.

I n this chapter we will begin to analyze the policy-making process as a
sequence of functional activities. Three aspects of policy formation are
discussed: the nature of public problems, agendas and the process of
agenda setting, and the formulation of policies to deal with problems. Before going on, the meaning of a couple of terms needs to be clarified. *Policy
formation* denotes the total process of creating or forming a policy. *Policy
formulation*, in contrast, refers more narrowly to the development of a proposed course of action for handling a problem.

The legislature will be the primary institutional focus of the chapter,
although the other branches of government are also involved in agenda
setting and the formulation of policy proposals. The U.S. Supreme Court,
for instance, sets its own agenda when it determines which of the cases
appealed to it will actually be heard and decided. Again, much policy (or
rule) formulation occurs in the context of the administrative process, as
agencies exercise their discretion to make rules.

It should be kept in mind that problem definition, agenda setting, and
proposal formulation, together with policy adoption, which is the subject of
the next chapter, are functional categories. Although they can be readily
separated for purposes of analysis, in actuality they frequently are interrelated and smudged together. For instance, those wanting action on a
problem may try to define it broadly, as affecting large numbers of people
to help ensure it gets on a legislative agenda. Again, those formulating a
policy proposal will often be at least partly guided in their efforts by the
need to win support for the adoption of their proposal. Particular provisions
may be included, modified, or excluded for this purpose.

POLICY PROBLEMS

Studies of policy formation often devote little if any attention to the nature
and definition of public problems. Instead, problems are taken as "givens,"
and analysis moves on from there. Yet, if policy study does not consider the
characteristics and dimensions of the problems that stimulate government
action, it is less than complete. It is important to know why some problems
are acted on and others are neglected. Moreover, whether a problem is
foreign or domestic, a new item or the outgrowth of an existing policy,
limited or sweeping in scope, helps to determine the nature of the ensuing
policy-making process. The evaluation of a policy also requires information
on the substance and dimensions of the target problem in order to appraise
the policy's effectiveness.

For our purposes, a *policy problem* can be defined as a condition or situation that produces needs or dissatisfaction on the part of people for which relief or redress is sought. Such matters as dirty air, unwholesome food, the practice of abortion, the actions of a foreign government, and criminal trial procedures may become problems if they produce sufficient anxiety or dissatisfaction as to cause people to seek a remedy. For this to happen there must be some criterion or standard by which the condition is adjudged to be both unreasonable or unacceptable and appropriate for government to handle. If people view a condition as normal, inevitable, or their own responsibility then nothing will likely happen because it is not perceived as a problem. If, for instance, a group of people is afflicted with depressed economic conditions but accepts these conditions as inevitable or legitimate and neither does anything about them, nor somehow elicits actions by others in their behalf, then according to the stated definition, no problem exists. Conditions do not become public problems unless they are defined as such, then articulated by someone, and then brought to the attention of government.

Conditions can be defined as problems and redress can be sought by persons other than those directly affected.[1] In the mid-1960s, poverty was defined as a public problem and a War on Poverty declared more because of the actions of public officials and publicists than because of the actions of the poor themselves. Legislators are frequently looking for problems that they can mitigate or solve. Of course, there is always the possibility that a problem will be defined differently by those directly affected than by others. Indeed, problems are often defined differently by individuals and groups holding varying interests and values.

While many problems are persistent, how they are defined may change over time as society changes. We can use alcoholism (drunkenness) as an illustration. In the nineteenth century, drunkenness was viewed as a personal problem, as the product of one's evil, wicked, or sinful ways, and therefore as one's just desserts. In the early decades of the twentieth century, it became more common to view drunkenness as a social problem that arose from the response of some individuals to the social, family, and other pressures that played upon them. Counseling and other social services were seen as appropriate responses. More recently, alcoholism (no longer called drunkenness) has been defined as an illness (i.e., a pathological condition) requiring medical treatment, whatever its immediate social causes. This medical definition reduces the individual's responsibility and the stigma attached to the condition. Public policy, however, has not fully caught up with the modern definition, and most problem drinkers continue to be dealt with through the regular law enforcement processes.

The definition of problems is often a political process whose outcome will help determine appropriate solutions. Is access to public transportation for the physically handicapped a transportation problem or a civil rights problem? Identification as a transportation problem means that the handicapped should have adequate transportation available to them, whether through regular modes of transportation or any practical means, such as special van service. However, definition as a civil rights problem means that the handicapped should have equal access to regular transportation facilities, which might require installing elevators at subway stations, fitting buses with loading ramps for wheelchairs, and making other expensive modifications. After some waivering between the two alternatives, public policy moved toward the availability of transportation solution in the 1980s under the Reagan administration.[2]

Another aspect of problem definition is causation. A condition may be defined as a problem, but what causes the condition? For example, inflation, the upward movement of prices at an unacceptable rate as measured by the consumer price index, is a public problem. But what is its cause? Is it the underproduction of goods and services? Excess demand for goods and services (i.e., too many dollars chasing too few goods)? Too much money in circulation? To deal effectively with a problem one must treat its causes rather than its symptoms. For many problems, their underlying causes can be neither easily diagnosed nor evaluated. Identifying the causes of a problem, and getting agreement on them may be a hard task for policy makers. Defining the problem then becomes itself a problem.

The nature and scope of some public problems may be difficult to specify because of their diffuse or "invisible" nature. Because measurement may be quite imprecise, policy makers may be uncertain about the magnitude of the problem and in turn about effective solutions. In the 1980s, growing numbers of homeless people were sleeping in public and private shelters, the streets, under bridges, and in other places not suitable for human habitation. Estimates of the number of homeless people in the United States ranged from 250,000 to 3 million.[3] Anywhere from 10 to 47 percent of them were thought to be chronically mentally ill. These wide ranges reflect the difficulties involved in getting an accurate count of the homeless and their characteristics. The Stewart B. McKinney Homeless Assistance Act of 1987 called for better data collection on the homeless by the states while also expanding federal assistance for services to this group. Other problems that are difficult to measure include child abuse, learning disabilities among school children, illegal immigration, and the amount of income not reported on tax returns.

Our concern is not merely with problems but with *public* problems, which leads to the question, What characteristics or qualities make a problem public? Most people would agree that the fact that John Smith's car is out of gasoline is a private problem, however disturbing to Smith it might be, whereas the widespread shortage of gasoline in a community or region is perceived as a public problem. What distinguishes private problems from public problems? Essentially, public problems are those that have a broad effect, including consequences for persons not directly involved.[4] Problems that have a limited effect, being of concern only to one or a few persons who are directly involved, can normally be viewed as private. Admittedly, this is not a very sharp set of definitions. An illustration may help convey the notion. Assume that Mary Smith is unhappy with her tax burden under the existing laws. Acting on her own, she may seek a favorable administrative ruling to reduce the burden or try to induce her representative in Congress to sponsor an amendment to the tax laws that will lessen her tax obligation. Our imaginary citizen has a problem, but it is essentially private. As another alternative, she may seek to publicize her problem and enlist the support of others in a similar situation. A bill may be introduced in the legislature and a campaign for its passage launched, which in turn will likely draw opposition. Directly or indirectly, many people become involved or perceive themselves as being affected. A public problem now exists.

Many of the problems that are acted on by governments, it should be noted, are really private problems. To a large extent, the micropolitical level of politics discussed in Chapter 2 is focused on private problems. Private bills passed by Congress that apply only to the persons that are named deal with private problems, such as immigration difficulties. Much of the time of many members of Congress and their staffs is also devoted to "case work," the provision of assistance to individual constituents in their personal dealings with administrative agencies. This activity does help "humanize" government by making it more responsive to the problems of private citizens.

Before leaving this discussion of problems, it should be stressed that whether a given condition or situation is regarded as a problem depends not only on its objective dimensions but also, and quite importantly, upon how it is perceived. Take as an illustration the "farm problem" in the United States during the 1980s. Essentially, the problem was the "surplus" production of some farm commodities with the consequence that they would not move in the market at prices acceptable to farmers. The commodities were not "surplus" in the sense that no one anywhere would not use them at some price. For many nations in the world, such as some in northern Africa, such abundance would be viewed as a blessing rather than a "problem."

Again, whether there was in fact an "energy crisis" in the form of a shortage of fuel, especially oil and natural gas, in the 1970s and whether this was a public problem requiring governmental action depended upon its being defined and accepted as such. Moreover, *how* it was defined helped determine what was viewed as an appropriate response. The Nixon, Ford, and Carter administrations, acting on the belief that here was indeed a crisis, took various actions to alleviate it, including petroleum price controls, conservation measures, the creation of programs to develop new sources of energy, and eventually deregulation of oil and most natural gas prices. The Reagan administration, in sharp contrast, denied the existence of an energy crisis and moved to dismantle many of the programs set up in the 1970s. Critics of the administration contend it took a short-sighted view of the problem.

This leads to another question: Why are some matters, apart from their scope or impact on society, seen as public problems requiring governmental action while others are not? Some answers to this question are provided in the following discussion of the policy agenda and the process of agenda setting.

THE POLICY AGENDA

One constantly reads about demands being made by this group or that individual or some public official for action by some governmental body on some problem, whether it be rough streets or crime therein, the disintegration of the family, or waste and fraud in defense contracting. Of the thousands and thousands of demands made upon government, only a small portion will receive serious consideration by public policy makers. Those demands that policy makers choose or feel compelled to act on at a given time, or at least appear to be acting on, constitute the *policy agenda*,[5] which is thus distinguishable from political demands generally. It should also be distinguished from the term *political* (or *policy*) *priorities*, which designates a ranking of agenda items, with some matters being considered more urgent or pressing than others. Sometimes a problem will be referred to as a "crisis," as in "the savings and loan crisis," in an effort to secure higher agenda status and help ensure action.

To achieve agenda status, a public problem must be converted into an *issue*, or a matter requiring public attention (see Figure 3.1). As political scientist Robert Eyestone states, "An issue arises when a public with a problem seeks or demands governmental action, and there is public disagreement over the best solution to the problem."[6] A rising crime rate may be defined as a public problem, but disagreement over what if anything government should do about it creates an issue. In recent years important public issues have included such matters as prayers in public schools, illegal drug traffic, illegal immigration, research on and treatment of AIDS, and support of the "Contras" (rebels) in Nicaragua. Many stands may be taken or alternatives proposed on such issues, thereby demonstrating the inadequacy of the old saw that "there are two sides to every issue."

Of the number of policy agendas that can be identified in a political system, professors Roger W. Cobb and Charles D. Elder have specified two

FIGURE 3.1   A Model of the Political System

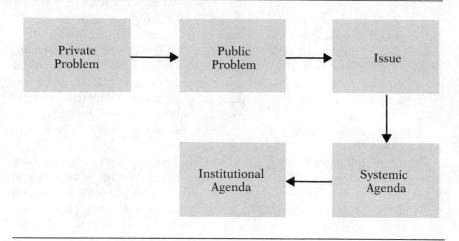

basic types: the systemic agenda and the institutional, or governmental, agenda. The *systemic agenda*, as they define it, "consists of all issues that are commonly perceived by members of the political community as meriting public attention and as involving matters within the legitimate jurisdiction of existing governmental authority."[7] A systemic agenda will exist for every national, state, and local political system. Some items may appear simultaneously on many systemic agendas, such as environmental protection, drug abuse, and crime in the streets. Other issues, such as the international trade deficit or the building of a new convention center in a given city, will appear only on the national and a local agenda, respectively.

The systemic agenda is essentially a discussion agenda. Most of the items on it will be general or abstract rather than specific or detailed in nature. Action on a problem requires that it be brought to the attention of a governmental body with authority to take appropriate measures. An *institutional* or *governmental agenda* consists of those problems to which legislators or public officials feel obliged to give serious and active attention. Only some of the issues that concern policy makers are likely to be widely discussed by the public. The public's cognizance of policy issues is often rather low, with awareness and information largely confined to a narrow segment of the population, that is, the "attentive public."

Because there are a variety of points at which policy decisions can be made, there are also several institutional agendas. At the national level one can identify legislative, executive, administrative, and judicial agendas. An institutional agenda is basically an action agenda and thus will be more specific and concrete than a systemic agenda. Whereas crime in the streets may be of systemic concern, Congress will be confronted with more fully developed proposals for action in this policy area, such as a program of financial aid to local law enforcement agencies or a proposal for the construction of additional prisons. Appearance on an institutional agenda does not guarantee that a topic will be acted upon, although it clearly increases its chances. Professor John W. Kingdon makes a useful distinction between subjects on the governmental (or institutional) agenda that are getting attention, and those on the "decision" agenda, which "are up for an active decision."[8]

Institutional agenda items can range from mandatory to discretionary in nature.[9] Congress can be used to illustrate this classification scheme. Much of its time is given to the consideration of matters which it is required to handle, including the reauthorization of public programs (such as the foreign aid program), consideration of the president's budget requests, and, for the Senate, the approval of treaties and presidential appointments. Other matters, notably proposals for new legislation, whether initiated by members themselves, pressure groups, or other sources, are discretionary. Choice exists as to whether they should be considered. Some matters, which technically are discretionary, may appear mandatory because of strong presidential pressure or the existence of a compelling crisis.

A policy agenda is not necessarily highly structured or organized. It would probably not be possible to secure complete agreement on the content of any agenda, at least if it is of some complexity, whether it is that of Congress or a city council. Clues to the content to the congressional agenda are provided by presidential messages, legislation singled out by party leaders for attention, issues discussed in the communications media, and the like. The inability to enumerate all the items on a policy agenda does not destroy the usefulness of the concept for policy study.

THE AGENDA-SETTING PROCESS

At any given time, many problems and issues will be competing for the attention of public officials, who will also have their own "pet" ideas to push. Only a portion of them will succeed in securing agenda status, however, because officials lack the time, resources, interest, information, or will to consider many of them. Agenda building is thus a competitive process, and a number of factors determine whether an issue gets on an agenda.

One factor is suggested by political scientist David B. Truman, who says that interest groups seek to maintain themselves in a state of reasonable equilibrium and that if anything threatens this condition, they react accordingly.

> When the equilibrium of a group (and the equilibrium of its participant individuals) is seriously disturbed, various kinds of behavior may ensue. If the disturbance is not too great, the group's leaders will make an effort to restore the previous balance. . . . This effort may immediately necessitate recourse to the government. Other behaviors may occur if the disturbance is serious to the point of disruption.[10]

Thus American steel producers and shoe manufacturers, seeing cheaper imported steel and shoes as contrary to a satisfactory price and profit situation, seek limitations on imports. Companies threatened by unfriendly take-overs have likewise sought governmental restrictions on corporate acquisitions. Moreover, when one group gets what it wants from government, this may cause a reaction by other groups, as in the case of organized labor's continued efforts to secure first the repeal of and then modifications in the restrictions imposed on them by the Taft-Hartley Act of 1947. Automobile manufacturers for years were similarly successful in delaying the imposition of fuel economy standards set by energy conservation legislation. Interest groups thus can place issues on an institutional agenda but by no means do they account for all issues achieving agenda status.

Political leadership is another important factor in agenda setting. Political leaders, whether motivated by considerations of political advantage, concern for the public interest, or an urge to enhance their political reputations, may seize upon particular problems, publicize them, and propose solutions. Of particular importance here is the president because of his prominent role as an agenda setter in American politics. Presidential legislative recommendations are almost automatically placed on the congressional agendas, as were Carter's proposals for energy legislation and economic deregulation, Reagan's tax reform proposals, and Bush's proposal for the rescue of failing savings and loan institutions.

In his study of presidential agenda setting, Professor Paul Light found that in selecting major domestic issues on which to advocate action, presidents are motivated by three primary considerations.[11] The first is electoral benefits, which are especially important during a president's first term. Certain issues are seen as critical to electoral success, and as vital in building and maintaining electoral coalitions. There is also a feeling that issues stressed during a campaign should be acted on. The second concern is historical achievement. Because history surrounds the office, and the Washington community and others constantly compare presidents, a president becomes concerned with greatness, with his place in history. Issues are singled out that they want to "mark" their administrations. The third consideration is good policy. Presidents enter office with ideological concerns and personal commitments that may dispose them to act on some matters even in the face of congressional hostility and bureaucratic resistance. The importance of some issues, moreover, makes such action imperative. As Light concludes, "Presidents do have notions of what constitutes good public policy."

Members of Congress also sometimes serve as agenda setters. In a study of agenda setting in the U.S. Senate, Professor Jack L. Walker concludes that there are some "activist legislators, motivated by a desire to promote social change, and anxious to gain reputations as reformers [who] constantly search for issues that might be transformed into new items on the Senate's discretionary agenda."[12] Senator Warren Magnuson (D, Washington), for example, was instrumental in putting consumer protection legislation on the congressional agenda in the 1970s, and programs to expand benefits for the elderly were long of concern to Representative Claude Pepper (D, Florida).

Government units also often serve as agenda setters for one another. Congress ensured that highway speed limits would appear on the agendas of state legislatures when, in 1974, it adopted the National Maximum Speed Law, providing that states would lose some of the federal highway funds if they did not reduce speed limits to 55 miles per hour. Supreme Court decisions have provided further impetus for congressional action.[13] Congress, for example, has tried (unsuccessfully) to overcome the Court's decision that prayers in public schools are unconstitutional by proposing a constitutional amendment. Several provisions have also been included in legislation to restrict the use of federal funds to pay for abortions as a consequence of the Court's decision in *Roe* v. *Wade* (see p. 59). More frequently Court decisions interpreting and applying legislation trigger congressional responses to overcome their effects.

Items may achieve agenda status and be acted upon as a result of some sort of crisis, natural disaster, or sensational event, such as a hurricane or an airplane disaster. This serves to dramatize an issue and attract wide attention, causing public officials to feel compelled to respond. There may be awareness, discussion, and continuing advocacy of action on some matter, but without broad interest being stirred, some sort of "triggering" even seems needed to push the matter onto a policy agenda for decision.[14] Thus the Soviet launching of the first Sputnik into orbit in 1957 helped push space research and exploration onto the policy agenda in the United States, notwithstanding the Eisenhower administration's initial professed lack of concern about this accomplishment. The killing of five school children and the wounding of several others in Stockton, California, in early 1989 by a deranged person wielding an assault rifle similarly sparked a public outcry against the sale of such weapons; President Bush subsequently acted to ban their importation.

Protest activity, which may include actual or threatened violence, is another means by which problems may be brought to the attention of policy makers and put on a policy agenda.[15] During the 1960s, such actions as the sit-in movement, the voters' rights march in Selma, Alabama (and the brutal reaction by the Selma police), and the 1963 march on Washington helped keep civil rights issues at the top of the national policy agenda. Riots in many northern cities were also contributory. In more recent years, groups concerned with women's rights have utilized various kinds of demonstrations in their efforts to move their concerns onto policy agendas, and with some success. Homosexuals have also taken to the streets to call attention to their problems.

Some problems or issues may attract the attention of the communications media and, through their reportage, either be converted into agenda items or, if already on an agenda, be given more salience. A classic example is the impact of the highly colored and often inaccurate reporting of the Pulitzer and Hearst newspapers in the 1890s in making Spain's treatment of its colonies, particularly Cuba, a major issue and thus doing much to cause the United States eventually to declare war on Spain.[16] More recently, the media have helped make nuclear safety a continuing concern by the extensive coverage of such major events as the melt-down at the Three-Mile Island nuclear power plant in Pennsylvania in 1979 and the explosion of a nuclear reactor at Chernobyl in the Soviet Ukraine in 1986 as well as many lesser nuclear safety incidents.

Whether the news media are motivated by a desire to "create" news, report all that is newsworthy, stimulate sales, or serve the public interest is not the concern here. Whatever their motives, as important opinion shapers they help structure policy agendas. While notions concerning proper news media operations and the compelling force of some events will limit somewhat the discretion the media have in selecting the events (the "news") they bring to the public's attention, they nonetheless do have much leeway.

Changes in statistical indicators may also produce awareness of problems and help move them onto agendas.[17] Governmental agencies and others collect data on many activities and events, such as consumer prices, the foreign-trade balance, highway deaths, disease rates, infant mortality rates, and industrial accident rates. Health care cost containment has been an important issue in Washington because the statistics indicate that health care costs are rising rapidly. Conversely, as the rate of increase in the consumer price index declined in the early 1980s, so did public concern about inflation. Although the Federal Reserve Board continued to worry about inflation (this reflects its policy orientation), most Washington officials were more concerned about other problems.

Political changes, including election results, changes in administrations, and shifts in the public mood, may make possible the movement onto an agenda of items that previously were unlikely candidates for inclusion.[18] Lyndon Johnson's landslide election in 1964, together with the election of favorable majorities in both houses of Congress, opened the doors for the enactment of a flood of social welfare legislation. These doors partly closed two years later when the voters, reacting negatively to the administration's ventures in Vietnam, turned many of Johnson's supporters out of office. Political change can also *reduce* the agenda opportunities for some items. The Reagan administration's preference for cutbacks in the government's role in society made major new spending and regulatory programs difficult to obtain, and few were proposed.

Although I have not presented all the alternatives, my purpose here has been to indicate a variety of ways in which problems can reach a policy agenda.[19] It should also be apparent that all public problems do not reach a policy agenda, because policy makers do not feel compelled to handle certain problems (or potential problems). To account for their inaction, the concept of *nondecisions* is a useful analytical and explanatory tool.

NONDECISIONS

Nondecision making has been defined by Professor Peter Bachrach and Morton S. Baratz as "a means by which demands for change in the existing allocation of benefits and privileges in the community can be suffocated before they are even voiced; or kept covert; or killed before they gain access to the relevant decision-making arena; or failing all these things, maimed or destroyed in the decision-implementing stage of the policy process."[20] There are various ways by which problems may be kept off a systemic or institutional agenda. At the local level, particularly, force may be utilized, as in the South during the 1950s and 1960s by various white groups to stifle black demands for equal rights. Another possibility is that prevailing values and beliefs—political culture—may also operate to deny agenda status to particular problems or policy alternatives. Public acceptance of the graduated income tax has operated to deny agenda status to demands of the radical right for its repeal. Our beliefs concerning private property and capitalism have kept the issue of railroad nationalization from ever becoming a real agenda item, even in the late nineteenth and early twentieth centuries, when railroad policy was being developed, except when particular facets of railroad operations, such as passenger service (witness Amtrak), become unprofitable for private enterprise.

A third possibility has been suggested by Professor E. E. Schattschneider. "The crucial problem in politics," he states, "is the management of conflict. No regime could endure that did not cope with this problem. All politics, all leadership, all organization involves the management of conflict. All conflict allocates space in the political universe. The consequences of conflict are so important that it is inconceivable that any regime would survive without making an attempt to shape the system." To survive, then, political leaders and organizations must prevent problems or issues that would threaten their existence from reaching the political arena (that is, from achieving agenda status). The kinds of problems that they resist will depend upon what kinds of leaders and organizations they are; whether, for example, they are conservative Republicans or independent commissions. They will in any case resist considering some problems, for, as Schattschneider contends, "all forms of political organization have a bias in favor of the exploitation of some kinds of conflicts and the suppression of others because *organization is the mobilization of bias*. Some issues are organized into politics while others are organized out."[21]

In the study of public policy making it is important to know why some problems are dealt with and others are neglected or suppressed. Recall that public policy is determined not only by what government does do but also by what it does not do. Take the situation of migratory farm workers, whose problems usually receive short shrift from the public officials. Why is this the case? What does an answer to this question tell us about who gets what and why from the policy process? Is the neglect of migrant workers at least partly due to nondecision making? Notwithstanding the somewhat imprecise nature of the concept of nondecision, it has utility for the analysis of the policy process.

Problems that may reach agendas may, of course, also disappear from agendas. Action may be taken on a problem, or a decision may be made not to act, not to have a law on a matter. Policymakers may then feel that the problem has been taken care of and turn their attention to other issues. In the late 1970s, for example, whether to impose charges on the commercial users of inland waterways, such as the Mississippi and Ohio rivers, was a hot issue.[22] However, once legislation imposing user charges was enacted, the issue quickly fell from sight. Other factors that may push items off an agenda include changes in the conditions that gave rise to a problem, the appearance of new and more pressing problems, or people may become accustomed to a condition and no longer label it as a problem (as in the instance of noise caused by the landings of Concorde airplanes around Washington, D.C.).

Policy analyst Anthony Downs has suggested that an "issue-attention cycle" causes problems to fade from public view.[23] The cycle, according to Downs, has five stages: (1) the preproblem stage; (2) alarmed discovery and euphoric enthusiasm for action on the problem; (3) realization of the high cost of significant progress on the issue; (4) gradual decline in the intensity of public interest in the problem; and (5) the postproblem stage, as the issue experiences "a twilight calm of lesser attention or spasmodic recurrences of interest," and may be left to a subsystem for further action. Downs further suggested that problems likely to go through this cycle all possessed in some degree three qualities: They mostly affected a numerical minority (for example, poverty); they involved social arrangements providing benefits to a majority or powerful minority (for example, the use of motor fuel taxes to finance public transit systems); and they lacked or no longer had exciting qualities (for example, NASA space shots). On the other hand, he thought that environmental protection was an issue likely not to fade because of its broad appeal. Time has validated his opinion.

TWO CASES IN AGENDA SETTING

To illustrate the agenda-setting process further, brief consideration will be given to how two problems of substantially different scope, content, and impact achieved agenda status. One is coal mine safety; the other is environmental pollution control.

Coal mining has long been a highly hazardous occupation marked by high rates of accidental injuries and deaths. Regulatory activity to protect miners was first undertaken by the state governments early in this century. However, because of dissatisfaction with the effectiveness of state regulation, federal regulation was sought by miners and their supporters, and was finally obtained with the Coal Mine Safety Act of 1952.

Enforcement of the act was handled by the Bureau of Mines in the Department of the Interior. The bureau, which also was concerned with promoting the mining industry, was often criticized as being too responsive to the interest of mine owners. Frequent accidents and deaths continued to occur in the coal mines. For nearly two decades nothing really effective was done to strengthen mine safety policy, even though the technology to improve safety conditions without a major decline in production was available. One reason for the inactivity was that underground coal mining is concentrated in a few areas of the country, such as West Virginia and southern Illinois, and most people are both relatively unaffected by and unaware of the problems of miners.

This changed, however, on November 20, 1968, with an explosion at the Consolidated Coal Company's No. 9 mine in Farmington, West Virginia. Seventy-nine miners were trapped below the surface, and all died before rescue workers could reach them. This tragedy, which was well reported by the national news media, focused the nation's attention on the miner's plight. This included not only explosions and other accidents but also black-lung disease, caused by the continued inhalation of coal dust. Demanding remedies, the miners staged protest meetings, engaged in wildcat strikes, and conducted other activities, including a march on the West Virginia state capitol. In March 1969 the West Virginia legislature enacted legislation providing compensation for victims of black-lung disease.

The miners and their leaders continued to press for national legislation as well, with a nationwide coal strike repeatedly being threatened if action was not forthcoming. President Nixon responded by sending Congress a special message, along with a draft bill, on coal mine safety. The bill was stronger than one proposed a year earlier, prior to the explosion, by President Johnson. In October 1969 the Senate passed a mine safety bill by a 73 to 0 vote, and a few weeks later the House did so by a 389 to 4 vote. It was signed into law by President Nixon. The federal Mine Safety and Health Act of 1969 provided for health standards and stronger safety standards for mines, as well as a black-lung compensation program. The Bureau of Mines continued to have responsibility for enforcing the health and safety standards.

Mine safety did not drop off the congressional agenda with the adoption of the new law, however, as is frequently the case in such matters. Some members of Congress continued to monitor its enforcement by the Bureau of Mines, which was criticized as being too close to the mining industry, too willing to trade safety for more production, and generally being lax in enforcing the law. In early 1973 several bills providing for transfer of the mine safety away from the Bureau of Mines were introduced in Congress. Before action could be taken on them, however, the Secretary of the Interior unexpectedly set up a new Mine Enforcement and Safety Administration (MESA) in the department to handle the mine safety program separately from the Bureau of Mines.[24] This was obviously intended to ward off congressional action.

Accidents and deaths continued to occur in the coal mines and some members of Congress transferred their unhappiness with the state of mine safety enforcement from the Bureau of Mines to MESA. The Department of the Interior was generally viewed as lax on health and safety matters. Discontent peaked in 1977, and mine safety returned to the active congressional agenda. Amendments to the federal Coal Mine Safety Act transferred mine safety enforcement from MESA to a new Mining Safety and Health Administration (MSHA) in the Department of Labor, which was viewed as a more hospitable locale for the program. The 1969 act was also revised in an effort to expedite the setting of health and safety standards and the imposition of penalties for their violation. Metal and nonmetallic mines were also put under the jurisdiction of MSHA. Strongly supported by organized labor, the 1977 legislation was strongly opposed by the coal mining industry.

Enforcement of the mine safety legislation, which was never stringent, waned in the 1980s under the Reagan administration.[25] A former coal mine operator was appointed to head MSHA, and revisions were made in mine safety regulations that were generally in accord with coal industry recommendations. Also, legislation was proposed by the administration that, it was said, would reduce the regulatory burdens on mine operators without reducing safety protection for workers. No action was taken on it in Congress.

In 1987, as a consequence of some multiple-death mine accidents and studies critical of mine safety enforcement, the issue once again hit the congressional agenda. Hearings were held by both House and Senate committees. At a hearing before the Senate Labor and Human Resources Committee, witnesses decried the laxity of enforcement and supported the creation of a new, independent agency to handle all mine-safety enforcement duties. The committee chair, Senator Orrin Hatch (R, Utah), and its ranking Democratic member, Senator Edward Kennedy (Massachusetts), joined in assailing MSHA for weakening safety standards and enforcement programs. No legislation resulted. The Reagan administration, however, did agree to hire about one hundred new mine inspectors, and a rule that had reduced criminal convictions of negligent operators was rescinded.[26]

The number of coal mine deaths has declined in recent years, in large part because the number of persons employed in underground mines has declined because a growing portion of the nation's coal is produced by surface (or strip) mining. Less hazardous for miners, surface mining is more hazardous for the environment, which is a problem that President Carter and Congress sought to deal with by the Surface Mining Control and Reclamation Act of 1977.

Environmental pollution is a long-standing feature in our society, but not until the 1960s did it become perceived as a major public problem. Where, for example, belching factory smokestacks were once regarded as a sign of progress, now they are generally viewed as problems requiring control. Both the national and state governments have enacted a variety of pollution-control legislation, and demands for additional, and stronger, legislation continue.

Several factors have contributed to making pollution control an important item on the policy agenda.[27] The affluence of American society contributes in several ways to the problem of pollution. As J. Clarence Davies explains:

> The increase in production has contributed to an intensification of the degree of actual pollution; the increase in the standard of living has permitted people the comparative luxury of being able to be concerned about this; and the availability of ample public and private resources has given the society sufficient funds and skilled manpower to provide the potential for dealing with the problem.

People who are compelled to be continually concerned with securing the necessities of life will probably have little time or inclination to worry about pollution. In the developing countries, one will note little concern for the problem. Indeed, it is probably not perceived as a problem. In an affluent society, on the other hand, the conditions of life contribute to concern over pollution. More leisure time leads to greater demands for recreational resources and aesthetic pleasures, while a high level of education enables people to understand better the nature and dangers of pollution. One can usefully regard pollution control as a "middle class issue," which helps ensure governmental attention to it.

Pollution control is an attractive public issue. It affects everyone, and a program that does something for everyone tends to be quite attractive politically. Moreover, it is difficult to oppose pollution control—except indirectly, by contending that pollution standards increase energy use and thus contribute to energy—because one cannot win many political allies by openly favoring dirty air and water. In addition, pollution control is often tied to public health, which is another popular concern. As the old song has it, "Everybody wants to go to heaven, but nobody wants to die."

Finally, when government acts on the pollution problem, it helps create a demand for additional action. The problem is publicized and given respectability, and the public learns that something can be done to alleviate the problem. Moreover, when agencies are established to administer pollution-control programs, they develop vested interests in drawing attention to the programs. This, in turn, may lead to the development of group support for the program, an institutionalization of concern, and a continuous demand for action.

The experience of the Environmental Protection Agency is a case in point. Because of strong political support for environmental protection both within Congress and among environmental groups, the Reagan administration had to back away from its effort in the early 1980s to reduce significantly the agency's pollution-control activities. In 1989 President Bush appointed a strong environmentalist to head the agency.

Environmental protection continued to occupy a prominent position on national systemic and institutional agendas throughout the 1980s. Acid rain and the "greenhouse effect" received much attention. In the same week in August 1988 both *Time* and *Newsweek* carried cover stories on the problem of ocean pollution.[28] The huge crude oil spill that occurred when an oil tanker ran aground in Alaska's Prince William Sound in March 1989 further focused public and official attention on the environment. Pollution control appears likely to remain on the policy agendas of all levels of government for years to come.

THE FORMULATION OF POLICY PROPOSALS

Policy formulation involves the development of pertinent and acceptable proposed courses of action for dealing with public problems. Several competing proposals for dealing with a given problem may be presented.

Policy formulation does not always culminate in a law, executive order, or administrative rule. Policy makers may decide not to take positive action on some problem, but instead decide to leave it alone, to let matters work themselves out. Or they may be unable to agree on what to do. For example, because Reagan administration officials were unable to agree on how to revise an executive order on affirmative action in hiring by governmental contractors, the existing order was left intact. In short, the fact that a public problem reaches a policy agenda does not mean that positive action will be taken or, if it is, that it will be soon in coming. Decades of complaints, recommendations, studies, and failed attempts preceded the enactment of legislation by Congress in 1988 to reform the nation's welfare system. Awareness of a problem does not guarantee positive governmental action, although unawareness or a lack of concern pretty much ensures inaction.

Who Is Involved?

In this discussion of who is involved in the development of policy proposals, attention will be focused primarily on the national level in the United States. In the twentieth century, the president, together with his chief aides and advisors in the Executive Office, has been the leading source of initiative in the formation of major policy proposals (at the state level, governors usually play the same role). In his annual State of the Union and budget addresses, and in special messages, the president lays out a comprehensive legislative program for Congress to act on.

The members of Congress and the public have come to expect the president to present policy recommendations to Congress for consideration. Moreover, the members of Congress have come to expect the chief executive to present them with draft bills embodying his recommendations. What the members of Congress want is "some real meat to digest," not merely some good ideas to consider. While this does not mean that Congress always acts positively on the president's proposals (which is far from the case), presidential recommendations do, among other things, help Congress set its agenda and indicate where the president stands on some major issues.

GOVERNMENTAL AGENCIES.   Many policy proposals are developed by officials—both career and appointed—in the administrative departments and agencies. Concerned with governmental programs in agriculture, health, welfare, law enforcement, foreign trade, and other areas, they become aware of policy problems and develop proposals to deal with them. These are then transmitted to the executive and, if in accord with the president's policies and programs, sent on to Congress. Agency officials, because of their specialization, expertise, and continued involvement in particular policy areas, are in a good position to engage in policy formulation.

Many agency proposals are designed to modify or strengthen existing laws. In the course of their administration loopholes, weaknesses, or omissions may have been identified. A large, complex piece of legislation, the Tax Reform Act of 1986 contained numerous technical errors when it was passed. This is typically the case with such legislation. Two years were required for Congress to pass "corrective" legislation: the Technical and Miscellaneous Tax Act of 1988. The reason for the delay lay not in correcting the technical errors, which were readily taken care of. Rather, problems arose in reaching agreement on substantive provisions, some raising revenue and others providing tax breaks for various individuals, companies, and groups, that Senators and Representatives wanted to put into the tax law. The need to correct the 1986 law provided them with a vehicle for additional tax action.

PRESIDENTIAL ORGANIZATIONS. Various temporary organizations, sometimes called "adhocracies," may be established by the president to study particular policy areas and to develop policy proposals.[29] These include presidential commissions, task forces, interagency committees, and other arrangements. With the exception of interagency committees, their memberships may include both legislative and executive officials as well as private citizens.

The President's Commission on Privatization, set up in 1987 by President Reagan, recommended that various services provided by the United States Postal Service and some federal prisons be turned over to private contractors. The commission also supported previous proposals by the administration to sell some governmental petroleum reserves and electric power marketing administrations. Advisory commissions of this sort are variously employed to develop policy proposals, to win support for those proposals through the endorsement of their usually prestigious members, or to create the appearance of government concern with some problem.

Presidential commissions, however, may not always produce the kind of report preferred by their appointer. The Brady Commission, for example, was appointed by the Reagan administration to investigate the stock market collapse of October 19, 1988, and to make recommendations for preventing future occurrences of this sort. The Commission, to the administration's surprise, recommended tighter governmental control, preferably by the Federal Reserve Board, of trading activities on the stock and futures markets. Finding such advice uncongenial, the administration appointed an interagency committee, composed of members from the various financial regulatory agencies, to review the recommendations of the Brady Commission and others. The interagency committee (formally, the White House Working Group on Financial Markets), composed of conservative administration officials, subsequently favored making only minimal changes in existing regulatory policies, which was in line with presidential preferences.[30]

President Lyndon Johnson made extensive use of task forces to develop legislative proposals, appointing over one hundred of these groups during his tenure.[31] He believed that task forces, composed of outstanding private citizens and top administration officials, would be more innovative and imaginative in developing proposals for new policies than would the national bureaucracy. He was quite pleased with the results. His successors in the 1970s and 1980s made little use of task forces, perhaps because they were less activist in their policy inclinations.

Another arrangement takes the form of a committee of executive officials and members of Congress appointed jointly by the president and legislative leaders to deal with a pressing problem. In 1987 such a committee worked out the Bipartisan Budget Agreement on budget deficit reduction. (This is discussed in Chapter 5.) This was a very informal arrangement. More formal and more publicized was the Budget Commission, composed of private citizens appointed by the House, Senate, and President Bush to develop a longer-term proposal for balancing the federal budget. The commission, however, was unable to agree on a plan, partly because it had to work in public sessions. Divided along party lines, it issued two reports. The Republican version supported President Bush's policies; the Democratic version said Bush's policies "lead nowhere." The impact of the commission was nil.

LEGISLATORS.   In the course of congressional hearings and investigations, through contacts with various administrative officials and interest-group representatives, and on the basis of their own interests and activities, legislators receive suggestions for action on problems and formulate proposed courses of action. The capacity of members of Congress to engage in policy formulation has been strengthened by the creation of the Office of Technology Assessment and the Congressional Budget Office, and the expansion of the activities of the Congressional Research Service (which is a part of the Library of Congress). Increased staff resources for both individual members and committees also have had a positive effect.

In some areas, Congress has done much of the policy formulation. Such is the case for air and water pollution control, where under the leadership of such individuals as Senator Edmund Muskie (D, Maine) and Representative Paul Rogers (D, Florida) in the 1960s and 1970s, Congress was willing to move more quickly and extensively than was the executive. This pattern has continued, even though policy leadership in this area has become more diffused. The Food Security Act of 1985, which continued income-support programs and production controls for various agricultural commodities, was also largely written in Congress, with the executive serving mostly as a source of restraint, trying to hold down the cost of the farm program. That the administration was not especially successful in this role is attested to by the fact that the costs of the farm program exceeded $20 billion in some years in the 1980s.

INTEREST GROUPS.   Interest groups play a major role in policy formation, often going to the legislature with specific proposals for legislation. Or they may also work with executive and legislative officials to develop and enact an officially proposed policy, perhaps with some modifications to suit their interests. Environmental, agricultural, and pesticide manufacturers were major players in the formulation of the legislation in 1988 that amended and reauthorized the Federal Insecticide, Fungicide, and Rodenticide Act (FIFRA). FIFRA is intended to protect the public against hazardous pesticides used on farm crops. Another example is the Israeli lobby, which consists of a number of groups, and has been very influential and successful in shaping American financial aid to Israel.

At the state level, interest groups often play an important role in the formulation of legislation, especially on complex and technical issues, because state legislators frequently lack the time and staff resources needed to cope with such matters. It is reported that the Illinois legislature customarily enacts legislation in the area of labor-management relations only after it has been agreed to by representatives of organized labor and industry.[32] Thus by custom private groups may become the actual formulators of policy.

Competing proposals for dealing with a given problem may come from all of these sources. Take the example of national health insurance in the early 1970s.[33] Under consideration off and on for decades, it seemed then like an idea whose time had finally come. The Nixon administration sent Congress a proposed National Health Insurance Partnership Act. It provided that employers should make approved health care plans available to their employees, that government-sponsored insurance would be available to low-income families with children who were not protected by employment-based insurance, and that health services should be improved through health maintenance organizations. Senator Edward Kennedy and Representative Martha Griffiths (D, Michigan) developed and introduced a bill providing for a comprehensive national health insurance system that would be financed partly by taxes on employers and beneficiaries, and partly by general revenue funds. The American Medical Association, long a strong opponent of national health insurance, proposed a Health Care Insurance Act. Referred to as "Medicredit," it provided for tax credits for the purchase of private health insurance along with federally subsidized health insurance for low-income people. The Health Insurance Association of America, an insurance company interest group, favored a national Health Care Act creating an insurance system in which costs would be met by employer and employee contributions; the poor would be covered by government-subsidized, state-sponsored programs. There were also other proposals in the arena.

Policy makers were thus not confronted simply with a choice between a governmental health insurance program and no program at all. Rather, private and official actors had developed a variety of proposals reflecting their interests and concerns that competed for acceptance. No proposal was adopted, however, because budgetary constraints developed which closed off the opportunity for policy innovation in the national health insurance policy area. Consequently, viewed as something the nation could not afford, national health insurance dropped off of the policy agenda. No further major action occurred in this area until 1988, when legislation to protect Medicare recipients against the costs of catastrophic (long-term or severe) illnesses was passed.

POLICY FORMULATION AS A TECHNICAL PROCESS

Policy formulation involves two markedly different sorts of activities. One is to decide generally what, if anything, should be done about a particular problem. Thus, in the above illustration there is the question, "What kind of national health insurance system should we have?" In other instances the questions may be: "What sorts of restrictions should be imposed on the practice of abortion?" or "What should be the minimum wage level and who should be covered by it?" Answers to these questions take the form of general principles or statements. Once such questions have been resolved, the second type of activity comes into play. Legislation or administrative rules must be drafted which, when adopted, will appropriately carry the agreed-upon principles or statements into effect. This is a technical and rather mundane but nevertheless highly important task. The way a bill is written and the specific provisions it contains can have a substantial effect on its administration and the actual content of public policy. Poor drafting can result in a statute like the one enacted by the Kansas legislature early in this century. It provided that when two trains met on the same track each should get off onto a siding until the other had passed.

An interesting illustration is provided by the National Defense Education Act of 1958, enacted after the launching of the Soviet Sputnik and intended to help the United States "catch up with the Russians" in scientific and engineering education. A provision in the act that stated that students receiving graduate fellowship assistance had to sign a noncommunist affidavit, or "loyalty oath," produced a great deal of controversy. Liberals criticized the oath requirement as an affront to the patriotism of students and as unnecessary, among other things. Conservatives defended it as a necessary means of preventing financial aid from going to communists (who were then much out of favor in the U.S.) and wondered why any loyal American would balk at signing such an oath. Some universities announced they would not participate in the fellowship program if the oath requirement was retained. Apparently few, if any, graduate students, practical souls that they are, who qualified for fellowships declined to sign the oath and give up the money. Eventually, the oath was replaced by a milder and more acceptable "loyalty affirmation." Symbolic language *is* important.

Despite the controversy sparked by the oath requirement, there had been no discussion of it either in the committee hearings or during the floor debates on the act. No one had advocated its inclusion. How, then, did it find its way into the law? The answer to this question is not very dramatic, but such is the case with answers to many public policy questions. The person drafting the formal language of the act copied some of its fellowship provisions from a 1950 statute; one of these provisions (it can be called "boilerplate") was the loyalty oath requirement. It had caused no dispute under the earlier law. But when it was discovered in the 1958 act, the fun began. One moral that can be drawn from the story is that it is easier often to get a provision into a law than it is later to remove it.

The writing of laws and rules has to be carefully done because, as soon as they go into effect, people will begin looking for loopholes or trying to bend the meaning of their language to their advantage. Clarity in phrasing and intent also may help protect laws and rules against unfavorable judicial interpretation and provide clear guidance to those assigned their implementation. Congress and most of the state legislatures now have bill-drafting services to assist them in writing legislation.

FORMULATING POLICY: THE ECONOMIC RECOVERY TAX ACT

The Economic Recovery Tax Act of 1981 was a central part of the Reagan administration's program to control inflation and reduce the size of the national government. Other parts of the Reagan program included the reduction of domestic expenditures, a monetary policy featuring gradual growth in the money supply, and economic regulatory reform. In this account our attention will be on the administration's 1981 tax cut, its roots, and the process by which it evolved and won adoption.

During his campaign for the Republican presidential nomination in the early months of 1980, Ronald Reagan became committed to the theory known as supply-side economics. Essentially, this theory held that many of the economic problems confronting the American people were the product of high income tax rates that reduced the incentive of people to work, save, and invest. Significant tax reduction was necessary to unleash the productive capacity of the economy. Supply-side economics thus stood in contrast to traditional Keynesian economics with its focus on influencing aggregate demand for goods and services.

A prominent feature of the supply-side strategy was the Kemp-Roth tax cut proposal, which was named after two of its leading advocates: Representative Jack Kemp (R, New York) and Senator William Roth (R, Delaware). The Kemp-Roth proposal, which had first been introduced in Congress in 1977, called for a 30 percent reduction in marginal income tax rates (the rate a person pays on the last dollar of income taxed) spread over a three-year period. The proposal attracted support from conservatives but until 1980, it never really came close to enactment by Congress. Support of the Kemp-Roth proposal by Reagan, however, resulted in its being written into the 1980 Republican Party platform.

In February 1981, a few weeks after taking office, President Reagan unveiled the tax reduction legislation which had been quickly put together by a few top administration officials. The administration's tax bill had two main features: (1) a 10 percent cut in income tax rates to take effect on July 1, 1981, with additional 10 percent cuts on July 1 of each of the two succeeding years; and (2) liberalized depreciation allowances for business investment, which permitted depreciation for tax purposes of vehicles over a three-year period, machinery and equipment over five years, and buildings over ten years. This was known as the "10-5-3" proposal. That the administration's tax proposal was based on supply-side economics and the Kemp-Roth proposal is quite evident.

Although there was pressure from various interest groups and congressional sources for other tax changes, these were resisted by the administration, which wanted to secure quick passage of its "clean" bill. Once that was done, the administration promised to introduce a second tax bill that might incorporate such other tax changes as tuition tax credits, the lowering of inheritance taxes, and the indexing of income tax rates to reduce the "bracket creep" caused by inflation.

The President initially barred any compromises on his tax proposal. In the Senate, where the Republicans were in the majority, there was never much doubt that his basic tax proposal would pass. However, the Senate has traditionally added special provisions called "sweeteners" to tax bills and there was ample interest in doing this. In the House, which had a Democratic majority, the administration needed to pick up some Democratic votes in order to put together a majority for its bill. Indeed, the Democratic leadership in the House disliked Reagan's approach to tax reduction, charging that the president's bill favored the wealthy and would result in large budget deficits.

The task of preparing a Democratic alternative to the Reagan tax proposal fell to Representative Dan Rostenkowski (D, Illinois), Chairman of the House Ways and Means Committee, and the committee's Democratic majority. They developed a proposal that included a 15 percent cut in income taxes spread over two years, with the cuts focused on low- and middle-income persons, increased business depreciations (but less than in the administration's proposal), and other changes in taxation. Generally, their proposal provided greater tax relief for individuals than for businesses.

In May, the administration sought to work out a compromise with Rostenkowski because it was uncertain that its "clean" bill could pass. Rostenkowski, however, was unable to get authorization to bargain from the Ways and Means Democrats. The administration, which was impatient to secure action on taxation, then turned its attention to the conservative Democrats (the "Boll Weevils") in the House. In fact, some White House aides had been talking with the Boll Weevils at the same time that other officials were dealing with Rostenkowski.

To win the support of the conservative Democrats, the administration offered to include some tax cuts in its proposal that had been targeted for the second bill. Examples included tax breaks for small oil and gas royalty holders, lower inheritance taxation, and savings incentives. Also, the income tax cut was scaled back to 25 percent, and business depreciation was reduced somewhat. Business groups remained unenthusiastic about the proposal, so a few days later the administration added some more special tax advantages for business.

In the meantime, the Democratic majority on the Ways and Means Committee had continued working on its alternative, which they hoped would defeat the administration proposal when the legislation reached the House floor. In mid-July, by an 18-to-17 vote, the Democratic majority approved a provision reducing the windfall profits tax on oil, which had been adopted in 1978. This represented an effort on their part to secure the support of the conservative Democrats, many of whom were from oil-producing states. Not to be outbid, the administration hastily revised its proposal. Added to it were more "sweeteners," including tax breaks for oil producers, increased charitable deductions, annual indexation of income tax rates, and relief from estate and gift taxes. Generally, these changes were intended to pick up a handful of swing votes. "Both Republicans and Democrats admitted that their bills were more products of a political bidding war than blueprints for sound economic policy."[34]

A couple of days before the House action on the tax legislation was scheduled to occur, President Reagan addressed the nation on television and urged the public to support his proposal. As a consequence, the members of Congress were inundated by a tidal wave of communications mostly supportive of the President's position. When the vote was taken in the House, the members voted 238 to 195 to adopt the Republican tax proposal rather than the Democratic alternative; 190 Republicans were joined by 48 conservative Democrats in support of the administration. (Only 1 Republican representative voted against the administration.)

The Senate completed its action on the administration's tax proposal on the same day as the House. Of the 118 amendments to the tax bill considered by the Senate, 80 were adopted. The special-interest nature of some of the amendments is illustrated by one that permitted taxpayers in southern Alabama to claim a $10 tax credit for every pecan tree planted to replace one destroyed by Hurricane Frederick in 1979. (This provision was later abandoned.) There were, however, only a few major differences between the House and Senate bills, such as the scope of tax breaks for oil producers and increases in tax credits for child care. Annual indexation of income tax rates, which appeared in both bills, was added at the insistence of Senator Robert Dole (R, Kansas), chairman of the Senate Finance Committee. According to one explanation, "Dole figured there was so much junk being put in the tax bill that there might as well be some real reform, too."[35]

The differences between the House and Senate tax bills were readily resolved by a conference committee. Signed into law by the President in mid-August, the Economic Recovery Tax Act of 1981 contained a three-year, 25 percent cut in income tax rates; indexation of tax rates after 1984; new business depreciation allowances; and an array of tax breaks on such items as oil production, estates and gifts, interest income, charitable contributions, deposits into retirement accounts, income from new tax-exempt savings certificates, foreign earned income, child care, and the income of two-earner married couples. It was estimated that the act would reduce federal tax revenues by amounts ranging from $39 billion in 1982 to $280–290 billion in 1987.[36]

In this case study, one sees how the policy formulation and adoption processes become interwoven in actuality. Formulation must be concerned not only with developing a preferred or satisfactory policy alternative but also with winning its approval. An affirmative decision is the payoff of the policy process; its price may be concession and compromise, taking less or more than what one would really prefer. In the instance of the Economic Recovery Tax Act, the Reagan administration's basic tax reduction proposal emerged relatively intact; however, to secure its adoption the administration had to agree to myriad amendments. To put it another way, the administration had to share the formulation function with Congress and a variety of interest groups. The result was tax legislation that reduced revenues substantially more than the administration had originally intended. In 1982 Congress, concerned about large prospective budget deficits, enacted legislation increasing taxes by $98 billion over a three-year period, in part by eliminating or reducing some of the 1981 tax cuts.

FORMULATING POLICY: SOCIAL SECURITY REFORM

Since its inception in 1935, the Social Security program has been greatly expanded in scope, coverage, and level of benefits. In 1982, over 35 million people received program benefits, and another 110 million paid payroll taxes to support the program. Although described as an "insurance" program, it is better viewed as a "pay-as-you-go program" under which money is taken from one generation to pay benefits to another generation. It has become a widely accepted, politically popular program.

In the early 1980s, however, in part because of unstable economic conditions, the Social Security program was in serious financial trouble. An effort to "fix" the program during the Carter administration failed because the assumptions made concerning future revenues and benefit payments were flawed. Benefits paid out were exceeding revenues, and the program's reserve funds were declining. It was obvious that action to strengthen the program and shore up its finances, in both the short and long run was needed.[37]

None of the obvious solutions drew broad support, although each had some supporters. The Democrats tended to favor tax increases, while the Republicans were inclined to go with benefit reductions. Opinion polls indicated that the public generally did not like either category of solutions. The political situation was further complicated by wide pressure-group participation, including the National Council of Senior Citizens, American Association of Retired People, AFL-CIO, Chamber of Commerce, Business Roundtable, and National Federation of Independent Business. Some group coalitions also were in action, such as, Save Our Security (SOS) and the Fund for Assuring an Independent Retirement (FAIR). The general stance of the various groups was to stoutly oppose options that they particularly disliked rather than to provide positive support for some alternative. This made public action to remedy the social security problem exceedingly difficult to achieve.

In the spring of 1981, David Stockman, director of the Office of Management and Budget, was desperately trying to reduce the Reagan administration's prospective large budget deficit. To this end, he put together a package of reductions in Social Security benefits, that would also have improved the financial condition of the program. Strong negative reaction to his proposal, which had the approval of President Reagan, was instantaneous, once it became public. Within a few days the Republican-controlled Senate passed a resolution condemning the proposal by a vote of 96 to 0. This marked the end of serious efforts to reform Social Security in 1981. Later in the year stopgap legislation was adopted to permit borrowing among the Social Security trust funds (for old-age benefits, Medicare, and disability benefits). This served to stave off the crisis until mid-1983.

In September 1981, in an effort to calm the acrimonious political conflict over Social Security, which included much partisan warfare, President Reagan secured the creation of a bipartisan National Commission on Social Security Reform. Five members each were appointed by the House, Senate, and the executive. The Commission began meeting in early 1982 but was not scheduled to report until after the congressional elections in November, so as to defuse the political implications of the issue.

In the meantime it had become apparent that bargaining between the President and Congress would be necessary to develop an adequate corrective for the Social Security crisis. Unless the negotiations were secret (which by law those of the commission could not be), however, interest-group pressures would likely make it politically impossible for them to reach an agreement. The device chosen to get around this problem was the "Gang of Seventeen": seventeen leaders, five Democrats and twelve Republicans, from the House, Senate, and executive branch. The two people who really mattered, though, were Reagan and the Democratic Speaker of the House, Thomas P. ("Tip") O'Neill. Their agreement was necessary if anything was to be accomplished.

The Gang of Seventeen held a number of meetings early in 1982. Convening in secret, they kept no records and all conversations were off the record. It was in essence an ad-hoc group operating outside the normal legislative and executive processes. Its efforts failed, however, because Reagan and O'Neill were unable to agree on how to handle the intertwined issues of tax increases and Social Security reform. An effort by the Senate Budget Committee to work out a short-term solution also failed.

The National Commission had held a number of meetings in 1982 and, right after the November elections, made a strong effort to reach agreement on a Social Security rescue plan. They did not succeed, however, again because Reagan and O'Neill refused to help them reach a settlement. Although the national commission was stalemated, it had helped delay any decision on the issue until after the elections, which both sides wanted.

In early 1983, another attempt to develop an acceptable proposal on Social Security was launched. Following quiet negotiations among some White House officials and members of Congress, yet another negotiating group—the "Gang of Nine"—was formed. It was composed of Stockman; White House aides James A. Baker III, Richard Darman, and Kenneth Duberstein; Robert Ball, a former Social Security Commissioner; Alan Greenspan, an economist and chairman of the National Commission; and three members of Congress—Representative Barber Conable (R, New York), Senator Dole, and Senator Daniel Moynihan (D, New York). Ball represented speaker O'Neill and Stockman represented President Reagan in the Gang of Nine's deliberations. Highly informed on Social Security matters, they were the crucial players in this quiet drama.

Meeting in secret, the Gang of Nine considered dozens of options. Over the course of a few days, differences were narrowed and compromises were made on various Social Security tax increases and benefit cuts. Most of the hard negotiating was done by Stockman and Ball on behalf of their principals (Reagan and O'Neill). In mid-January, agreement was reached on a Social Security package. Major components included increases in Social

Security taxes, reductions in cost-of-living adjustments (COLAs) for retirement benefits, extension of program coverage to all nonprofit employees and new federal employees, and taxation of the Social Security benefits of upper-income retirees. Some pain was inflicted on a lot of people. The package would raise an estimated $168 billion during the next few years and was expected to keep the Social Security program solvent well into the twenty-first century.

The Gang of Nine's proposal was then submitted to the National Commission for its approval, which was to build support for the package. Strong White House pressure was exerted on some of the Commission's Republican members to get their support, and consequently a favorable report came from the commission. The National Commission also unanimously recommended that the Congress "not alter the fundamental structure of the Social Security program or undermine its fundamental principles." This knocked radical reform (e.g., making Social Security voluntary) off of the agenda. Both Reagan and O'Neill agreed to support the package.

Legislation embodying the reform package was considered, passed by Congress, and signed into law by the President in April, 1983. Although a variety of minor changes and additions were made by Congress, the only major change was to increase the retirement age gradually from sixty-five to sixty-seven (by the year 2027).

The National Commission is sometimes credited with working out the agreement on the Social Security problem. In reality, it did not. Rather it served as a shield for secret negotiations, bargaining, and compromise among a few high-level officials. They, not the commission, were the actual policy formulators of the overall structure of Social Security reform. Congress in turn handled the more detached aspects of formulation and put the package into final legislative form.

Problem identification, agenda setting, and policy formulation constitute the predecision segment of the policy process in that they do not involve formal decisions on what will become public policy. They are important, however, because they help to determine which issues will be considered, which will be given further examination, and which will be abandoned. They thus involve political conflict and help set the terms for additional conflict. As E. E. Schattschneider comments,

> Political conflict is not like an inter-collegiate debate in which the opponents agree in advance on the definition of the issues. As a matter of fact, the definition of the alternatives is the supreme instrument of power.... He who determines what politics is about runs the country, because the definition of the alternatives is the choice of conflicts, and the choice of conflicts allocates power.[38]

In actuality it is often difficult if not impossible to separate policy formulation from policy adoption, which is the subject of the next chapter. Analytically, they are distinct functional activities that occur in the policy process. They do not, however, "have to be performed by separate individuals at different times in different institutions."[39] Those who formulate courses of action in most instances will be influenced by the need to win adoption of their proposals. Some provisions will be included, others excluded, and particular words and phrasing will be used in an attempt to build support for a proposed policy. Looking further ahead, the formulators may also be influenced by what they think may happen during the administration of the policy once adopted. Possible reactions may be anticipated and taken into account in an effort to ensure that the policy will accomplish its intended purposes. Such actions help tie together the different stages of the policy process.

Notes

1. David G. Smith, "Pragmatism and the Group Theory of Politics," *American Political Science Review*, LVIII (September, 1964), pp. 607–610.
2. Robert A. Katzmann, *Institutional Disability* (Washington, D.C.: Brookings Institution, 1986).
3. General Accounting Office, *Homeless Mentally Ill: Problems and Options in Estimating Numbers and Trends* (Washington, D.C.: General Accounting Office, 1988).
4. See John Dewey, *The Public and Its Problems* (Denver: Swallow, 1927), pp. 12, 15–16.
5. Cf. Layme Hoppe, "Agenda-Setting Strategies: The Case of Pollution Problems." Unpublished paper presented at the annual meeting of the American Political Science Association (September, 1970).
6. Robert Eyestone, *From Social Issues to Public Policy* (New York: Wiley, 1978), p. 3.
7. Roger W. Cobb and Charles D. Elder, *Participation in American Politics: The Dynamics of Agenda-Building*, 2d ed. (Baltimore: Johns Hopkins University Press, 1983), p. 85.
8. John W. Kingdon, *Agendas, Alternatives, and Public Policies* (Boston: Little, Brown, 1984), p. 4.
9. See Jack L. Walker, "Setting the Agenda in the United States Senate: A Theory of Problem Selection," *The British Journal of Political Science*, VII (October, 1977), pp. 423–446.
10. David B. Truman, *The Governmental Process* (New York: Knopf, 1951), p. 30.
11. Paul Light, *The President's Agenda* (Baltimore: Johns Hopkins University Press, 1982), chap. 3. The quotation is on p. 67.
12. Walker, *op. cit.*, p. 431.

13. Beth M. Hensikin and Edward I. Sidlow, "The Supreme Court and the Congressional Agenda-Setting Process." Unpublished paper presented at the annual meeting of the Midwest Political Science Association (April, 1989).

14. Cf. Cobb and Elder, *op. cit.*, pp. 24–25.

15. See Michael Lipsky, "Protest as a Political Resource," *American Political Science Review*, LXII (December, 1968), pp. 1144–1158.

16. This is discussed in fascinating style in W. A. Swanberg, *Citizen Hearst* (New York: Scribner's, 1961), pp. 79–169.

17. Kingdon, *op. cit.*, pp. 95–99.

18. *Ibid.*, pp. 152–160.

19. Those wishing to pursue this topic further should consult the highly informative study by Cobb and Elder, *op. cit.*

20. Peter Bachrach and Morton S. Baratz, *Power and Poverty* (New York: Oxford University Press, 1970), p. 44.

21. E. E. Schattschneider, *The Semi-Sovereign People* (New York: Holt, Rinehart and Winston, 1960), p. 71.

22. T. R. Reid, *Congressional Odyssey: The Saga of a Senate Bill* (San Francisco: W. H. Freeman, 1980).

23. Anthony Downs, "Up and Down with Ecology: The Issue-Attention Cycle," *Public Interest*, XXXII (Summer, 1972), pp. 38–50.

24. *The New York Times*, May 8, 1973, p. 21.

25. Laurence E. Lynn, Jr., *Managing Public Policy* (Boston: Little, Brown, 1987), pp. 254–256.

26. *The New York Times*, March 12, 1987, p. 11; *The Wall Street Journal*, June 1, 1987, pp. 1, 10.

27. This discussion is based on J. Clarence Davies III, *The Politics of Pollution* (Indianapolis: Bobbs-Merrill, 1970). The quotation is on p. 21.

28. "Our Filthy Seas," *Time*, Vol. 132 (August 1, 1988), pp. 44–50; and "Don't Go Near the Water," *Newsweek*, Vol. 112 (August, 1988), pp. 42–47.

29. Francis E. Rourke and Paul R. Schulman, "Adhocracy in Policy Development." Unpublished paper presented at the annual meeting of the American Political Science Association (September, 1988).

30. *Congressional Quarterly Weekly Report*, Vol. 46 (February 6, 1988), pp. 243–245.

31. Emmette S. Redford and Richard T. McCulley, *White House Operations: The Johnson Presidency* (Austin: University of Texas Press, 1986), chap. 5.

32. Gilbert Y. Steiner and Samuel K. Gave, *Legislative Politics in Illinois* (Urbana: University of Illinois Press, 1960), p. 52.

33. See Anne R. Somers, *Health Care in Transition: Directions for the Future* (Chicago: Hospital Research and Educational Trust, 1971).

34. *Congressional Quarterly Weekly Report*, Vol. 39 (July 25, 1981), p. 1323.

35. Steven R. Weisman, "Reaganomics and the President's Men," *The New York Times Magazine* (October 24, 1982), p. 90.

36. John L. Palmer and Isabel V. Sawhill (eds.), *The Reagan Experiment* (Washington: The Urban Institute Press, 1982), pp. 111–115. For a partial summary of the 1981 act, see Joseph A. Pechman (ed.), *Setting National Priorities:*

The 1983 Budget (Washington: The Brookings Institution, 1982), pp. 251–262. See also *Congressional Quarterly Weekly Report*, Vol. 31 (August 8, 1981), pp. 1431–1438.

37. This account is based on an outstanding study by Paul Light, *Artful Work: The Politics of Social Security Reform* (New York: Random House, 1985). For a summary of the 1983 legislation see *Congressional Quarterly Weekly Report*, Vol. 41 (March 26, 1983), pp. 596–600.
38. Schattschneider, *op. cit.*, p. 68.
39. Charles O. Jones, *An Introduction to the Study of Public Policy* (Belmont, Calif.: Wadsworth, 1970), p. 53.

4

POLICY ADOPTION

The finishing touch: President Bush signing the natural-gas deregulation bill.

A policy decision involves action by some official person or body to adopt, modify, or reject a preferred policy alternative. In positive fashion it takes such forms as the enactment of legislation or the issuance of an executive order. It is helpful to recall the distinction made in Chapter 1 between policy decisions, which significantly affect the content of public policy, and routine decisions, which involve the day-to-day application of policy. Furthermore, a policy decision is usually the culmination of a variety of decisions, some routine and some not so routine, made during the operation of the policy process.

What is typically involved at the policy adoption stage is not selection from among a number of full-blown policy alternatives but rather action on a preferred policy alternative for which the proponents of action think they can win approval, even though it does not provide all that they might like. As the formulation process moves toward the decision state, some provisions will be rejected, others accepted, and still others modified; differences will be narrowed; bargains will be struck, until ultimately, in some instances, the policy decision will be only a formality. In other instances, the question will be in doubt until the votes are counted or the decision is announced.

Although private individuals and organizations also participate in making policy decisions, the formal authority rests with public officials: legislators, executives, administrators, judges. In democracies, the task of making policy decisions is most closely identified with the legislature, which is designed to represent the interests of the populace. One frequently hears that a majority of the legislature represents a majority of the people. Whatever its accuracy as a description of reality, such a contention does accord with our notion that the people should rule in a democracy. Policy decisions made by the legislature are usually accepted as legitimate, as being made in the proper way and hence binding on all concerned. Generally, decisions made by public officials are regarded as legitimate if the officials have legal authority to act and meet accepted standards in taking action.

Legitimacy is a difficult concept to define. It is not the same as legality, although legality can contribute to a belief in legitimacy, which focuses attention on the rightness or appropriateness of government and its actions. With respect to policy making, legitimacy involves both *how* something is done (i.e., whether proper procedures are used) and with *what* is being done. Some actions of government, even when within the legal or constitutional authority of officials, may not be regarded as legitimate because they depart too far from prevailing notions of what is acceptable. Thus many Americans never accepted the legitimacy of the Vietnam War. Other people do not accept the legitimacy of a constitutional right to privacy as a barrier to some governmental actions. Legitimacy is an important consideration in public support for both government and the policies that it adopts, and public officials must be cognizant of this. When legitimacy erodes, governments and their policies diminish in effectiveness.

There is much disagreement among political and social scientists over political decision making, including how to study it, how decisions are actually made, and what constitutes a decision. I shall make no attempt to resolve any of these controversies. What I will do, rather, is discuss some topics which will help the reader get a handle on decision making, including decision theories, criteria, and styles; the process of majority building (or decision making) in Congress; and presidential decision making. The chapter ends with a case study of the national regulation of natural gas prices to provide an integrated view of the process of policy adoption.

THEORIES OF DECISION MAKING

Decision making, as noted in Chapter 1, involves making a choice from among alternatives. Many highly formal, quantitative models of decision making exist, including linear programming, game theory, and the Monte Carlo method. These are often grouped under the rubric "decision sciences." There are also some very informal and nonrational ways to make decisions, including palmistry, dart throwing, and reflection on one's belly button. None of these genres of decision making will come under review here.

Three theories of decision making that emphasize the procedure and intellectual activities involved in making a decision will be presented: the rational-comprehensive theory, the incremental theory, and mixed scanning. To the extent they may describe how decisions are *actually* made by individuals and groups, they are empirical. Viewed as statements of how decisions *should* be made, they become normative. It is not always easy to separate these two qualities in decision making theories and studies, as we will discover.

The Rational-Comprehensive Theory

Perhaps the best-known theory of decision making is the *rational-comprehensive theory*. It draws considerably from the economists' view of how a rational person would make decisions as well as from theories of rational decision making developed by mathematicians, psychologists, and other social scientists. The rational-comprehensive theory usually includes the following elements:

1. The decision maker is confronted with a given problem that can be separated from other problems or at least considered meaningfully in comparison with them.
2. The goals, values, or objectives that guide the decision maker are clarified and ranked according to their importance.
3. The various alternatives for dealing with the problem are examined.
4. The consequences (costs and benefits, advantages and disadvantages) that would follow from the selection of each alternative are investigated.
5. Each alternative, and its attendant consequences, can be compared with the other alternatives.
6. The decision maker will choose that alternative, and its consequences, that maximizes the attainment of his or her goals, values, or objectives.

The result of this process is a rational decision, that is, one that most effectively achieves a given end.

The rational-comprehensive theory has had substantial criticism directed at it. Professor Charles Lindblom contends that decision makers are not faced with concrete, clearly defined problems. Rather, they have first of all to identify and formulate the problems on which they make decisions. For example, when prices are rising rapidly and people are saying "we must do something about the problem of inflation," what is the problem? Excessive demand? Inadequate production of goods and services? Administered prices by powerful corporations and unions? Inflationary psychology? Some combination of these? One does not, willy-nilly, attack inflation but the causes of inflation, and these may be difficult to determine. Defining the problem is, in short, often a major problem for the decision maker.

A second criticism holds that rational-comprehensive theory is unrealistic in the demands it makes on the decision maker. It assumes that he or she will have enough information on the alternatives for dealing with a problem, will be able to predict their consequences with some accuracy, and will be capable of making correct cost-benefit comparisons of the alternatives. A moment's reflection on the informational and intellectual resources needed for acting rationally on the problem of inflation posed above should indicate the barriers to rational action implied in these assumptions—lack of time, difficulty in collecting information and predicting the future, complexity of calculations. Even use of that modern miracle, the computer, cannot fully alleviate these problems. There is no need to overload the arguments, as some do, by talking of the need to consider all possible alternatives. Even a rational-comprehensive decision maker should be permitted to ignore the absurd and far-fetched.

The value aspect of the rational-comprehensive theory also receives some knocks. Thus, it is contended that the public decision maker is usually confronted with a situation of value conflict rather than value agreement, and that the conflicting values do not permit easy comparison or weighing. Moreover, the decision maker might confuse personal values with those of the public. In addition, the rationalistic assumption that facts and values can be readily separated does not hold up in practice. Some may support a dam on a stream as demonstrably necessary to control flooding while others may oppose it, preferring a free-flowing stream for aesthetic and ecological reasons. Recourse to the "facts" will not resolve such controversies.

There is also the problem of "sunk costs." Previous decisions and commitments, investments in existing policies and programs, may foreclose many alternatives from consideration on either a short- or a long-run basis. A decision to institute a system of socialized medicine represents a commitment to a particular mode of medical care that is not easily reversed or significantly altered in the future. An airport, once constructed, cannot be easily moved to the other side of town.

Finally, the rational-comprehensive model assumes the existence of a unitary decision maker. This condition cannot be met by legislative bodies, plural-headed agencies, or multiple-member courts.

The Incremental Theory

The *incremental theory* of decision making is presented as a decision theory that avoids many of the problems of the rational-comprehensive theory and, at the same time, is more descriptive of the way in which public officials actually make decisions.[1] Incremental decisions involve limited changes or additions to existing policies, such as a small percentage increase in an agency's budget or a modest tightening of eligibility requirements for student loans. Incrementalism can be summarized in the following manner:

1. The selection of goals or objectives and the empirical analysis of the action needed to attain them are closely intertwined with, rather than distinct from, one another.
2. The decision maker considers only some of the alternatives for dealing with a problem, which will differ only incrementally (i.e., marginally) from existing policies.
3. For each alternative, only a limited number of "important" consequences are evaluated.
4. The problem confronting the decision maker is continually redefined.

Incrementalism allows for countless ends-means and means-ends adjustments that have the effect of making the problem more manageable.

5. There is no single decision or "right" solution for a problem. The test of a good decision is that various analysts find themselves directly agreeing on it, without agreeing that the decision is the most appropriate means to an agreed objective.

6. Incremental decision making is essentially remedial and is geared more to the amelioration of present, concrete social imperfections than to the promotion of future social goals.[2]

Lindblom contends that incrementalism represents the typical decision-making process in pluralist societies such as the United States. Decisions and policies are the product of "give and take" and mutual consent among numerous participants ("partisans") in the decision process. Incrementalism is politically expedient because it is easier to reach agreement when the matters in dispute among various groups are only modifications of existing programs rather than policy issues of great magnitude or of an "all-or-nothing" character. Since decision makers operate under conditions of uncertainty with regard to the future consequences of their actions, incremental decisions reduce the risks and costs of uncertainty. Incrementalism is also realistic because it recognizes that decision makers lack the time, intelligence, and other resources needed to engage in comprehensive analysis of all alternative solutions to existing problems. Moreover, people are essentially pragmatic, seeking not always the single best way to deal with a problem but, more modestly, "something that will work." Incrementalism, in short, yields limited, practical, acceptable decisions.

Various criticisms have been directed at incrementalism. One is that it is too conservative, too focused on the existing order; hence, it is a barrier to innovation, which is often necessary for effective public policies. Another is that in crisis situations (such as the Cuban missile crisis or the 1981 air traffic controllers' strike), incrementalism provides no guidelines for handling the tasks of decision. Third, geared as it is to past actions and existing programs, and to limited changes in them, incrementalism may discourage the search for or use of other readily available alternatives. Fourth, incrementalism does *not* eliminate the need for theory in decision making, as some of its more enthusiastic advocates contend. For, unless changes in policy (increments) are to be made simply on a random or arbitrary basis, some theory (of causation, relationships, etc.) is needed to guide the action and to indicate what the likely effect of given changes will be. Notwithstanding reservations of these sorts, incrementalism has become a form of conventional wisdom.

Mixed Scanning

Sociologist Amitai Etzioni agrees with the criticism of the rational-comprehensive theory but also suggests there are some shortcomings in the incremental theory of decision making.[3] For instance, he says that decisions made by incrementalists would reflect the interests of the most powerful and organized interests in society, while the interests of the underprivileged and politically unorganized would be neglected. Great or fundamental decisions, such as a declaration of war, do not come within the ambit of incrementalism. Although limited in number, these fundamental decisions are highly significant and often provide the context for numerous incremental decisions.

Etzioni accordingly presents *mixed scanning* as an approach to decision making that takes into account both fundamental and incremental decisions and provides for "high-order, fundamental policy-making processes which set basic directions and . . . incremental processes which prepare for fundamental decisions and work them out after they have been reached." He offers the following illustration:

> Assume we are about to set up a worldwide weather observation system using weather satellites. The rationalistic approach would seek an exhaustive survey of weather conditions by using cameras capable of detailed observations and by scheduling reviews of the entire sky as often as possible. This would yield an avalanche of details, costly to analyze and likely to overwhelm our action capacities (e.g., "seeding" cloud formations that could develop into hurricanes or bring rain to arid areas). Incrementalism would focus on those areas in which similar patterns developed in the recent past and, perhaps, on a few nearby regions; it would thus ignore all formations which might deserve attention if they arose in unexpected areas.
>
> A mixed-scanning strategy would include elements of both approaches by employing two cameras: a broad-angle camera that would cover all parts of the sky but not in great detail, and a second one which would zero in on those areas revealed by the first camera to require a more in-depth examination. While mixed-scanning might miss areas in which only a detailed camera could reveal trouble, it is less likely than incrementalism to miss obvious trouble spots in unfamiliar areas.[4]

Mixed scanning permits decision makers to utilize both the rational-comprehensive and incremental theories in different situations. In some instances, incrementalism will be adequate; in others, a more thorough approach along rational-comprehensive lines will be needed. Mixed scanning also takes into account differing capacities of decision makers. Generally speaking, the greater the capacity of decision makers to mobilize power to implement their decisions, the more scanning they can realistically engage in, and the more encompassing the scanning, the more effective the decision making.

Mixed scanning is thus a kind of "compromise" approach that combines use of incrementalism and rationalism. It is not really clear from Etzioni's discussion, however, just how it would operate in practice. This is something on which the reader can ponder and speculate. Certainly, though, Etzioni does help alert us to the significant facts that decisions vary in their magnitude (e.g., scope and impact) and that different decision processes may be appropriate as the nature of decisions varies.

DECISION CRITERIA

Decision making can be studied either as an individual or as a collective process. In the first instance, the focus is on the criteria used by individuals in making choices. In the latter, the concern is with the processes by which majorities are built, or by which approval is otherwise gained, for specific decisions. Individual choices, of course, are usually made with some reference to what others involved in the decisional situation are likely to do.

An individual may be subject to a variety of influencing factors when deciding how to vote on or resolve a particular policy question. Which of these forces is most crucial, so far as her choice is concerned, is often hard to assess. Public officials frequently make statements explaining their decisions in the *Congressional Record,* constituency newsletters, speeches, press conferences, court opinions, memoirs, and elsewhere. The reasons they give for their decisions may be those that were really controlling or may be those that are thought to be acceptable to the public at large or to important constituents, while the actual bases for choice go unstated. Nonetheless, it is often possible, through careful observation and analysis, to determine which factors were operative in a given situation, if not necessarily to assign them specific weights. A number of criteria that may influence policy choice are discussed here. They include values, party affiliation, constituency interests, public opinion, deference, and decision rules. The concept of the public interest will be scrutinized in the following section.

Values

In our concern with the broader social and political forces that impinge on decision makers, there is a tendency to neglect their own values (or standards or preferences). These may be difficult to determine and impossible to isolate in many instances. Decision-making persons, however, are not simply pieces of clay to be molded by others. Rather, their values may be important or even determinative in shaping their behavior. Some decision makers may come under criticism if they insist too strenuously on the primacy of what they personally value. Here I will comment on five categories of values that may guide the behavior of decision makers: organizational, professional, personal, policy, and ideological.

ORGANIZATIONAL VALUES.   Decision makers, especially bureaucrats, may be influenced by organizational values. Organizations, such as administrative agencies, utilize many rewards and sanctions to induce their members to accept and act on the basis of organizationally determined values. To the extent this succeeds, an individual's decisions may be guided by such considerations as the desire to see the organization survive, to enhance or expand its programs, and to maintain its powers and prerogatives. Bureaucratic struggles between rival agencies, such as the Army Corps of Engineers and the Bureau of Reclamation in the water-resource policy, may stem from their desire to protect or expand their respective programs and activities, and a belief in their necessity and appropriateness.

PROFESSIONAL VALUES.   The professional values of agency personnel may be important. Professions tend to develop distinctive preferences as to how problems should be handled. Professionally trained people carry these preferences or values with them into organizations, some of which become dominated by particular professions. Such is the case with the Occupational Safety and Health Administration (OSHA). Dominated by industrial hygienists, OSHA's industrial health and safety rules reflect their preference for using engineering or design standards rather than performance standards to protect workers against hazards. Economists, with their preference for market solutions and efficiency held sway in the Federal Trade Commission during the 1980s. Consequently, the agency was disinclined to intervene in many merger and trade-practice cases.

PERSONAL VALUES.   Decision makers may also be guided by their personal values, or by the urge to protect or promote their own physical or financial well-being, reputation, or historical position. The politician who accepts a bribe to make a particular decision, such as the awarding of a license or contract, obviously has personal benefit in mind. On a different plane, the president who says that he is not going to be "the first president to lose a war" and thus acts accordingly is also being influenced by personal values, such as concern for his place in history. Personal values are important, but the rational-choice theorists go much too far when they try to explain the behavior of officials totally on the basis of self-interest. The location of public buildings is probably better explained by self-interest than is the adoption of civil rights policies.

POLICY VALUES.   Policy values are also significant. Neither the discussion to this point nor cynicism should lead us to assume that decision makers are influenced only by personal, professional, and organization considerations. Decision makers may well act on the basis of their perceptions of the public interest or their beliefs concerning what is proper, necessary, or morally correct public policy. Legislators may vote in favor of civil rights legislation because they believe that it is morally correct and that equality of opportunity is a desirable policy goal, notwithstanding that their vote may place them in political jeopardy. Studies of the Supreme Court also indicate that the justices are infleunced by policy values in deciding cases.

IDEOLOGICAL VALUES.   Finally, we come to ideological values. Ideologies are sets of coherent or logically related values and beliefs that present simplified pictures of the world and serve as guides to action for believers. In the Soviet Union, for instance, Marxist-Leninist ideology has served at least in part as a set of prescriptions for social and economic change. Although the Soviets have sometimes deviated from this body of beliefs, as in their use of economic incentives to increase production, Marxist-Leninist ideology still serves as a means of rationalizing and legitimizing policy actions by the regime. In the twentieth century, nationalism— the desire of a nation or people for autonomy and deep concern with their own characteristics, needs, and problems—has been an important factor shaping the actions of many nations, especially developing countries in Asia, Africa, and the Middle East.

During the Reagan years, conservative ideology and notably its intense variant known as "movement conservatism," influenced the actions of many Reagan administration members. Devout believers in individualism, minimal government, and the free market, they strongly supported deregulation, privatization, and reduced governmental spending. For movement conservatives, their ideology was both their beacon and their shepherd. For some, it was more important to be right, which meant to be true to their ideology, than to win on some legislative issue by compromising their principles. To them, "pragmatist" was a pejorative label, the American cultural preference for practicality notwithstanding.

Political Party Affiliation

Party loyalty is a significant decision-making criterion for most members of Congress, although it is difficult to separate party loyalty from such other considerations as leadership influence and ideological commitment. Relatively few votes on legislation in Congress meet the stringent "90 percent versus 90 percent" definition of a party vote, in which 90 percent or more of the Democrats are arrayed against 90 percent or more of the Republicans. In the nineteenth century, this type of party voting was at its peak during the McKinley era, when approximately 50 percent of the House votes fit the definition.[5] Since then, however, the parties have lost strength, and party voting has declined. In recent years only a handful of House roll-call votes have been party votes.

If, however, the measure of a party vote is relaxed to include situations in which a majority of one party opposes a majority of the other party, then in any given year during the 1970s and 1980s somewhere between one-third and one-half of the House and Senate roll-call votes fit the definition.[6] In comparison, it may be noted that most of the votes in the British House of Commons meet the "90 percent versus 90 percent" party vote standard. On many government proposals, formal votes, or divisions, are not taken. Although dissenting votes to party positions have increased since 1970, they usually involve only a handful of a party's members.[7]

Party affiliation does remain the best predictor of how members of Congress will vote on issues. If one knows the member's party affiliation, and the party positions on issues, and then uses party affiliation as the basis for predicting votes, he or she will probably be correct more often than when using any other single indicator. If the political parties in Congress are not strong, disciplined parties, neither are they unimportant in their impact on legislative decision making.

Party loyalties or attachments vary in importance among issue areas. Party conflict has developed most consistently on such matters as agricultural price supports, business regulation, labor, and social welfare. In the agricultural area, for example, Democrats have tended to favor high price supports and production controls, while Republicans have preferred lower price supports and fewer controls. Again, Democrats have been more inclined to support the development of new welfare programs, such as Medicare, and the expansion or increased funding of existing ones, such as public assistance, than have Republicans. In other issue areas, such as civil rights, veterans' benefits, public works, and foreign policy, it has often been difficult or impossible to delineate distinct and persistent party differences.

Constituency Interests

A bit of conventional wisdom in Congress holds that, when party interests and constituency interests conflict on some issue, members should "vote their constituency." It is, after all, the voters at home who hold the ultimate power to hire and fire. In acting for their interests, representatives may act as either a delegate, carrying out their instructions, or a trustee, exercising judgment in their behalf when voting on policy questions.[8] Of course, representatives may try to combine these two styles, acting as a delegate on some issues and as a trustee on others.

In some instances, the interests of constituents will be rather clear and strongly held, and representatives will act contrary to them at their own peril. In the past, for example, southern members of Congress were well aware of the strong opposition among their white constituents to civil rights legislation and voted accordingly. A legislator from a strong labor district will likewise probably have little doubt concerning the constituents' interests on minimum-wage and right-to-work legislation. On a great many issues, however, a representative will be hard put to determine what the voters want. Large portions of the electorate have little, if any, knowlege of most issues. How, then, do representatives measure which way the wind is blowing from each district if no air currents are moving? In such situations, legislators must make a decision on the basis of their own values or on other criteria, such as recommendations from party leaders or the chief executive.

Nonelected public officials, such as administrators, may also act as representatives. Agencies often have well-developed relationships with particular interest groups and strive to represent their interests in policy formation and administration. The Department of Agriculture is especially responsive to the interests of commercial farmers, while the Federal Maritime Commission has viewed itself as the representative of international shipping interests in the national administrative system. The decision and actions of the two agencies have reflected the interests of their constituents. Some commentators have contended that administrative agencies may in fact be more representative of particular interests in society than are elected officials.[9] Whatever the validity of this contention, it is clear that legislators are not the only officials influenced by the need or desire to act representatively in making decisions.

Public Opinion

Political scientists have devoted much time and effort to studying the formation, content, and change of public opinion on political issues. The more philosophically inclined have been concerned with what should be the role of public opinion in the governmental process. Our concern here is with the effect of public opinion on the actions of policy makers. Are the choices of policy makers shaped or determined by public opinion? Does public opinion serve as a decision criterion? It is well to proceed tentatively in answering such questions, bearing in mind Professor V. O. Key's comment that "to speak with precision of public opinion is a task not unlike coming to grips with the Holy Ghost."[10]

A useful way to approach the problem of the effect of public opinion on policy making is to distinguish between decisions that shape the broad direction, or thrust, of policy and the day-to-day, often routine decisions on specific aspects of policy. Public opinion is probably not a significant decision criterion in the second category. To draw on Key again, "Many, if not most, policy decisions by legislatures and by other authorities exercising broad discretion are made under circumstances in which extremely small proportions of the general public have any awareness of the particular issue, much less any understanding of the consequences of the decision."[11] The legislator deciding how to vote on a particular tax amendment or public-works bill, for example, will probably be unaffected in any direct sense by public opinion. Of course, he may try to anticipate the reaction of the public to such votes, but this will leave him with substantial latitude, given the lack of awareness mentioned above.

Nonetheless, the general boundaries and direction of public policy may be shaped by public opinion. Given existing public attitudes, such actions as the nationalization of the steel industry, the repeal of the Sherman Act, or a major revision of the Social Security program appear highly unlikely. Conversely, officials may come to believe that public opinion demands some kind of policy action, as was the case with labor-reform legislation in 1959 and tax-reduction legislation in 1981. These were generalized rather than specific demands, which left much discretion on details to Congress. In the area of foreign policy, public opinion appears to accord wide latitude to executive officials, as the conduct of American intervention in Vietnam during the 1960s clearly indicates. Ultimately, however, growing public opposition to the Vietnam war seems to have contributed to President Johnson's decision not to run for re-election in 1968 and to begin to "wind down" the war and withdraw.[12]

In summary, policy makers do not appear unaffected in their choices by public opinion. The relationship between public opinion and policy actions, however, is neither as simple nor as direct as was once assumed. But the elected public officials who totally ignore public opinion and do not include it among their decision criteria, should there be officials so foolish, are likely to find themselves out of luck at the polls.

Deference

Officials confronted with the task of making a decision may decide how to act by deferring to the judgment of others. The "others" to whom deference is given may or may not be hierarchical superiors. Administrative officials often do make decisions in accordance with the directives of department heads or chief executives. This is how we expect them to act, especially when the directives of superiors are clear in meaning, which, it must be added, they sometimes are not. Administrators may also defer to the suggestions or judgments of members of Congress, as Department of Agriculture officials did when receiving advice from Congressman Jamie Whitten (D, Mississippi), who chaired the House of Agricultural Appropriations Subcommittee and later the full Appropriations Committee. Because of his position and influence, Whitten was sometimes referred to as the "permanent Secretary of Agriculture."[13]

Members of Congress often have to vote on issues that are of little interest to them because they do not affect their constituents, on which they have little information, or that are highly complex in nature. On such matters, they often decide how to vote by seeking the advice of other legislators whose judgment they trust, whether party leaders, committee chairs, or policy experts. When members are unable to decide how to vote on the basis of their own analysis of an issue, deference to someone whose judgment they trust is a reasonably rational, low-information strategy for making decisions. Political scientist Donald R. Matthews argues that, because of the widespread practice of deference to policy experts, "few institutions provide more power to the exceptionally competent member than does the House of Representatives."[14]

Judges, too, make decisions by deference. For example, when they interpret a statute, in the course of either applying it to a particular case or determining its constitutionality, they often defer to the intent of the legislature.[15] Statutory language is often ambiguous and unclear. In trying to determine what the legislature intends by particular phrases such as "restraint of trade" or "all lawful means," they may refer to such materials as committee hearings and reports and floor debates on the law in question. In the course of debate on bills, legislators often strive to build a record of legislative intent to inform both courts and administration on their intended meaning. Those who argue that legislative debates are meaningless ignore this function of debate, among other things.

Decision Rules

Those confronted with the task of making many decisions often develop rules of thumb, or guidelines, to focus attention on particular facts and relationships and thereby both simplify and regularize the decision-making process. There is no set of decision rules common to all decision makers, although some may be widely utilized. What guidelines, if any, apply in a particular situation is a matter to be determined by empirical investigation. A few examples will be presented here to illustrate the concept.

The rule of *stare decisis* (in effect, "let the precedents stand") is often used by the judiciary in deciding cases. According to this decision rule or principle, current cases should be decided in the same way as similar cases were in the past. The use of precedents to guide decision making is by no means limited to the judiciary. Executives, administrators, and legislators also frequently make decisions on the basis of precedents. They are often urged to do so by those who would be affected by their actions, particularly if this will help maintain a desired status quo. Those adversely affected by existing precedents are likely to find them lacking in virtue and utility.

In the antitrust area, some *per se* rules have been developed. Certain actions, such as price fixing and market allocation, have been held to be *per se* (in effect, "as such") violations of the Sherman Act. If the action is found to exist, this is sufficient to prove violation, and no effort is made to inquire into the reasonableness or other possible justifications of the action. *Per se* rules thus add simplicity and certainty to antitrust decision making.

Professor Richard F. Fenno, Jr., in his study of a number of congressional committees, has found that each committee has some decision rules that help shape its decision-making activities. Thus, the House Appropriations Committee, seeking independence from the executive, has a "rule" that it should reduce executive budget requests, and in fact most requests are reduced. Again, the House Post Office and Civil Service Committee has a decision rule, in Fenno's words, "to support maximum pay increases and improvement in benefits for employee groups and to oppose all rate increases for mail users."[16] Fenno points out that every committee has decision rules, although some rules are easier to discover than others.

THE PUBLIC INTEREST

The task of government, it is often proclaimed, is to serve or promote the public interest. Statutes sometimes include the public interest as a guideline for agency action, as when the Federal Communications Commission is directed to license broadcasters for the "public interest, convenience, and necessity." In this section, I will discuss this rather elusive normative concept and its usefulness as a criterion for decision making.

Most people, I am certain, if asked whether public policy should be in accord with the public interest or with private interests (the latter could further be described as narrow, selfish, greedy, and the like, but I see no need to overload the argument), would opt for the former. Difficulty arises, however, when one is asked to define the public interest. Is it the interest of the majority? If so, how do we determine what policy the majority really wants? Is it the interest of consumers, who are a rather large group? Is it what people would want if they "thought clearly and acted rationally"? How do you define the public interest?

Many people, including most political scientists, would say that it is not possible to provide a universally accepted or objective definition of the concept, especially in substantive terms.[17] Some would contend that whatever results from the political struggle over policy issues is the public interest. If all groups and persons had an equal chance to engage in that struggle, which in fact they do not, this notion of the public interest might be more appealing. I, for one, do not care to define a multitude of tax loopholes or inaction that permits the wanton destruction of natural resources as in the public interest. (By making that statement I indicate a normative bias, which will be especially disturbing to those who hold that "one person's opinion is as good as another's.") Sometimes the public interest is depicted as a myth by which policy, however particularistic, can be rationalized as being in the general interest and hence made more publicly acceptable. This, of course, is attempted or done with regularity (just as scoundrels sometimes wrap themselves in the flag or cite scripture to justify their predations). Beyond that, however, I think that the concept can be given enough content to render it a useful general standard for decision making on public policy. When evaluating policy, we need to be able to state not only whether the policy is acomplishing its asserted objectives but also whether the objectives are worthy of accomplishment. In this latter regard, a standard of more noble quality than "it is (or is not) in *my* interest" seems needed.

The question now arises about how to determine the nature of the public interest. Professor Emmette S. Redford has suggested three approaches to this task.[18] One is to look at policy areas where there is much conflict among group interests, as in agriculture, labor relations, energy, and transportation. In some instances, the direct interests of one or another group may prevail and become accepted as the public interest. There is no reason to assume that private interests and the public interest must always be antithetical. For example, if it is in the private interest of medical doctors to prevent the practice of medicine by various "quacks," so it is in the public interest not to have unqualified people practicing medicine. (It would seem difficult to argue the contrary position reasonably.) However, in the struggle among private group interests, it may become apparent that others are indirectly involved and have interests that should be considered in policy making. These "public interests," while not represented by organized groups, may be responded to by decision makers and thus influence the outcome. In the conflict between labor and management over the terms and conditions of employment, it becomes apparent that the public has an interest in maintaining industrial peace, preventing disruptions of the flow of goods and services, and the like. The result has been the development of various procedures for the settlement of labor disputes. In a particular dispute, such as one involving the railroad industry, a public interest may clearly emerge along with those of the railroad companies and labor unions.

A second approach is to search for widely and continuously shared interests that, because of these characteristics, can be called public interests. Illustrative are the interests of people in such matters as world peace, education, clean air, the avoidance of severe inflation, and an adequate traffic control system. Here the public interest appears as public needs. Clearly, especially in large cities, there is a public interest in having a traffic control system to facilitate the safe, orderly, and convenient movement of pedestrians and vehicles. The fact that there are various alternatives for meeting this need can be taken to mean that more than one way exists to meet the public interest; it does not negate its existence. Nor does the concept, to be meaningful, need to be so precise as to indicate whether the traffic flow on a given street should be one-way or two-way. Must a concept, to be useful, always yield an answer to the most minute questions?

There is nothing very mystical in talking about the public interest as a widely shared interest. We speak, for example, of the shared interests of wheat farmers in higher wheat prices or of sport fishermen in an adequate fish-stocking program, and attribute much reality to such interests. The public interest differs only in its wider scope. There is no way to determine precisely at what point an interest is sufficiently widely shared as to become a public interest. Few interests, indeed, would be shared by everyone. The survival of the nation-state may be opposed by the advocate of world government; even at old-time western rustler lynchings there was at least one dissenter. Qualitative judgments are obviously called for in determining the existence of a public interest, as in many areas of political life and academic activity. They should be made with as much care and rigor as possible.

A third approach to determining the public interest is to look at the need for organization and procedure to represent and balance interests, to resolve issues, to effect compromise in policy formation, and to carry public policy into effect. There is, in short, a public interest in fair, orderly, and effective government. The focus here is on process rather than policy content. As the noted columnist Walter Lippmann once wrote,

> The public is interested in law, not in the laws; in the method of law, not in the substance; in the sanctity of contract, not in a particular contract; in understanding based on custom, not in this custom or that. It is concerned in these things to the end that men in their active affairs shall find a *modus vivendi;* its interest is in the workable rule which will define and predict the behavior of men so that they can make their adjustments.[19]

Although the public is obviously interested in particular laws as well as *the* law, Lippmann's statement well points up the concern with adequate process. How things are done, moreover, often affects the attitudes of the public concerning their acceptability.

The public interest is thus diverse in nature and must be searched for in various ways. While it probably cannot be converted into a precise set of guidelines to inform the action of decision makers, neither can it fairly be described as merely a myth. It directs attention beyond the more immediate toward broader, more universal interests. It also directs attention toward unorganized and unarticulated interests that otherwise may be ignored in both the development and evaluation of policy. It is an ideal, like justice and equality of opportunity, to which all can aspire.

STYLES OF DECISION MAKING

Most policy decisions of any magnitude are made by coalitions, which often take the form of numerical majorities, whether one's attention is on Congress, the Michigan State Legislature, the Oakland City Council, or the Danish Folketing. Even when a numerical majority is not officially required, the support (or consent, which is much the same thing) of others is needed to ensure that the decision is implemented and compliance is achieved. The president, for example, is often vested with the final authority to make decisions, as on budget recommendations to Congress and tariff reductions. However, he will need to gain the cooperation or support of other officials if his decisions are to be effective. As political scientist Richard E. Neustadt, an astute observer of the presidency, has remarked, "Underneath our images of Presidents-in-boots, astride decisions, are the half-observed realities of Presidents-in-sneakers, stirrups in hand, trying to induce particular department heads, or Congressmen or Senators, to climb aboard."[20] President Kennedy sometimes told friends who offered policy suggestions or criticism, "Well, I agree with you, but I'm not sure the government will."[21] These comments point up the coalitional nature of much presidential decision making and the President's need to induce others to go along if he is to be successful.

Although coalition building is necessary in all democratic legislative bodies, it is especially notable in multiparty legislatures. This is well illustrated by the Danish Folketing, whose 179 seats are divided among nine or ten parties, none of which holds close to a majority of seats. To take office, a Danish prime minister must put together a majority coalition, which involves considerable negotiation and bargaining. Once in office the prime minister, in taking policy actions, must always be concerned with holding the coalition together, lest he lose his majority and thus the power to govern.

In this section our focus will shift from individuals' decision making to decision making as a social or collective process. Three styles of collective decision making will be examined: bargaining, persuasion, and command. Each involves action to reach agreement and induce others to comply.

Bargaining

The most common style of decision making in the American political system is bargaining. Bargaining can be defined as a process in which two or more persons in positions of power or authority adjust their at least partially inconsistent goals in order to formulate a course of action that is acceptable but not necessarily ideal to the participants. In short, bargaining involves negotiation, give-and-take, and compromise in order to reach a mutually acceptable position. In the private realm, it is epitomized in collective bargaining over the terms of work by union leaders and management officials. For bargaining to occur, the bargainers must be willing to negotiate, they must have something to negotiate about, and each must have something (i.e., resources) that others want or need.

Two factors seem especially important in making bargaining the dominant mode of decision making in our society. One is social pluralism, or the presence of a variety of partially autonomous groups such as labor unions, business organizations, professional associations, farm organizations, environmental groups, sportsmen's clubs, and civil rights groups. Although partially autonomous, they are also interdependent and "must bargain with one another for protection and advantage."[22] The second factor is the use of such constitutional practices as federalism, the separation of powers, and bicameral legislatures, which serve to fragment and disperse political power among many decision points. Major policy decisions at the national level often require the approval of all branches of government plus acceptance by state or local governments and affected private groups. Such is the case with many current federal aid to education and environmental pollution-control policies.

Bargaining may be either explicit or implicit in nature. When bargaining is explicit, the bargainers (group leaders, party officials, committee chairmen, department heads, executives, and so on) state their agreements (bargains) clearly to minimize the likelihood of misunderstanding. The U.S. Constitution is a good illustration of explicit bargaining between large and small states, North and South, and other interests. An explicit bargain was struck by Wilbur Mills (D, Arkansas) Chairman of the House Ways and Means Committee, and President Johnson in 1968 when Mills agreed to go along with the administration's income-tax increase proposal only after the President had agreed to a reduction in expenditures.[23] In international politics, treaties exemplify explicit bargains. Here we can note that bargaining in international politics is widely accepted because the idea of national interests is well accepted. In domestic politics, bargaining, however necessary and prevalent, is often looked upon as incompatible with a quest for the "public interest" or, in more crude language, as a "sell out."

More frequently, however, bargaining is probably implicit in nature. In implicit bargaining, the terms of agreement among the bargainers are often vague or ambiguous, and may be expressed in such phases as "future support" or "favorable disposition." Such bargaining frequently occurs in Congress, where one member will agree to support another on a given bill in return for "future cooperation." Understandings or gentlemen's agreements may be developed by administrators concerning their responsibilities for the administration of particular programs so as to eliminate conflict among themselves. In some instances, implicit bargaining may be sufficiently nebulous so that it is unclear whether an agreement actually exists. In Congress, bargaining frequently occurs on procedural actions intended either to slow down or to accelerate the handling of legislation as well as on the substance of legislation.

Three common forms of bargaining are logrolling, side payments, and compromise. *Logrolling*, which is a way of gaining support from those who are indifferent to or have little interest in a matter, usually encompasses a straightforward mutual exchange of support on two different topics. This is a common form of bargaining because every item on an agenda is not of interest to all decision makers. The classic example of logrolling is the appropriations bill for rivers and harbors legislation, which funds a variety of separate river, harbor, and flood-control projects. Members of Congress care mainly about the projects in their own districts, so those who want a particular project in effect agree to support the projects for all the other members' districts. Logrolling is usually implicit in nature.[24]

Side payments are rewards offered to prospective supporters or coalition members that are not directly related to the decision at hand, or at least its main provisions, but are valued for other reasons. Legislative leaders may use committee assignments, allocation of office space, campaign assistance, and support for members' "pet" bills as means of securing their support for legislation. During consideration of the 1986 tax-reform legislation, the chairman of the House Ways and Means Committee, Dan Rostenkowski (D, Illinois) used "transition rules" to gain support for it.[25] Supposedly, these rules ease the transition between existing tax law and a new tax law for various taxpayers. However, transition rules also become legislative favors that can be doled out to win votes. Because they provide millions of dollars of tax benefits to companies and others in legislators' home states or districts they are highly valued. The chairman of the Senate

Finance Committee also used this form of bargaining to elicit support for the tax-reform proposal. In all, about 340 transition rules were included in the Tax Reform Act of 1986 at an estimated total cost of $10.6 billion over five years.[26]

Compromise typically involves explicit bargaining, is normally centered on a single issue, and involves questions of more or less of something. Here the bargainers regard "half a loaf as better than none" and consequently adjust their differences by each giving up something so as to come into agreement. This contrasts with logrolling, in which no change in the bargainers' original positions is necessary. A fine historical example is the Missouri Compromise of 1820, which temporarily settled the conflict between North and South over the extension of slavery into the Louisiana Territory. To simplify, the North wanted slavery excluded from the territory, while the South wanted no such prohibition. It was finally agreed that slavery would be prohibited in the territory except in Missouri, north of latitude 36'30. The Civil Rights Act of 1964 also involved many compromises between those favoring stronger legislation and those wanting weaker or no legislation, especially on the provisions pertaining to public accommodations, equal employment opportunity, and judicial enforcement. On equal-employment opportunity, for instance, it was provided that the Federal Equal Employment Opportunity Commission could handle discrimination cases only after existing state equal opportunity agencies had an opportunity to act and even then could only use voluntary means to reach settlements. This was done to reduce conservative opposition to the legislation. Issues involving money, such as budgets, are probably the easiest matters on which to compromise because they are readily amenable to the splitting of differences.

Persuasion

Attempts to convince others of the correctness or value of one's position, and thereby cause them to adopt it as their own, involve persuasion. Unlike bargainers, persuaders seek to build support for what they want without having to modify their own position.[27] This may involve trying to convince others of the merits of one's position or of the benefits that will accrue to them or their constituents if they accept it, or some combination of the two. Persuaders thus try to induce others "to do it their way." Attorneys who argue cases before the Supreme Court not only present their side of the issue but seek to persuade a majority of the Court of the correctness of their position. Presidential meetings with congressional leaders are often sessions in which presidential programs are explained, their benefits for members of Congress and their constituents outlined, and appeals made for congressional leaders' support. Within Congress, appeals by party leaders to the rank and file to the effect that "Your party needs your support on this issue, can't you go along?" are essentially persuasive in content. Statements by officials to the public explaining and justifying particular programs, such as a price freeze, represent efforts to convince the public to comply with them.

Command

Bargaining involves interaction among peers; command involves hierarchical relationships among superordinates and subordinates. It is the ability of those in superior positions to make decisions that are binding upon those who come within their jurisdiction. They may use sanctions in the form of either rewards or penalties—although usually sanctions are thought of as penalties—to reinforce their decisions. Thus, the subordinate who faithfully accepts and carries out a superior's decision may be rewarded with favorable recognition or a promotion, while the one who refuses to comply may be fired or demoted. President Nixon's decision to institute a price-wage freeze in August 1971, on the basis of authority granted by the Economic Stabilization Act of 1970, was essentially one of command. The Office of Management and Budget engages in command behavior when it approves, rejects, or modifies agency requests for appropriations and proposals for legislation prior to their transmittal to Congress. On the whole, however, command is more characteristic of decision processes in dictatorial rather than democratic societies and in military rather than civilian organizations because of their greater hierarchical qualities. Command is the primary style of decision making in many Latin American and African countries.

In practice, bargaining, persuasion, and command often become blended in a given decisional situation. The president, although he has authority to make many decisions unilaterally, may nonetheless also bargain with subordinates, modifying his position somewhat and accepting some of their suggestions, for more ready and enthusiastic support.[28] Within agencies, subordinates often seek to convert command relationships into bargaining relationships. A bureau that obtains considerable congressional support may thus put itself into position to bargain with, rather than simply be commanded by, the department head. A pollution-control agency may have the authority to set emission standards and act to enforce them on the basis of its statutory authority. It may, however, bargain with those potentially affected in setting the standards in hope of gaining easier and greater compliance with the standards set. Presidential and gubernatorial efforts to win support for legislative proposals also typically involve a combination of persuasion and bargaining.

In summary, bargaining is the most common form of decision making in the American policy process. Persuasion and command are supplementary, being "better suited to a society marked by more universal agreements on values and a more tightly integrated system of authority."[29] Nowhere is the bargaining process better illustrated than in Congress, to which we now turn our attention.

MAJORITY BUILDING IN CONGRESS

The enactment of major legislation by Congress requires the development of a numerical majority or, more likely, a series of numerical majorities, which are most commonly created by bargaining. Even if a majority in Congress are agreed on the need for action on some issue, such as labor-union reform, they may not agree on the form it should take, thereby making bargaining essential.

A highly important characteristic of Congress, which has much importance for policy formation, is its decentralization of political power. Three factors contribute to this condition. First, the political parties in Congress are weak, and party leaders have only limited power to control and discipline party members. In contrast with party leaders in the British House of Commons, who are strong and have a variety of means to ensure support of party policy proposals by party members, congressional leaders, such as the floor leaders, have few sanctions with which to discipline or punish recalcitrant party members. The party leadership has only "bits and fragments" of power, such as desired committee assignments, office space, use of the rules, and the ability to persuade, with which to influence the rank and file. The member who chooses to defy party leadership can usually do so with impunity, and, indeed, not a few people will probably applaud such independence.

Second, the system of geographical representation and decentralized elections contributes to the decentralization of power in Congress. Members of the House and Senate are nominated and elected by the voters in their constituencies and owe little or nothing for their election to the national party organizations or congressional leaders. It is their constituencies that ultimately possess the power to hire and fire them, and it is therefore to their constituencies that they must be responsive, at least minimally, if they wish to remain in Congress. From time to time, important constituent interests in a district may be adversely affected by party programs. Conventional congressional wisdom holds that, when party and constituency interests conflict, members should "vote their constituency," as their reelection may depend upon it.

A third factor contributing to the decentralization of power in Congress is the committee system. There are twenty-two standing committees in the House and sixteen in the Senate, with jurisdiction over legislation in such areas as agriculture, appropriations, energy and natural resources, international relations, and human resources. Traditionally, these committees have done most of the legislative work in Congress. Almost all bills are referred to the appropriate standing committees for consideration before being brought to the floor of the House or Senate for debate and decision. The standing committees possess vast power to kill, alter, or report unchanged bills sent to them. Most bills sent to committees are never heard from again. The committee chairs, who gained their positions on the basis of seniority, had much power over the operation of their committees. They selected the committee staff, scheduled and presided over meetings, set the agenda, scheduled hearings and chose witnesses, and decided when votes would be taken. Through long experience, they were often highly knowledgeable on the policy matters within the jurisdiction of their committees. Because of the fairly large number of interests that came within their jurisdiction, the chairs could act as brokers to build compromises among conflicting or differing interests.

During the 1970s, various reforms to reduce the power of committee chairs and other changes occurred in Congress. As a consequence, much of the power of many of the standing committees has shifted to their subcommittees, of which there are over 220, and the subcommittee chairs. The subcommittees, whose jurisdictions are of course more specialized or narrowly focused than the parent committees, now handle most of the legislative activity and make many of the decisions on legislation. In the House, for example, almost all legislative hearings are now conducted by the subcommittees. The subcommittee chairs can act with substantial independence in the conduct of their subcommittees. As a consequence of this shift to "subcommittee government," more members of the House and Senate are now importantly involved in the policy-making process and have an opportunity to make policy innovations. Another consequence is that the committees have lost much of their role as arenas in which interests could be mediated and compromised. The subcommittees are also more responsive to particularized interests and single-interest groups, thereby further fragmenting the legislative process. The standing committees of course have not lost all their importance but they are no longer the "feudal baronies" they were once depicted as being.

The decentralization of power in Congress, together with the complexities of its legislative procedures, usually requires the formation of a series of majorities for the enactment of major legislation. There are a number of decision stages through which a bill must pass in the course of becoming a law.[30] Briefly, in the House, these are subcommittee, committee, Rules Committee, and finally floor action; and in the Senate, subcommittee, committee, and floor action. Assuming the bill is passed in different versions by the two houses, a conference committee must agree on a compromise version, which then must be approved by the two houses. If the president approves it, the bill becomes law; if, however, he vetoes it, the bill becomes law only if it is passed again by a two-thirds majority in each house. There are thus 10 or 12 stages at which a bill requires the approval of some kind of majority. If it fails to win majority approval at any one of these stages, it is probably dead. Should it win approval, its enactment is not assured; rather, its supporters face the task of majority building at the next stage.

Extraordinary majorities are sometimes needed to get bills through some stages of the legislative process. Reference has already been made to the two-thirds majorities needed to override a presidential veto. Only infrequently are bills able to secure these majorities. During the period from 1954 to 1988, of the 694 bills vetoed by the president, only 44 were subsequently enacted into law. In the Senate, debate on a bill can be effectively terminated only by unanimous consent agreement or by the imposition of cloture. The cloture rule provides that debate may be terminated upon a motion signed by sixteen senators that is then approved by three-fifths of the entire membership (60 senators). Since a single senator who is so inclined can block the closing of debate by a unanimous consent agreement, this leaves cloture as the only alternative for shutting down a filibuster. Because of the difficulties in obtaining cloture in times past, southern Democrats were consistently able to block the enactment of major civil rights legislation through filibusters or threats thereof until the adoption of the 1964 Civil Rights Act. Since then resistance to the use of cloture has weakened and the procedure has been used dozens of times to close off filibusters on a variety of bills. Still, filibusters have sometimes been used successfully to block legislation, such as a campaign finance reform bill and a measure banning aid to the Nicaraguan rebels, both in 1987.

The multiplicity of stages, or decision points, in the congressional legislative process provides access for a variety of groups and interests. Those who lack access or influence at one stage may secure it at another stage. It becomes quite unlikely that a single group or interest will dominate the process. The complexity of the process, however, has a conservative effect in that it gives an advantage to those seeking to block the enactment of legislation. And it is well to remember that many groups are more concerned with preventing than with securing the enactment of legislation. All they have to do to achieve their preference is to win the support of a majority, or at least of a dominant actor, at one stage of the process. Here is support for the familiar generalization, that procedure is not neutral in its impact.

Much bargaining is necessary for the enactment of legislation by Congress. Those who control each of the decision points may require the modification of a bill as a condition for their approval, or they may exact future support for some item of interest to themselves. Bargaining is facilitated not only by the many decision points but also by the fact that legislators do not have intense interest in many of the matters on which they must decide. It is no doubt easier for them to bargain on such issues than on issues on which they have strong feelings. At this point, however, it does not seem necessary to elaborate further upon the ubiquity of bargaining in Congress.

PRESIDENTIAL DECISION MAKING

Apart from his integral role in the legislative process, the president can be viewed as a policy adopter in his own right. In foreign affairs, much policy is a product of presidential actions and decisions, based either on the president's constitutional authority or broad congressional delegations of power. Decisions to recognize foreign governments and to establish formal diplomatic relations with them, as the Nixon and Carter administrations did with the People's Republic of China, are in the president's domain. Treaties with other nations are made and entered into on behalf of the United States by the president, subject to approval by the Senate. One can cavil on whether the president is the true decision maker here. In the case of executive agreements, which have the same legal force as treaties, and which are used much more frequently than treaties in foreign relations, there can be no doubt. The president makes the decisions on executive agreements. Executive agreements have been used to end wars, establish or expand military bases in other countries, and limit the possession of offensive weapons by the United States and the Soviet Union. They are also often used for such routine purposes as customs enforcement.[31]

For over a half-century international trade policies have been primarily a construct of president action, albeit based on congressional authorizations. Through the time of the Smoot-Hawley Tariff of 1930, by which Congress in an orgy of logrolling elevated tariffs to an all-time high, this issue area had been dominated by Congress. Change set in with the New Deal and the enactment of the Reciprocal Trade Agreements Act of 1935. This statute authorized the president to enter into agreements with other nations to lower tariff and other trade barriers (e.g., import quotas). Since then, under the guidance of presidential leadership and decisions, the United States has continually advocated and moved in the direction of free trade. All presidents since the Great Depression have been advocates of the reduction of trade barriers. By the late 1980s, United States tariffs averaged less than 5 percent of the value of imported products.

In domestic matters, Congress often delegates discretionary authority to the president or to agencies under his direction and control. Executive orders, which are not mentioned in the Constitution, are also used by presidents for making domestic policies.[32] Executive orders have been promulgated to desegregate the armed services, establish loyalty-security programs, require affirmative action by government contractors, classify and withhold government documents from the public, and provide for presidential control of agency rule making. Presidents Johnson and Carter used executive orders to establish systems of voluntary wage and price controls to combat inflation. Nothing in the Constitution or laws specifically authorized them to so act. On the other hand, nothing prohibited them from so doing. Operating with a broad view of presidential power, they responded to necessity as they saw it.

By considering some of the general factors that shape and limit presidential decision making, we not only can gain useful insight into presidential decision making but also can discover another perspective from which to view decision making in general. Before proceeding further, it must be remembered that presidential decision making is an institutional process. A variety of agencies, aides, and advisors (both official and unofficial) assist the president in the discharge of his responsibilities. But whether he simply approves a recommendation from below or makes his own independent choice, the president alone has the ultimate responsibility for decision.

What factors help shape and limit presidential decision-making?[33] One is permissibility, an aspect of which is legality. The president is expected to act in conformity with the Constitution, statutes, and court decisions. The lack of a clear constitutional basis certainly contributed to congressional criticism of the Nixon administration's Cambodian bombing policy in the summer of 1973 and to an agreement by the administration to cease bombing after August 15, 1973, in the absence of congressional authorization. Another aspect of permissibility is acceptability. Foreign policy decisions often depend for their effectiveness upon acceptance by other nations, while domestic policy decisions, such as that by President Reagan to recommend elimination of the Department of Energy, may depend upon their acceptance by Congress, executive-branch officials and agencies, or the public.

A second factor is available resources. The president does not have the resources to do everything he might want to do, whether by resources one means money, manpower, patronage, time, or credibility. Funds allocated to defense are not available for education or medical research. Only a limited number of appeals to the public for support for his actions can be made without the possibility of diminishing returns. Time devoted to foreign policy problems is not available for domestic matters. While the president has considerable control over the use of his time, he does not have time to concern himself with everything that he might wish.[34] A lack of credibility may also limit the president, as the experiences of Presidents Johnson and Nixon attest.

A third factor is available time, in the sense of timing and the need to act. A foreign policy crisis may require a quick response, as was the case with the Cuban missile crisis of 1962, without all the time for deliberation and fact-gathering one might prefer. Domestic policy decisions may be "forced," as by the need to submit the annual budget to Congress in January or the constitutional requirement to act on a bill passed by Congress within ten days if the president wishes to veto it (barring the possibility of a pocket veto). As former White House aide Theodore C. Sorensen states,

> There is a time to act and a time to wait. By not acting too soon, the President may find that the problem dissolves or resolves itself, that the facts are different from what he thought, or that the state of the nation has changed. By not waiting too long, he may make the most of the mood of the moment, or retain that element of surprise which is so often essential to military and other maneuvers.[35]

President Reagan demonstrated the importance of timing when he moved quickly and decisively in the first months of his term to secure adoption of his economic program of tax cuts and domestic expenditure reductions. By so doing he was able to capitalize on the euphoria and political support that attend the early days of a new administration. As time goes on, these decline, and the political life of a president becomes more difficult.

Previous commitments are a fourth factor that may shape presidential decisions. These commitments may be personal, taking the form, for instance, of campaign promises or earlier decisions. While too much emphasis can be placed on the need for consistency, the president must avoid the appearance of deception or vacillation if he is to retain his credibility and political support. Jimmy Carter suffered from a reputation (not fully deserved) for indecisiveness, as when in 1977 he proposed a tax rebate to stimulate the economy and then reversed himself a few months later. Campaigning for the presidency in 1980, Ronald Reagan pledged to eliminate the Department of Energy. He, however, neither made good on the pledge nor suffered much in reputation as a consequence. People were often more attentive to and influenced by his words than by his actions.

Commitments may also take the form of traditions and principles, such as those that hold the United States meets its treaty obligations and engages in military action only if attacked. During the Cuban missile crisis, for example, an air strike without warning on the Soviet missile sites was rejected by the Kennedy administration as a "Pearl Harbor in reverse," a naval blockade of Cuba was chosen instead. A "first-strike" strategy generally has been excluded from American foreign policy.

Finally, available information can be an important influence on presidential decisions. Many sources of information—official and unofficial, overt and covert—are available to the president. At times, particularly with respect to domestic policy, he may be subject to drowning in a torrent of words and paper. Still, the president at times may be confronted by a shortage of reliable information, especially in the area of foreign affairs. Reliable information on the possible reactions to a Berlin airlift, the resumption of nuclear testing, or a strategic Defense Initiative ("Star Wars") may be scarce because of the need to predict what will happen in the future. Predicting the future is an uncertain task, except perhaps for a few who claim a sixth sense or a clear crystal ball.

Domestic policy decisions may also involve some uncertainty. This is quite obvious when economic stability policy is under consideration. Will a reduction in income taxes encourage higher levels of investment and economic growth? How much restraint must be imposed on the economy to "break the back" of the inflationary psychology contributing to inflation? When all the advice is in, the president has to make a choice, a calculated one based on limited information, that the alternative chosen will produce the desired result.

Uncertainty may contribute to delay and a lack of action on some matters. Given doubts as to what needs to be done, or what the impact of action may be, the decision may be to hold off, to see whether things will not work themselves out or to let the situation "clarify itself" (i.e., to give oneself more time to gather information on conditions and alternatives).

As a leader in policy formation, the president is subject to a variety of political pressures and constraints, however great his legal powers may appear to be. Legal authority by itself often does not convey the capacity to act effectively. Thus the president may have to persuade because he cannot command; he may have to bargain because he cannot compel action. President Truman once remarked, "I sit here all day trying to persuade people to do the things they ought to have sense enough to do without my persuading them. . . . That's all the powers of the Presidency amount to."[36] An overstatement, perhaps, yet a remark worth reflecting upon.

THE DYNAMICS OF POLICY DEVELOPMENT: THE CASE OF NATURAL GAS

The regulation of the natural gas industry, especially as this entailed the regulation of the field price of natural gas, provides an instructive example of the policy-making process. Beginning with the adoption of the Natural Gas Act of 1938, a half-century of policy developments and controversies will be traced. Few economic issues have been the focus of more macropolitical struggle in the last several decades than has national regulation of the field price of natural gas. The discussion will illustrate many of the aspects of policy making discussed in previous chapters, demonstrate the often continuous nature of the policy process, and indicate how the different levels and branches of government can become involved in a policy area. It is not a simple story, but then policy making in actuality is often a complex and arcane process.

There was once a time when natural gas had little commercial value. Usually discovered in the course of exploration for oil, natural gas was regarded as a nuisance, and most of it was either vented (released into the atmosphere) or flared (burned) to dispose of it. In the late 1920s, however, the development of seamless pipe made it possible to move gas over long distances, as from producing areas in the Southwest to consuming cities in the Midwest and Northwest. In time, natural gas became a major source of energy because of its clean, efficient nature. In the 1980s, natural gas accounted for over 20 percent of national energy production.

The natural gas industry encompasses three basic economic functions: the production and gathering of gas in the field, transportation to the market, and distribution to the ultimate consumers.[37] A series of Supreme Court decisions placed the first and third functions within the scope of state regulatory power. Most of the transportation of gas, however, takes place in interstate commerce (that is, across state lines) and therefore falls under the jurisdiction of the national government. State utility commissions can regulate the prices charged to local consumers, but not the wholesale prices at which gas is sold to local distributing companies by interstate pipeline companies. As large quantities of natural gas began to move across state lines, the problem of regulating this traffic gained in importance. It was argued that the states could not effectively regulate gas prices for local consumers as long as wholesale prices were uncontrolled.

The jurisdictional gap that existed was filled without much controversy when Congress enacted the Natural Gas Act of 1938. Gas pipeline companies were directed to file rate schedules with the Federal Power Commission (FPC) and could not alter their rates without its approval. The FPC was empowered to set "just and reasonable" rates and to exercise broad control over pipeline companies, including control of entry into the business. Production and gathering of gas, direct sales to industrial users, and the local distribution were exempted from control by the commission. A problem soon arose, however, because the act was not clear as to whether field prices of gas—the prices charged by processors and gatherers to pipeline companies—were sales in interstate commerce and thus subject to regulation by the FPC. Gas producers, it should be noted, had not opposed the enactment of the Natural Gas Act, as they assumed they were exempt from its control.

At first the FPC held that it did not have jurisdiction over the field prices of gas. Then, in 1943, the commission reversed itself and held that it *did* have such jurisdiction. In 1947 the Supreme Court upheld the commission, and ruled, in effect, that all sales to interstate pipeline companies were sales in interstate commerce and thus within the jurisdiction of the FPC. The Court declined to accept the contention that such sales were part of the processing and gathering function and thus exempt from national regulation. To say the least, the Court's interpretation of the Natural Gas Act differed considerably from that of the gas interests and their supporters.

Even before the Supreme Court issued its 1947 decision, a move started in Congress, led by members from the South and Southwest and supported by oil and gas interests, to amend the Natural Gas Act. One bill, introduced by Representative Ross Rizley (D, Oklahoma), would have exempted sales by both integrated and independent producers from FPC regulation. (An integrated producer is one that has its own pipelines or is affiliated with a pipeline company. An "independent" is the value-laden title given to a company, regardless of size, that does not control its own pipelines.) The FPC opposed the Rizley bill but gave its support to another bill designed to exempt only independent producers. Further by a 4-to-1 decision in 1947, the FPC issued its Order No. 139, by which it interpreted the Natural Gas Act as denying it power to regulate prices charged by independent producers. This, however, did not abate the congressional effort to amend the act. Moreover, by 1949 the position of the commission had shifted, and three of the five members now opposed exemption of independents. Leland Olds, the FPC chairman, was especially strong in his opposition.

Activity now began to pick up in Congress, and natural gas legislation became an important item on its policy agenda. In 1949, Democratic Senator Robert Kerr of Oklahoma introduced a bill to exempt sales by independent producers. The House had earlier passed a similar bill by a 183-to-131 vote. At first the Senate Committee on Interstate and Foreign Commerce refused to report out the Kerr bill, partly because of the strong opposition of FPC Chairman Olds. About this time Olds's term on the commission expired, and his name came before the Senate for renomination. A bitter attack against his renomination was launched by oil and gas interests, senators from major gas-consuming states, and consumer interests. His renomination was rejected by a 51-to-15 vote.[38] With Olds out of the way, the Senate turned its attention to the Kerr bill and passed it by a vote of 44 to 38. Most of the opposition to it came from the gas-consuming states in the North and East. Former Senator Mon Wallgren, who had been appointed to take Olds's place on the FPC, now joined with two "consumer-minded" incumbent commissioners to recommend a presidential veto. Following President Harry Truman's veto of the Kerr bill, the commission repealed its Order No. 139.

The FPC now became the primary location of the policy struggle. While the Court had held that the commission possessed the power to regulate independent producers, it had not said the commission was *required* to do so. In 1951, in the Phillips Petroleum Company case, the commission again changed its mind, deciding by 4 to 1 that the Natural Gas Act's exemption of production and gathering from regulation included the sale of gas by independents to pipeline companies. This was of course unsatisfactory to proponents of regulation, and the commission's action was challenged judicially. In 1954 the case reached the Supreme Court. Allied in support of the commission's position were the FPC itself, the Phillips Petroleum Company, and the State of Texas. In opposition were the State of Wisconsin and several cities acting in support of consumers' interests. The Court reversed the FPC decision and held that the commission was required to regulate independent producers' prices.[39] The Court said this was consistent with the legislative history of the 1938 act, even though the FPC had relied heavily on the same history in reaching the opposite conclusion. The effect of the Court's action was to increase the responsibility of a reluctant commission for balancing consumer and producer interests through regulation.

Following the Court's 1954 decision, the struggle over exemption of independents shifted back to Congress. Much pressure was exerted on Congress by oil and gas interests to amend the 1938 act to exempt independents. An intensive public relations campaign was started to convince the public that such exemption was necessary to free independents from regulation and to insure adequate supplies of gas at reasonable prices for consumers. Thousands of gas producers gave their support to the exemption campaign. Further support came from President Eisenhower, who favored exemption of independents from national regulation as a means of reducing excessive centralization in government. Strong opposition to exemption came from cities in the North and East, labor groups, gas consumers, and local utility companies, who feared exemption would increase the prices they paid for gas. Coal interests also opposed exemption in an attempt to protect their competitive position vis-à-vis the gas industry in the sale of fuel.

Identical bills to exempt all independents from national regulation were introduced in the House and Senate by two Arkansas Democrats, Representative Oren Harris and Senator William Fulbright. The House passed the bill toward the end of 1955 by a 209-to-203 vote, which is indicative of the closeness and intensity of the struggle over the bill. The next February the bill came before the Senate for floor consideration. During the Senate debate, Senator Francis Case (R, South Dakota) announced that he would vote against the bill, although he previously had favored it. In explanation he stated that an oil company lawyer had offered him a $2500 campaign contribution on the condition that he vote for the measure. The Senate was undeterred by the publicity and controversy that this disclosure touched off and subsequently passed the bill by a 53-to-38 vote. Voting in both houses was based on regional and economic conditions rather than party lines. In the House, for example, representatives from gas-producing states tended to favor it, while representatives from northern gas-consuming areas tended to oppose it, regardless of their party affiliation.

This legislative effort came to naught when President Eisenhower, who had favored the bill, vetoed it because of the "Case incident." In his veto message, the president stated,

> Since the passage of this bill a body of evidence has accumulated indicating that private persons, representing only a very small segment of a great and vital industry, have been seeking to further their own interests by highly questionable activities. These include efforts I deem to be so arrogant and so in defiance of acceptable standards of propriety as to risk creating doubt among the American people concerning the integrity of governmental process.[40]

In other words, those involved in the "Case incident" had violated the basic "rules of the game" governing the political struggle. The exertion of pressure is one thing, bribery quite another.

To add another dimension to our study, I should mention that the gas interests also attempted to overcome the 1954 decision by action in the state policy-making arena. In the fall of that year, the Oklahoma Corporation Commission acted to set minimum field prices for natural gas. This move, had it been ruled constitutional, would have prevented the FPC from setting lower prices. A somewhat similar ploy was attempted in Texas, where it was presented as necessary for conservation of natural gas. This stratagem failed when the United States Supreme Court declared that it was unconstitutional for Oklahoma to regulate the field prices of natural gas moving in interstate commerce. The Court thus invoked the Constitution on the consumer side of the conflict. Its decision meant that policy on natural gas prices would continue to be developed in the national arena.

In 1958, another effort was made in Congress to amend the Natural Gas Act. A bill to exempt several thousand *small* independent gas producers from price regulation was introduced. Although it was sponsored by senators from both gas-producing and gas-consuming states, it never really got off the ground. This bill was unappealing to the large independent gas companies, who produce most of the supply of natural gas, as exemption of the "little fellow" did not really help them. After 1958, natural gas disappeared from the legislative agenda for a decade.

After 1954, the task of reconciling producer and consumer interests through the medium of rate regulation rested directly with the Federal Power Commission. At first, the commission sought to handle the problem by setting rates through adjudication based on the traditional individual company cost of service methods used in public utility regulation. This alternative proved unsatisfactory, however, because of the complexity of the problem, the large number of gas producers involved (over 18,000), and the commission's own lethargy. In 1960, the FPC ceased its efforts to set gas rates on a case-by-case basis and moved to a system of area pricing, under which the country was divided into twenty-three gas-producing regions for rate-making purposes.

In August 1965, the FPC completed action in the first area rate case, involving the Permian Basin area of western Texas and eastern New Mexico. The commission's decision was regarded as a victory for consumer interests. Ceilings of 16½ and 15½ cents per thousand cubic feet (mcf) were set for gas produced in Texas and New Mexico, respectively. Higher rates were permitted for "old" gas (from wells in production before 1961) than for "new" gas (from wells starting production after January 1961 or from wells also producing oil). The higher price for new gas was intended to stimulate production and move more gas into the interstate market. Gas producers had argued for a 20-cent ceiling, while the going market price was 17 to 18 cents per mcf. The area-pricing action was unsuccessfully challenged in the federal courts by the gas industry. Subsequently, rate proceedings were completed for other areas. Intense struggles occurred over whether gas prices should be a penny or two higher or lower per mcf than proposed by the FPC.

The consumption of natural gas increased at a rapid pace during the 1960s, stimulated by such factors as low prices; convenience in the use of gas; its cleanliness, which helped industrial users meet air quality standards; and the absence of any regulation of the end-uses of gas.[41] By the early 1970s a shortage in the supply of natural gas had emerged. Existing users were not always able to get all the gas they wanted, while prospective new users were sometimes denied access to gas by gas companies. What had produced this situation? Generally, two conflicting explanations have been advanced for the gas shortage. The critics of rate regulation, including the gas producers, contended that the low gas rates set by the FPC were the problem, having operated to discourage exploration and production and to divert gas into the intrastate (and unregulated) market where prices were higher. Deregulation of the price of natural gas was necessary in their view to call forth adequate supplies. Those who supported gas regulation contended that the gas shortage was a product of two factors: greatly increased demand for natural gas and the possibility of deregulation and higher prices for gas, which was said to have caused gas companies both to produce less gas and to sell less gas in the interstate market. They contended that eliminating uncertainty over the continuation of regulation would help to eliminate the shortage of gas. Notice how policy evaluation and policy advocacy were blended in this situation.

In 1975, natural gas deregulation again became a major item on the national policy agenda. With the support of the Ford administration, a strong effort was made in 1975 and 1976 to enact legislation repealing the FPC's authority to regulate the field price of interstate gas. The repeal legislation was passed by the Senate fairly readily. It ran into difficulty in the

House, however, where supporters of continued regulation were able to amend the bill to retain regulation of large gas producers and to extend federal regulation to intrastate sales while removing most small producers from control. This of course was not acceptable to the gas industry and its supporters, who insisted on total deregulation. No conference committee action was taken on the bill, and it died.

Now let us return to the Federal Power Commission and, to begin, backtrack a bit. Under the Nixon administration the FPC had become pro-industry in orientation, in contrast to its consumer orientation through most of the 1960s. In 1974 the commission abandoned its area-pricing scheme and, through a rule-making proceeding, adopted a single *national* price of 52 cents per mcf for all "new" natural gas (that is, all gas sold after 1972). When it became apparent in the summer of 1976 that Congress was not going to end natural gas regulation, the commission made a drastic change in gas rates, setting a nationwide price of $1.42 per mcf with annual escalation.[42] According to the commission majority, this higher rate was added in order to get producers to increase exploration, production, and sale of gas, although they did not guarantee that production would actually increase. In effect, the commission had substantially done what Congress refused to do: deregulate the price of natural gas. The new price for gas was seven times higher than what it had been in 1968 at the end of the Johnson administration. Whereas previously rates had been kept low for consumer protection, now they were set in the interest of gas production (and producers).

This shift in policy did not do much to lessen the demand of the gas industry for total deregulation. In the winter of 1976–77, the price of gas in the intrastate market was higher than the new FPC rate, running over $2 per mcf in Texas, for example. The industry and its supporters continued to proclaim the virtues of an unregulated market and to present it as a solution for the gas problem. They were disappointed in the spring of 1977, however, when President Carter, who along with Gerald Ford had favored deregulation during the 1976 presidential campaign, unveiled his comprehensive energy policy proposal. In apparent contradiction of a campaign pledge made to Texas petroleum interests, he recommended continued regulation of natural gas prices, albeit with an increase to $1.75 per mcf. An energy bill passed by the House in September that included provisions both for this price and for its extension to intrastate sales. The gas industry still wanted total deregulation, while consumer spokespersons protested that $1.75 per mcf was too high. A few weeks later, however, the Senate passed a bill by a 50-to-46 vote that provided for an end to federal regulation of natural gas sales. Contributing to the Senate action was the fact that the Senate leadership was much less supportive of President Carter than was the House leadership.

A House-Senate conference, set up to resolve differences between the two bills, quickly reached agreement on most issues. However, the conferees where deadlocked on how to handle natural gas price deregulation, and negotiations to resolve their differences stretched on for a year. In an effort to get an agreement, President Carter personally met several times with the conferees. He also held many meetings with businesses to win their support so that they would exert pressure on senators to back the administration bill. In October 1978, following an intensive White House lobbying effort the bill was finally agreed to and enacted,[43] although even its supporters were not very pleased with its contents.

The Natural Gas Policy Act contained several important provisions:

1. The maximum price of new natural gas was set at $1.75 per mcf and could rise about 10 percent annually.
2. The pricing system for old gas (gas discovered before April 1977) was quite complicated and included numerous categories, depending upon such factors as when the gas was committed to the interstate market and whether it was produced onshore or offshore, by small or large producers, and so on.
3. Federal regulation was for the first time extended to intrastate gas (that gas produced and sold in the same state).
4. Rate regulation for all new gas was to be added by January 1, 1985.

Implementation of the act was assigned to the Federal Energy Regulatory Commission (FERC), which in 1977 had been created to replace the FPC. President Carter had wanted natural gas rate-making authority to be vested in the Secretary of Energy when the Department of Energy was established in 1978. Congress was unwilling to vest this authority in a single official, however, so it set up a new regulatory commission in place of the FPC. Formally located within the Department of Energy, the FERC operates independently of departmental controls. Given the complexity of the new law, it confronted a large task.

The Reagan administration, which advocated the total deregulation of natural gas rates, did not actively push the issue during its first two years in office. In 1981 the energies of the administration were concentrated on its economic program. Moreover, a windfall profits tax then seemed to be a condition for deregulation, and in his efforts to win votes for his economic program the president had pledged to veto a windfall profits tax on decontrolled gas. Congressional elections then made 1982 politically unpropitious for launching a deregulation effort. Other priorities thus kept natural gas off the administration's active policy agenda.

In 1983, however, the administration did recommend the deregulation of all natural gas. Neither the House nor the Senate, however, was able to reach agreement on a natural gas bill. Because the Congress was split by regional (i.e., consumer versus producer areas) and ideological differences, confronted with a gas industry that was somewhat divided, and uncertain as to the consequences of both deregulation and continued regulation, majority coalitions could not be formed. Moreover, the appearance of an at least temporary glut in the supply of gas, with some market prices being below the regulated price, reduced the urgency for action by those favoring the continuation of regulation to protect consumers. Consequently, the deregulation of new gas went into effect on January 1, 1985.

Natural gas prices peaked in 1984 and then began to decline; by 1989 the market price for gas was substantially below its 1984 level. According to one study, the 1988 average price was $1.71 per mcf, compared to $2.69 per mcf in 1984.[44] Only 6 percent of the natural gas sold was held below the market price by regulation, although 40 percent was still subject to controls. In some instances gas prices were propped up above the market price by controls. This changed market situation helped defuse the conflict over regulation.

Legislation providing for the total deregulation of natural gas prices was introduced in Congress in 1989 and quickly passed with minimal conflict.[45] Signed into law by President Bush in July, the act provides that gas from new wells will be decontrolled on May 15, 1991, and gas from existing wells by 1993.

Why did the 1989 legislation produce so little controversy in contrast to the bitter conflicts that occurred in the late 1970s and mid-1980s? One factor seemed to be the general public acceptance of economic deregulation. Another was that a coalition of gas producers, pipeline companies, distributors, and industrial users remained unified in supporting the bill, whereas consumer-group opposition was scarce. Most important, however, was the fact that natural gas price regulation, as a result of market changes, had lost its redistributive quality. It no longer involved any significant allocation of wealth and resources among producers and consumers. The market, at least for the time being, appeared to be an adequate protector of consumer interests. In the House, for instance, members who had earlier strongly opposed deregulation took the lead in securing enactment of the 1989 law.

A half-century of struggle over natural gas price regulation has come to an end. However, should natural gas prices rise substantially in the future, the issue of natural gas price regulation will predictably be restored to the national policy agenda.

Notes

1. The leading proponent of incrementalism undoubtedly in Charles Lindblom. See his "The Science of 'Muddling Through,'" *Public Administration*

Review, XIX (1959), pp. 79–88; *The Intelligence of Democracy* (New York: Macmillan, 1964); *The Policy-Making Process* (Englewood Cliffs, N.J.: Prentice-Hall, 1968); and, with David Braybrooke, *The Strategy of Decision* (New York: Free Press, 1963).

2. This summary draws primarily on Lindblom's "The Science of 'Muddling Through,'" *op. cit.*, and *The Intelligence of Democracy, op. cit.*, pp. 144–148.

3. Amitai Etzioni, "Mixed-Scanning: A 'Third' Approach to Decision-Making," *Public Administration Review*, XXVII (December, 1967), pp. 385–392.

4. *Ibid.*, p. 389.

5. David W. Brady, "Congressional Leadership and Party Voting in the McKinley Era: A Comparison to the Modern House," *Midwest Journal of Political Science*, XVI (August, 1972), pp. 439–441.

6. Norman J. Ornstein, et al., *Vital Statistics on Congress, 1984–1985 Edition* (Washington, D.C.: American Enterprise Institute, 1984), p. 182.

7. Richard Rose, *Do Parties Make a Difference?* 2d ed. (Chatham, N.J.: Chatham House, 1984), pp. 74–91; and Edward Crowe, "Consensus and Structure in Legislative Norms: Party Discipline in the House of Commons," *Journal of Politics*, XLV (August, 1983), pp. 907–931.

8. A thorough discussion of the concepts of representation can be found in John C. Wahlke et al., *The Legislative System* (New York: Wiley, 1962).

9. See, e.g., Peter Woll, *American Bureaucracy*, 2d ed. (New York: Norton, 1977).

10. V. O. Key, Jr., *Public Opinion and American Democracy* (New York: Knopf, 1961), p. 14.

11. *Ibid.*, pp. 81–90.

12. Cf. John E. Mueller, "Trends in Popular Support for the Wars in Korea and Vietnam," *American Political Science Review*, LXV (June, 1971), pp. 358–375.

13. Nick Kotz, *Let Them Eat Promises: The Politics of Hunger in America* (Englewood Cliffs, N.J.: Prentice-Hall, 1969).

14. Donald R. Matthews and James A. Stimson, "The Decision-Making Approach to the Study of Legislative Behavior." Unpublished paper presented at the annual meeting of the American Political Science Association (September, 1969), p. 19.

15. Robert H. Salisbury, *Governing America: Public Choice and Political Action* (New York: Appleton-Century-Crofts, 1973), p. 237. Chap. 13 contains a very useful treatment of decision making.

16. Richard F. Fenno, Jr., *Congressmen in Committees* (Boston: Little, Brown, 1973), pp. 48, 64.

17. See Glendon Schubert, *The Public Interest* (New York: Free Press, 1960).

18. Emmette S. Redford, *Ideal and Practice in Public Administration* (Tuscaloosa: University of Alabama Press, 1957), chap. 5.

19. Walter Lippmann, *The Phantom Public* (New York: Harcourt, Brace, 1925), p. 105. Cf. Frank J. Sorauf, "The Public Interest Reconsidered," *Journal of Politics*, XIX (November, 1957), pp. 616–639.

20. Richard E. Neustadt, "White House and Whitehall," *The Public Interest*, II (Winter, 1966), pp. 55–69.

21. As quoted in Roger Hilsman, *The Politics of Policy Making in Defense and Foreign Affairs* (New York: Harper & Row, 1971), p. 1.
22. Robert A. Dahl and Charles E. Lindblom, *Politics, Economics, and Welfare* (New York: Harper & Row, 1953), p. 328. Chaps. 12 and 13 present a thorough and insightful discussion of bargaining in American politics.
23. See the discussion of this episode in Lawrence C. Pierce, *The Politics of Fiscal Policy Formation* (Pacific Palisades, Calif.: Goodyear, 1971), chap. 7.
24. Lewis A. Froman, Jr., *People and Politics* (Englewood Cliffs, N.J.: Prentice-Hall, 1962), pp. 56–57.
25. Jeffrey H. Birnbaum and Alan S. Murray, *Showdown at Gucci Gulch* (New York: Random House, 1987), pp. 146, 240–243.
26. *The New York Times*, September 20, 1986, p. 24.
27. Peter Burnell and Andrew Reeve, "Persuasion as a Political Concept," *British Journal of Political Studies*, XIV (October, 1984), pp. 393–410.
28. Cf. Richard E. Neustadt, *Presidential Power* (New York: Wiley, 1980).
29. Dan Nimmo and Thomas D. Ungs, *American Political Patterns*, 2d ed. (Boston: Little, Brown, 1969), p. 367.
30. A good discussion of congressional procedures can be found in Walter J. Oleszak, *Congressional Procedures and the Policy Process*, 2d ed. (Washington, D.C.: The Brookings Institution, 1984).
31. George C. Edwards III and Stephen J. Wayne, *Presidential Leadership* (New York: St. Martin's, 1985), pp. 290–293.
32. Cf. Ruth P. Morgan, *The President and Civil Rights: Policy-Making by Executive Order* (New York: St. Martins, 1970).
33. In this discussion I will depend substantially on an insightful little book by Theodore C. Sorensen, *Decision-Making in the White House* (New York: Columbia University Press, 1963). Sorensen served as Special Counsel to President Kennedy.
34. Cf. George Reedy, *The Twilight of the Presidency* (New York: World, 1970).
35. Sorensen, *op. cit.*, p. 29.
36. As quoted in Neustadt *Presidential Power, op. cit.*, pp. 9–10.
37. See Ralph K. Huitt, "National Regulation of the Natural-Gas Industry," in Emmette S. Redford (ed.), *Public Administration and Policy Formation* (Austin: University of Texas Press, 1958), pp. 53–116, for further discussion and background on gas regulation.
38. Joseph P. Harris, "The Senatorial Rejection of Leland Olds," *American Political Science Review*, XXV (September, 1951), pp. 674–693.
39. *Phillips Petroleum Company* v. *State of Wisconsin*, 347 U.S. 672 (1954).
40. Carl Solberg, *Oil Power* (New York: New American Library, 1976), chap. 8.
41. Richard Corrigan, "FPC's Gas Price Ruling Leaves Consumers Out in the Cold," *National Journal*, Vol. 8 (November 13, 1976), pp. 1626–1631.
42. See M. Elizabeth Sanders, *The Regulation of Natural Gas: Policy and Politics, 1938–1978* (Philadelphia: Temple University Press, 1981).
43. Pietro S. Nivola, "Energy Policy and the Congress: The Policy of the Natural Gas Policy Act of 1978," *Public Policy*, XXVIII (Fall, 1980), pp. 491–543.
44. *The Washington Post National Weekly Edition*, July 3–9, 1989, p. 20.
45. *Congressional Quarterly Weekly Report*, Vol. 47 (June 17, 1989), p. 1467; (June 24, 1989), p. 1538.

5

BUDGETING AND PUBLIC POLICY

The Stealth bomber: The degree to which Congress funds it can affect American defense policy for decades.

F ew public policies can be put into effect without the expenditure of money. Many programs, such as Social Security, Medicare, Aid to Families with Dependent Children (AFDC), and unemployment compensation, primarily entail the transfer of funds from taxpayers to the government to individual recipients. The effectiveness of other programs is often greatly affected by the adequacy of the funding for their conduct and implementation.

At an extreme, a policy without funding will become a nullity. Thus in 1973 Congress eliminated the Subversive Activities Control Program not by repealing the legislation upon which it was based but by ceasing to appropriate money for its administration. Although the agency (the Subversive Activities Control Board) administering the program had never succeeded in registering a single subversive person or organization (e.g., the Communist Party), the program was of symbolic importance to some conservatives and a source of employment to a few others for over two decades.

It is also possible for a department or agency to be better funded than necessary. Thus the Reagan administration sought and obtained increased funding for defense programs in the early 1980s. Some observers were doubtful that the Defense Department could wisely use all of the additional funds, or that they would strengthen defense capabilities. Stories of cost overruns and waste were numerous, and many questions were raised concerning the necessity or capabilities of various weapons systems.

Some of the major aspects of the national budgetary process will be sketched in this chapter. This will not be done in great detail because the major purpose here is to indicate how the budgetary process helps shape the nature and implementation of public policies.

THE BUDGET AND PUBLIC POLICY

The national budget has increased greatly in size and complexity in the last few decades. In 1960 federal expenditures totaled $92.2 billion; by 1988 they had increased to more than $1.1 *trillion.* Even when inflation is taken into account, the budget has quadrupled in size. Many new policies and programs have been added and others have been expanded during these decades. Much of the expenditure growth here, however, is accounted for by a few programatic areas: national defense, social and income security, Medicare (which began operating in 1966), and interest payments on the national debt. Table 5.1 portrays expenditure patterns for several functional areas from 1960 to 1990.

Most governmental expenditures in 1960 went to pay the direct costs of

TABLE 5.1   National Governmental Expenditures for Selected Functions and Years, 1960–90 (Billions of Dollars)

Function	1960	1965	1970	1975	1978	1980	1981	1982	1983	1984	1985	1986	1987	1988	1989*	1990*
National defense	45.9	49.6	81.7	86.5	105.2	134.0	157.5	185.3	201.9	227.7	252.7	273.4	282.0	290.4	298.3	303.0
Income security†	3.7	9.1	15.6	50.2	61.5	86.5	99.7	107.7	122.6	112.7	128.2	119.8	123.2	129.3	136.9	136.8
Social Security	4.3	16.4	30.3	64.7	93.9	118.5	139.6	156.0	170.7	178.2	188.6	198.8	207.4	219.3	232.3	246.7
Medicare	—		6.2	12.7	22.8	32.1	39.1	46.6	52.6	57.5	65.8	70.2	75.1	78.9	86.7	94.9
Agriculture	3.3	4.8	5.2	3.0	7.7	8.8	11.3	15.9	22.9	13.6	25.6	31.4	26.6	17.2	20.9	15.9
Natural resources	1.0	2.1	3.1	7.3	10.9	13.9	13.6	13.0	12.7	12.6	13.4	13.6	13.4	14.6	16.5	14.4
Energy	0.5	0.7	1.0	2.9	5.9	10.2	15.2	13.5	9.4	7.1	5.7	4.7	4.1	2.3	4.1	2.3
Veterans' benefits	5.4	5.1	8.7	16.6	19.0	21.2	23.0	24.0	24.8	25.6	26.3	26.4	26.8	29.4	29.2	29.9
Interest on debt	8.3	10.4	14.4	23.2	44.0	52.5	68.7	85.0	89.8	111.1	129.4	136.0	138.6	151.7	165.7	170.1
All other‡	9.8	17.1	29.4	65.2	79.9	113.2	110.5	98.7	100.9	105.7	110.6	115.7	106.7	130.9	146.4	139.8
Total	92.2	118.3	195.6	332.3	450.8	590.9	678.2	745.7	808.3	851.8	946.3	989.8	1003.9	1064.0	1137.0	1151.8

* Estimates.
† This includes public assistance, food stamps, railroad and governmental employee retirement benefits, and unemployment compensation.
‡ This includes international affairs, science, space, transportation, education, commerce, community development, justice, and general government.

Source: Statistical Abstract of the United States (Washington, D.C.: Government Printing Office, 1980, 1989). The United States Budget in Brief, Fiscal Year 1990 (Washington, D.C.: Government Printing Office, 1989).

operating government agencies and programs. Consequently, most people were only indirectly affected by budget decisions, such as whether appropriations were increased for the Department of Commerce or sharply cut for the foreign aid programs. This is no longer the case. Now a large portion of the budget goes directly to provide income support for retired persons, veterans, farmers, the needy, and others. Many corporations have also become reliant upon defense spending (or contracting) for their continued prosperity.

These changes in the composition of the budget reflect changes in national priorities. They also have important consequences for the budgetary process. Those directly affected by governmental programs have organized to defend and increase their benefits and have become important participants in the budgetary process. This has made budget decision making both more political and more difficult. Even in an age of trillion dollar budgets, there is not enough money to meet all demands. As elsewhere in the political process, those who are organized tend to fare better.

The budget conveys a good view of the government's total set of policies for the fiscal year it covers. In the budget one can find answers to such policy issues as the balance between private and governmental (national) spending, the balance between civilian and military spending, whether medical research (including AIDS) will be accelerated or slowed, whether welfare spending in general as well as spending for particular welfare programs will be expanded or contracted, whether there will be greater or lesser regulation of surface or strip mining, and whether more or less emphasis will be given to environmental protection. This happens because the budgetary process, within the framework of existing substantive law, is a process for making choices among competing social values and allocating resources for their attainment. The budget is not simply a financial statement; it is also a policy statement. Conflicts over money are in reality conflicts over policy.

The content and effectiveness of public policies often depend considerably upon the amount of funds provided for their enforcement or implementation. The rigorousness of antitrust enforcement, the number of children enrolled in Headstart programs, the number of illegal aliens apprehended, and the availability of housing subsidies for low-income people are all matters very much affected by appropriations. The Occupational Safety and Health Administration, for example, has funding to hire only enough inspectors to permit the inspection of covered work places on the average of once every ten years. Obviously this limits the impact of the program. This is in line with the Reagan administration's goal of reducing the amount of regulations by reducing the number of regulators by restricting the funds of regulatory agencies. On the other hand, increased funding for the National Institutes of Health means an expansion of basic health-related research, about 85 percent of which is financed by the national government.

In addition to being used to finance the government's various activities and policies, the budget can also be used to stabilize the economy, to help prevent inflation or recession. Fiscal policy involves the discretionary use of the government's taxing and spending powers to stimulate or restrain the economy through budget deficits or surpluses, respectively. Briefly stated, according to Keynesian economic theory, a budget deficit adds to the total demand for goods and services in the economy, thereby stimulating the economy. Conversely, a budget surplus will reduce the total demand for goods and services, thereby imposing restraint on the economy. Fiscal policy was relied heavily upon in the 1960s and 1970s by presidential administrations in their efforts to stabilize the economy. The large, annual budget deficits incurred by the government during the Reagan years can be viewed as either "neutralizing" fiscal policy or as providing a continual stimulus to the economy. Regardless of the interpretation, the budgetary situation meant that the task of stabilizing the economy fell largely upon the Federal Reserve Board and its use of monetary policy (which involves control of the interest rate and money supply).

Finally, the budgetary process provides the president and Congress with an opportunity to review periodically the various policies and programs of the government, to assess their effectiveness, and to inquire into the manner of their administration. Every policy and program will not be examined in detail every year, but over a period of a few years most if not all will come under scrutiny. Thus the budgetary process provides a continuing opportunity for the exertion of presidential and congressional influence and control over the implementation of policies. Favored agencies and programs will likely prosper; those under attack, whether for wasting money, harassing citizens, or misconstruing policies, may suffer cutbacks and restraints. Thus, in 1989 congressional conservatives attacked the appropriation for the National Endowment for the Arts because they considered a couple of art exhibitions sponsored by the agency to be pornographic. Although most of the budget decisions made in a given year will be marginal, involving limited increases or decreases in agency funds, this does not diminish their importance.

THE NATIONAL BUDGETARY PROCESS

The budget submitted by the president to Congress in January of each year is for a single fiscal year, which extends from October 1 of one calendar year through September 30 of the following year. It takes its name from the calendar year in which it ends. Thus the period from October 1, 1981, through September 30, 1990, is designated fiscal year (FY) 1990.

The national budgetary process, like state and local budgetary processes, can be divided into four stages: preparation, authorization, execution, and audit. Auditing, which involves checking on expenditures to determine whether illegality, waste, or extravagance was involved, will not be discussed here.

Executive Preparation

The annual task of preparing a budget and submitting it to Congress for approval was assigned to the president by the Budget and Accounting Act of 1921. To assist the president in this task, the act established the Bureau of the Budget, now called the Office of Management and Budget (OMB). Prior to 1921, the president had been only marginally involved in the budgetary process; the departments and agencies acted largely on their own and sent their budget requests directly to Congress.

Preparation of the national budget within the executive branch begins nine months or so before it is sent to Congress in January of a given year. Most of the day-to-day work in developing the budget is handled by the OMB and the executive departments and agencies. The OMB provides instructions, policy guidance, and tentative budget ceilings to help the departments and agencies develop their budget requests. The latter, who are directly and specifically affected by budget decisions, and who are usually believers in the value and necessity of their programs, are expected to act as the advocates of increased spending (appropriations). What they request is subject to review and revision by OMB in accordance with the policies and programs of the president. Agencies sufficiently aggrieved by OMB decisions may try to appeal them to the president, who more often than not will uphold the OMB. Some presidents have discouraged the appeal of OMB decisions, however.

During the early years of the Reagan administration a "top down" budgetary process overlaid the traditional (or "bottom up") budgetary pattern, except for the Department of Defense. Basic budget decisions were made at the presidential level by the OMB director and others and, in effect, imposed on the departments and agencies. This in turn meant that they had less budgetary influence and discretion than under the former "bottom up" process. As time went on, however, the centralization of executive authority and ideological unity necessary to make top down budgeting workable and acceptable waned within the administration. As this happened, the budgetary process inched back toward the traditional "bottom up" pattern. Whether subsequent presidential administrations will be able to duplicate the early Reagan administration's budgetary control is problematical.[1]

The budget sent to Congress will reflect the president's decisions and priorities on such matters as its overall size, its possible effects on the economy, its major directions in public policy, and its allocation of funds among the various agencies and programs. Lyndon Johnson in 1967 wanted both "guns and butter"—increased spending for both the Vietnam war and the social welfare programs of his Great Society. Ronald Reagan, on the other hand, in the 1980s wanted less spending for a variety of welfare and domestic programs and more spending for national defense. President Bush's budget priorities in his first year in office were unclear. Campaigning for the presidency, he had advocated a "flexible freeze" on spending, no new taxes, and a reduction in the budget deficit. Although these goals were perhaps sufficient for campaign purposes, they did not amount to a real set of priorities. Once in office he initially did little to clarify them.

The discretion of both the president and Congress in making budget decisions is reduced by the fact that around three-quarters of national expenditures are "uncontrollable," at least in the short run. Based on existing law, uncontrollable expenditures represent continuing obligations and commitments that can be modified or eliminated only if the statutes authorizing them are changed. Examples include entitlement programs such as Social Security, Medicare, veterans' pensions, Guaranteed Student Loans, and agricultural price-support payments; grant-in-aid payments to the states; and interest on the national debt. Entitlement payments are so called because everyone who meets the eligibility criteria is entitled to benefits on the basis of a formula in the law. Appropriations for entitlements are made on an open-ended basis. Much of the spending that is controllable falls within the national defense area, which, as a practical matter, is not subject to extensive alteration. Since substantial reductions in military payrolls and weapons procurement would adversely affect defense preparedness, there is not much public or official support for such action.

Many of the entitlement programs are indexed to the consumer price index so that expenditures for them increase automatically during inflationary periods. This further inhibits the ability of the president and Congress to control expenditures or change budget priorities. Sometimes called "automatic government," indexation is a technique that, whatever its other uses, policy makers can use to avoid having to make tough decisions on program benefit levels, and to avoid the blame for potentially unpopular decisions.[2]

Congressional Authorization

The Constitution in Article I provides that "no money shall be drawn from the treasury, but in consequence of appropriations made by law," which means appropriations legislation enacted by Congress. To begin, it is important to note that two distinct steps are usually involved in the funding of public policies and programs. First, substantive legislation has to be enacted establishing a policy or program (e.g., the Clean Water Act) and authorizing the expenditure of money in its support. Second, money actually has to be made available for the policy or program through the adoption of appropriations legislation. The House has had a rule since 1833 that states that "no appropriation shall be reported in any general appropriations bill, or be in order as an amendment thereto, for any expenditure not previously authorized by law." Authorization legislation is handled by the various substantive or legislative committees (such as Agriculture, Energy and Commerce, and Armed Services), while appropriations legislation is the domain of the House and Senate Appropriations Committees. It is not uncommon for programs for which funding is authorized either to go unfunded or to be funded at levels lower than those authorized. Different committees, members, and processes in Congress can produce different policy results.

The legislative committees have sometimes circumvented the appropriations committees and the obstacles they represent by resorting to "backdoor spending." This may involve authorizing an agency to borrow money from the Treasury, which the agency can then spend. Or it may involve authorizing an agency to contract for the purchase of goods and services. Subsequently, funds will have to be appropriated to cover the borrowing or contracts. The House Appropriations Committee has been especially opposed to such practices because they effectively limit the committee's authority over spending.

For purposes of legislative enactment, the president's budget, which comes to Congress as a single document several hundred pages in length, is divided into thirteen appropriations bills (e.g., for defense, energy and water development, interior and related agencies, and foreign operations). These are then referred to the House Appropriations Committee, which by longstanding custom acts first on the budget. Its subcommittees hold hearings at which agency officials and others testify on budget requests and otherwise do most of the detailed legislative work on the budget. In reviewing agencies and their programs, the members of Congress may focus on topics such as the following:[3]

1. *Existence:* Is the agency or program necessary? Should it be retained?
2. *Objectives:* What are the goals of the agency or program? Are they the correct ones?
3. *Results:* What is the program accomplishing? Can the agency demonstrate benefits? Why are there complaints about the agency or program?
4. *Line-item changes:* Why does the agency need more money for person-

nel, equipment, or other matters? Why does it cost so much to run the program? What will a new program cost?

Hearings often focus on the fourth item, which involves changes in program funding. This is more determinate in nature than is deciding whether a program is necessary or what a program has accomplished. Members appear more comfortable in dealing with the financial aspects of agency operations.

What the subcommittees recommend is usually accepted with minimal change by the full Appropriations Committee. Its recommendations are in turn customarily approved with few changes by the House. As a consequence of this pattern, detailed decision making on appropriations is handled by small groups of House members.

The Senate Appropriations Committee, to which appropriations bills passed by the House are sent, does not engage in as intensive examinations of budget requests as does the House. Rather, the Senate Appropriations Committee tends to focus on "items in dispute," and serves as an appellate body to which agencies who have had their budget requests cut in the House can appeal for restoration of at least part of the cuts. The Senate frequently responds positively to such pleas.

Conference committees are used to resolve the differences between the House and Senate versions of appropriations bills. Often this involves "splitting the difference" between the two bills. Compromises are considerably easier to reach on money matters than on social issues such as abortion, school prayers, or gun control. These latter involve "moral" choices on which it is hard to compromise or divide up the difference.

Following the completion of congressional action, appropriations bills go to the president for approval. Once described as "veto proof" because the continued operation of the government depends on the spending they authorize, recent presidents have invalidated this bit of conventional wisdom. A number of appropriations bills viewed as "budget busting" or inflationary, or including funding for purposes not favored by the executive, have been turned down. Congress must then either rework the appropriations bill to meet presidential objections or seek to override the veto. Three of four appropriations bills vetoed by President Ford as inflationary were enacted into law by the Democratically controlled Congress by overriding the vetoes.

Presidents may also use their veto power more positively by threatening to wield it on an appropriations bill under congressional consideration. This may induce Congress to tailor the bill to fit presidential objectives and avoid the veto, especially if congressional leaders think the votes are not available for an override. This is really a form of strategic bargaining in which the possibility of future action is used in an effort to influence current action.

TABLE 5.2 Department of Transportation Appropriation,
Fiscal Year 1989 (Thousands of Dollars)

Item	President's Request	House Bill	Senate Bill	Enacted
Office of the Secretary	$ 68,610	$ 90,444	$ 89,890	$ 88,342
Coast Guard	2,970,306	2,632,750	2,699,616	2,696,216
Federal Aviation Administration	5,236,057	4,862,460	4,815,390	4,891,128
Federal Highway Administration	24,577	118,605	91,204	166,229
National Highway Traffic Safety Administration	94,538	99,800	96,180	98,650
Federal Railroad Administration	56,107	662,050	668,070	666,186
Urban Mass Transportation Administration	128,000	2,139,053	1,905,382	2,014,882
St. Lawrence Seaway	11,500	11,360	10,806	11,100
Research and Special Programs Administration	25,282	23,830	24,600	24,100
Office of the Inspector General	29,639	29,000	29,200	29,000
	$8,644,616	$10,669,352	$10,430,338	$10,685,833

Source: *Congressional Quarterly Weekly Report,* Vol. 46 (October 1, 1988), p. 2691.

The total amount of funds appropriated by Congress for a fiscal year will not deviate greatly from what is recommended in the president's budget. A change of 4 or 5 percent, up or down, would be exceptional. For fiscal year 1989, for example, President Reagan requested a total of $1,233.2 billion; Congress appropriated $1,272.7 billion. For particular agencies and programs, however, congressional action may differ substantially from presidential recommendations. As shown in Table 5.2, in 1989 Congress appropriated much more for the Department of Transportation than the President sought, most notably for urban mass transportation and Amtrak (in the Federal Railroad Administration item), programs that Reagan wanted to eliminate.

Action on all of the appropriations bills, including presidential approval, is supposed to be completed before the start of the fiscal year on October 1. It is quite common, however, for some or all of the bills to be pending on that date. When this occurs, a continuing resolution, which enables the affected agencies to continue operating on the basis of last year's budget, will be adopted. In 1987, none of the appropriations bills for fiscal year 1988 had been enacted when it began. Agencies operated on the basis of continuing resolutions for nearly three months before the budget was finally adopted in the form of an omnibus continuing resolution, which incorporated all of the appropriations bills.

At this point, a matter of terminology needs to be handled. Appropriation acts create *budget authority,* which permits agencies to obligate themselves for the expenditure or loan of money. When the money is actually paid out or expended, it is called an *outlay.* An agency must have budget authority before it can make an outlay. When Congress considers and acts on presidential budget requests, the focus is on budget authority (or appropriations). However, discussions of budget deficits and surpluses focus on outlays (or expenditures). Money that an agency obligates itself to spend in a given fiscal year, however, may not actually be paid out until a subsequent year, as is the case with many Defense Department purchases of weapons systems. Because of this, outlays or expenditures for a given fiscal year must be estimated; they cannot be precisely known until after the year is over.

In the immediate post–World War II decades, the budgetary process was somewhat disjointed and chaotic. Appropriations and revenues were considered separately by different committees and processes. The budget surplus or deficit for a fiscal year was an "accidental figure," determined only when all the appropriations bills, considered separately, were enacted, totaled, and compared with available revenue. Dissatisfaction with this situation, plus concern over the rapid growth of governmental spending and continued budget deficits, and a desire for greater congressional attention to the fiscal policy implications of the budget, contributed to the adoption of the Congressional Budget and Impoundment Control Act of 1974.[4]

The budgetary reform provisions of the act provide for a congressional budget process to coordinate the decentralized process by which budget decisions in Congress had been made. This involves setting overall levels of revenues and expenditures and the establishment of priorities (and spending limits) among functional areas (such as agriculture, international relations, and transportation) included in the budget. New Budget Committees were created in the House and Senate to handle these tasks. To assist them in their work, and to provide Congress with its own source of budgeting data and studies, a Congressional Budget Office (CBO) was set up.

The timetable for the congressional budget process, as it currently exists, is set forth in Table 5.3. (One should not assume that the various deadlines are precisely met.) The concurrent budget resolution developed by the Budget Committees sets targets for both overall revenues and expenditures (and thus indicates whether the budget will be balanced or in deficit). It also sets limits for each of the various functional areas. The Appropriations Committees are expected to work within the policy framework provided by the budget resolution.

If the appropriations and revenues limits set by the budget resolution are not met, reconciliation legislation is called for. The reconciliation process, under the control of the Budget Committees, involves action directing the legislative committees to make changes in substantive laws so as to

TABLE 5.3   Congressional Budget Process, 1989–93*

Early January	President submits his budget to Congress.
February 15	CBO reports to the Budget Committees on fiscal policy and budget priorities.
February 25	Congressional committees submit views and estimates on spending to the Budget Committee.
April 1	Senate Budget Committee reports its budget resolution. (There is no similar requirement for the House Budget Committee.)
April 15	Congress acts on the concurrent budget resolution.
June 10	House Appropriations Committee completes action on regular appropriations bills.
June 15	Congress passes a reconciliation bill.
June 30	House completes action on all appropriations bills.
August 20	CBO reports on estimated deficit and needed reductions in spending.
August 25	OMB estimates budget deficit and orders any necessary budget cuts.
October 1	New fiscal year begins.
October 15	"Automatic" budget cuts by OMB become effective if Congress has not adopted an alternative. President issues a sequestration order.
November 15	General Accounting Office issues compliance report on the sequestration order.

*This schedule reflects changes in the regular budget schedule made by the Gramm-Rudman-Hollings Act of 1985, as amended in 1987.

bring the spending (usually for entitlement programs) or the taxes that they authorize into line with the totals in the budget resolution. This legislation, unlike the congressional budget resolution, requires the approval of the president. First used on a limited basis by the Carter administration in 1980, the reconciliation process was utilized in 1981 by the Reagan administration to cut $35 billion from the budget.

Observers seem to agree that the new budgetary process has improved the quality of congressional decision making on the budget. More and better budgetary information is available to Congress. Budget decisions are more fully considered and debated, and members of Congress are compelled to heed the overall dimensions of the budget. The budget decision-making process has also become more complex with the new procedures and the participation of the Budget Committees. Conflict sometimes occurs between the Budget Committees, and the Appropriations and Tax Committees. The House Appropriations Committee, once famed for its role as "guardian of the treasury," and its subcommittees have consequently become more protective of their members' favorite agencies and programs.

Budget Execution

The obligation and actual expenditure (or outlay) of funds, once appropriated, rests with the various departments and agencies. To begin spending, however, they must first secure an apportionment from the OMB. An apportionment distributes "appropriations and other budgetary resources" (e.g., the authority to borrow money) to an agency "by time periods [usually quarterly] and by activities in order to ensure the effective use of available resources and to preclude the need for additional appropriations."[5] The OMB may also direct agencies to set aside funds for contingencies or not to spend funds when greater efficiency in operations or altered needs permit savings to be achieved without restricting the accomplishment of agency goals.

The amount of discretion that the president and agency officials have in spending funds and achieving objectives is significantly affected by the language of the appropriations laws. Executive officials would prefer to have broad discretion in deciding whether to spend funds or to shift funds among programs. However, Congress often includes considerable detail in appropriations legislation to reduce agency discretion and compel adherence to congressional preferences. Specific restrictions or instructions may be included, as when an amendment to an appropriations bill required the Occupational Health and Safety Administration to get rid of "nuisance standards." The committee reports accompanying appropriations bills may also specify how funds should be spent. Although these reports are not legally binding, it is impolitic for officials to disregard them, because members of Congress may subsequently call officials to account for ignoring such instructions. On the other hand, Congress may sometimes provide agencies with "lump sum" or very broad appropriations that confer much spending discretion, albeit within the boundaries provided by substantive legislation pertaining to agency action.

The practice of the presidential impoundment of funds has produced much controversy in recent years.[6] Presidents have long claimed and exercised authority to prevent the expenditure of funds for purposes they disagreed with on budgetary or policy grounds. Presidents Truman and Eisenhower, for example, refused to spend funds for military programs that they had not requested. President Lyndon Johnson impounded billions of dollars to combat inflation, although much of what he held back was subsequently released. Impoundment up until the 1970s was usually done on a selective and limited basis; and, although some dissatisfaction in Congress was created, major confrontations were avoided.

President Nixon, however, precipitated a major conflict over impoundment. Following his reelection in 1972, he decided to "take on the Congress and take over the government." This effort included the extensive impoundment of funds for water pollution control, mass transit, food stamps, medical research, urban renewal, agricultural programs, and highway construction. Numerous rationales were given, including the need to prevent the inflationary effects of "reckless" spending. In various instances, however, it was clear that the administration was using impoundment to reduce or eliminate congressionally authorized programs of which it disapproved. Most of the impoundments were challenged by adversely affected parties and were held to be illegal by the federal courts.

Congress too was stirred to action by the Nixon impoundments and included some controls on impoundment in the 1974 budget law. Under the act a *deferral* of expenditures, in which the executive seeks to delay or stretch out spending until a future point in the fiscal year when it is needed, could be done unless or until either house of Congress voted to disapprove. In contrast, an executive *rescission* of funds, which cancels existing budget authority and thus stops the expenditure of funds, becomes effective only if, within forty-five days of notification, both houses pass a rescission bill. It is, in actuality, not always easy to distinguish deferrals from rescissions. Overall, the effects of the new impoundment procedures were to give Congress more (and the executive less) authority over spending and to make appropriations legislation more of a mandate for agencies to spend allocated funds.

In *Immigration and Naturalization Service* v. *Chadha* of 1983,[7] a case involving a minor immigration matter, the Supreme Court declared unconstitutional the use of the legislative veto. The legislative veto permitted Congress or its committee to disapprove particular rules or actions of executive agencies and officials, such as the deferral of spending. Did this mean, then, that the president could still engage in the deferral of spending although Congress, if it so desired, could not veto the actions? The issue came to a head in 1986, when President Reagan acted to defer the expenditure of $5.1 billion for housing and related aid to low-income people. This action was quickly contested in the courts. In May 1986, a federal district court, later upheld by an appeals court, ruled that the president did not have deferral authority under the 1974 budget law. Both courts took the view that Congress would not have given deferral authority to the president without retaining a legislative veto for itself. Hence, when the legislative veto perished, so did deferral authority.

The problem pointed up in the controversy over deferral applies to the budgetary process generally: What is the appropriate balance between presidential discretion and congressional control in spending? In cases of

TABLE 5.4   Budget Receipts, Outlays, Surplus or Deficit, and Total
National Debt for Selected Years from 1940 to 1988 (Billions of Dollars)

Year	Receipts	Outlays	Surplus or Deficit	National Debt
1940	6.5	9.5	−2.9	50.7
1945	45.2	92.7	−47.6	260.1
1950	39.4	42.6	−3.1	256.8
1955	65.5	68.4	−4.1	274.4
1960	92.5	92.3	0.3	290.9
1965	116.8	118.2	−1.4	325.2
1969	186.9	183.6	3.2	367.1
1970	192.8	195.6	−2.8	382.6
1975	279.1	332.3	−53.2	544.1
1980	517.1	590.9	−73.8	914.3
1985	734.1	946.3	−212.3	1827.5
1988	908.9	1064.0	−155.1	2581.6*

*Estimated.

Source: *Annual Report of the Council of Economic Advisers* (Washington, D.C.: Government Printing Office, 1988), p. 374.

conflict, whose judgment should prevail? It would be much easier to answer these questions if only managerial matters were at stake. However, as we have seen, the budget is a policy document that reflects major policy values and priorities. This makes budgetary decision making much more contentious.

FIGHTING BUDGET DEFICITS

The national debt of the United States rapidly increased during the late 1970s and 1980s because of rising expenditures for entitlement programs and national defense, and declining revenues stemming from the 1981 tax cut and the recession of the early 1980s. Annual budget deficits reached what many considered alarming proportions; some said the budget was "hemorrhaging." The deficit for fiscal year 1986 reached a figure of minus $220.1 billion. The size of the national debt tripled during the 1980s (see Table 5.4). In this section some efforts to fashion and implement policy for budget deficit reduction are treated.

The Balanced Budget and Emergency Deficit Control Act (better known as the Gramm-Rudman-Hollings Act) was enacted by Congress in December 1985. Public and congressional concern over the large budget deficits of the 1980s provided the context and motivation for it. Efforts to reduce the budget deficit by conventional budgetary procedures had been unsuccessful because of strong partisan differences between members of Congress (especially the Democrats) and the Reagan administration on military and social welfare spending as well as tax increases.

The Gramm-Rudman-Hollings proposal was introduced in the Senate in late September 1985 as an amendment to a bill authorizing an increase in the size of the national debt, which was required to enable the government to continue borrowing money to meet its spending obligations. The amendment never received committee hearings or consideration in either house, however, although these are customary for legislation of such importance. The proposal required the president and Congress to eliminate the budget deficit within five years, either through the use of regular budget procedures or, if these were unavailing, through automatic, uniform, across-the-board budget cuts implemented by the CBO and the OMB. Described by Senator Warren Rudman (R, New Hampshire) as "a bad idea whose time had come," within a couple of weeks the Republican-led Senate had passed the measure by a 75-to-24 vote. This is indicative of how strongly the Senate felt compelled to do something about the deficit.

The House, under control of the Democrats, was now faced with the need to deal with the Gramm-Rudman-Hollings proposal.[8] Essentially, the House had three alternatives: ignore the proposal, explicitly reject it, or seek to modify it to make it more palatable. The Democratic leadership opted for modification of the proposal as the only politically viable alternative, given the public concern over the budget deficit. Negotiations with the Senate were entered into through the use of bipartisan conference task forces, rather than a regular conference committee. A compromise version of the Gramm-Rudman-Hollings bill was passed by the House, only to be rejected by a 24-to-74 Senate vote. The Senate then approved a version of the bill that was much the same as what it had originally passed. This in turn was quickly rejected by the House by a 117-to-239 party-line vote, the Democrats being in the majority. Momentarily, stalemate loomed.

Important issues in dispute between the two houses (and the political parties) included the timetable for deficit reduction, the number and nature of the programs to be exempted from automatic budget cuts, and the procedure to be used in making the automatic cuts. Questions were also raised about the constitutionality of the legislation. Negotiations between the House and the Senate were resumed, now handled by a small group of leaders meeting in private sessions rather than the conference committee. They succeeded in hammering out an agreement that was adopted by both houses in mid-December 1985 and signed into law by the president.

As originally enacted, the Gramm-Rudman-Hollings Act required that federal budget deficits be reduced to $171.9 billion in fiscal year 1986, $144 billion in 1987, $108 billion in 1988, $72 billion in 1989, $36 billion in 1990, and zero in 1991. A number of programs were exempted from the automatic budget cuts, including Social Security, veterans' pensions, Medicaid, food stamps, Aid to Families with Dependent Children (AFDC), child nutrition, and interest on the national debt. Cuts were limited in amount for five health programs, including Medicare. (These exemptions can be viewed as indicating congressional priorities on spending.) If regular budget and appropriations action failed to reach the deficit targets, then uniform and across-the-board reductions, divided equally in amount between nonexempt domestic programs and defense programs, would be made. This meant that across-the-board cuts would hit hard on nonexempt programs, because a substantial portion of the budget was immune from reductions.

The amount of any automatic reductions required, called a *sequester*, was to be determined by joint action by the CBO, OMB, and General Accounting Office (GAO), with the final decision resting with the GAO, a congressional agency headed by the comptroller general, who can be removed from office only by Congress. Although this would be put into effect by a presidential sequestration order, an overall effect of the act was to give the president little or no discretion in imposing the automatic budget cuts. There were doubts concerning the constitutionality of the act because of the involvement of the GAO in making the automatic budget cuts. Consequently, the Act provided that if the courts struck down the procedure for making automatic cuts, the reductions would have to be approved by both houses of Congress and the president, which meant that they were no longer automatic.

Several members of Congress immediately brought suit challenging the constitutionality of the act because of the role of the GAO and the comptroller general. The Reagan administration also questioned its constitutionality. In July 1986 the United States Supreme Court, by a 7-to-2 vote, determined that the automatic spending reduction procedure was unconstitutional while leaving the remainder of the law intact. The majority held that by giving final responsibility to the comptroller general, "who is subject to removal only by itself, Congress in effect has retained control over the execution of the act and has intruded into the executive function. The Constitution does not permit such intrusion."[9] The minority thought that this took too narrow a view of what was permissible under the separation of powers principle. The Court's decision removed from the statute its vital, action-forcing core.

Efforts to restore the vitality of the act were quickly begun but initially came to naught. However, in late summer 1986 the CBO and OMB issued a report stating that $45.4 billion in budget cuts were needed to meet the Gramm-Rudman-Hollings Act's target for fiscal year 1988. Cuts of this magnitude were unacceptable to most members of Congress, and also to the Reagan administration because of the reduction in defense spending they would entail. Consequently, pressure intensified to amend the act to ease the time schedule for reducing the debt and to provide again for an automatic budget reduction mechanism. Legislation for this purpose was adopted in late September 1987 and includes the following provisions:

1. The CBO and OBM are both directed to issue reports on the estimated budget deficit and the uniform percentage that program accounts must be reduced to meet the deficit reduction targets. The OMB is further directed to "give due regard" to the CBO report in deciding how much spending must be cut.
2. New budget deficit targets were set: $144 billion for fiscal year 1988, $136 billion for 1989, $100 billion for 1990, $64 billion for 1991, $28 billion for 1992, and zero for 1993.
3. A spending reduction of $23 billion was provided for 1988. (This was less than the original act required.)
4. The manner of calculating the spending total used in estimating the deficit from which cuts were to be made was revised. The effect of this was to ease the impact of cuts by expanding the base to which they would be applied.
5. The president was given some discretion to deviate from uniform reductions in military spending accounts.
6. No change was made in the programs protected against automatic reductions by the original act.

From a congressional perspective, the legislation was intended to push the president into negotiations on tax increases, defense spending restraints, and domestic spending cuts as part of a budget deficit reduction plan. Otherwise, the president would have to accept the consequences of the automatic, across-the-board cuts called for by the amended Gramm-Rudman-Hollings Act. However, because of slowness by Congress in taking action, in October 1987 the president moved to put into effect the $23 billion in across-the-board cuts the act specified for fiscal year 1988. This was intended to put pressure on Congress to reduce spending through regular budget procedures.

A few days later on October 19, the stock market collapsed, and the Dow Jones Industrial Average, a leading stock market indicator, fell by 508 points. Many wondered whether this was the precursor of a stock-market crash like that of 1929. Many attributed the collapse, at least in part, to concern by the financial communities, both in the United States and abroad, over the size of the budget deficit and the government's ability to control its finances. This created a crisis atmosphere that quickly produced negotiations between Democratic and Republican leaders in

Congress, the secretary of the Treasury, and other high-level Reagan administration officials to reduce the budget deficit.

A few weeks of closed-door meetings resulted in a Bipartisan Budget Agreement, which called for budget deficit reductions of $30 billion in 1988 and $46 billion in 1989. Included in the package were $9 billion in new tax revenues for 1988 and another $14 billion for 1989. These taxes represented a retreat for both House Democrats, who had advocated twice as much in increased taxes, and President Reagan, who had opposed any new taxes. Defense spending was increased somewhat, but not as much as the president wanted, and some entitlements were to be reduced. Legislative action was required to put the Bipartisan Budget Agreement into effect.

Strong pressure from congressional leaders of both parties was necessary to get the balky members of Congress to approve an omnibus appropriations resolution (which incorporated all thirteen annual appropriations bills) and a reconciliation bill providing for tax increases and expenditure reductions to implement the bipartisan agreement. Their enactment was marked by long bargaining sessions, partisan conflicts, and disagreement over what had been agreed to in the Bipartisan Budget Agreement, because no records had been kept and the participants had different recollections as to what they had agreed. Many members of Congress were dissatisfied with the entire process and felt excluded from real involvement. "That feeling of disfranchisement was aggravated by the way those two decisions were enacted: in two massive omnibus bills, each beyond the comprehension of any single member."[10]

As a consequence of the Bipartisan Budget Agreement and the implementing legislation, the automatic spending cuts initiated in October under the Gramm-Rudman-Hollings Act were rescinded. Regular budgetary procedures had proved sufficient. However, given the crisis-like conditions under which they were exercised, one hesitates to designate them as "normal."

What has been the impact of the Gramm-Rudman-Hollings Act on budget deficit reduction? An easy answer is not possible because of the complexity of budgetary policy and politics, and because of such actions as the Supreme Court's decision that the first automatic procedure was unconstitutional, and the Bipartisan Budget Agreement. Table 5.5 compares the Gramm-Rudman-Hollings Act budget deficit goals with the actual deficits for a few years. It does not portray success, although one could argue that the situation would have been worse without the Gramm-Rudman-Hollings Act.

What the act represents is an effort to use procedural rules to solve a substantive problem. The large budget deficits of the 1980s reflected strong differences between the president and Congress (mostly the Democrats) on issues of taxing and spending. President Reagan favored increased defense spending and lower domestic spending, and was adamantly opposed to

TABLE 5.5   The Gramm-Rudman-Hollings Act Deficit Goals
and Actual Deficits (Billions of Dollars)

Year	1985 Deficit Goals	1987 Revision of Deficit Goals	Actual Deficits
1986	171.9	—	221.2
1987	144	—	150.4
1988	108	144	155.1
1989	72	136	152.1
1990	36	100	
1991	0	64	
1992		28	
1993		0	

increasing taxes. The Democrats, who controlled the House of Representatives throughout Reagan's term and the Senate for his final two years in office, favored the maintenance of domestic spending and a reduction in defense spending. They contended that a major tax increase was needed to help balance the budget. The consequence was a stand-off. In this sort of situation, adopting some new rules is unlikely to be very effective in resolving conflict, especially when many of the participants do not like the rules.

Moreover, rules made by Congress can be changed by Congress, as the differences between the 1985 and 1987 versions of the Gramm-Rudman-Hollings Act well indicate. The rules are also open to manipulation and avoidance, as was done in 1986 and subsequently. Whether the deficit target is met at the beginning of a fiscal year involves estimating revenues and expenditures (outlays) for the year. This estimate in turn is based on a forecast of economic conditions, such as the rates of unemployment and economic growth, that will affect revenue and spending levels. Congress, on the basis of an economic forecast that was widely acknowledged to be overly optimistic, declared that it had met the target for fiscal year 1987 and that no sequestration resolution was needed. The OMB's assumption of future economic conditions was also optimistic.

Rules, as Professor Aaron Wildavsky has noted, "might help enforce a political consensus on the budget if there was one."[11] This, however, was lacking in the Reagan years. Large budget deficits were the consequence. It is unlikely that the important policy disagreements involved in the budget deficit struggle can be solved by procedural tinkering. In early 1989, a budget agreement between the Bush administration and Congress to meet the deficit reduction target was again freighted with rosy assumptions and budgetary "gimmickry." The agreement proved unworkable and a budget had not been agreed to when the fiscal year began on October 1. Subsequently, the president issued a sequestration order, cutting agency expenditures for fiscal year 1990 by $16.1 billion. Congress and the administration continued to struggle to adopt a budget that might permit rescinding the automatic reductions.[12] There was also talk of again revising the Gramm-Rudman-Hollings Act to ease the deficit reduction task.

Notes

1. Hugh Heclo, "Executive Budget Making," in Gregory B. Mills and John L. Palmer (eds.), *Federal Budget Policy in the 1980s* (Washington, D.C.: Urban Institute Press, 1984), pp. 255–291.
2. R. Kent Weaver, *Automatic Government: The Politics of Indexation* (Washington, D.C.: Brookings Institution, 1988).
3. Lance L. LeLoup, *Budgetary Politics*, 2d ed. (Brunswick, Ohio: King's Court Communications, 1980), p. 200.
4. John W. Ellwood and James A. Thurber, "The Politics of the Congressional Budget Process Re-Examined," in Lawrence C. Dodd and Bruce I. Oppenheimer (eds.), *Congress Reconsidered*, 2d ed. (Washington, D.C.: Congressional Quarterly Press, 1981), pp. 247–251.
5. *Budget of the United States Government, Fiscal Year 1989* (Washington, D.C.: Government Printing Office, 1988), p. 6e-6.
6. For fuller discussions, see Louis Fisher, *Presidential Spending Power* (Princeton, N.J.: Princeton University Press, 1975), chaps. 7–8; and James P. Pfiffner, *The President, the Budget, and Congress: Impoundment and the 1974 Budget Act* (Boulder, Colo.: Westview Press, 1979).
7. *Immigration and Naturalization Service* v. *Chadha*, 462 U.S. 919 (1983).
8. Darrell M. West, *Congress and Economic Policymaking* (Pittsburgh: University of Pittsburgh Press, 1987), chap. 7.
9. *Bowsher* v. *Synar* (1986). Reported in *Congressional Quarterly Weekly Report*, Vol. 44 (July 12, 1986), p. 1582.
10. *Congressional Quarterly Weekly Report*, Vol. 45 (December 26, 1987), p. 3184.
11. Aaron Wildavsky, *The New Politics of the Budgetary Process* (Glenview, Ill.: Scott, Foresman, 1988), p. 253.
12. *Congressional Quarterly Weekly Report*, Vol. 47 (October 21, 1989), pp. 2772–2773.

6

POLICY
IMPLEMENTATION

*Policy implementation at the most basic level:
cleanup operations at a hazardous waste site.*

Once the adoption stage of the policy process has been completed, we can begin to refer to something called *public policy*, even though it may exist only in rudimentary form and be subject to much further development. Our attention then turns to policy implementation or administration, which involves those players, organizations, procedures, and techniques concerned with carrying policies into effect in an endeavor to attain their goals. In actuality, however, it is often quite difficult if not impossible to differentiate neatly the adoption of policy from its implementation. Once again, the line between functional activities is smudgy.

Sometimes statutes do little more than to establish some policy goals and, within a framework of guidelines and restrictions, authorize the executive or an agency to fill in the details of policy through the issuance of rules or orders on the matter in question. The Occupational Safety and Health Act of 1970 is illustrative. Concerned with protecting the health and safety of workers in the workplace, it contains no substantive safety and health standards itself. Rather it authorizes the Occupational Safety and Health Administration (OSHA) in the Department of Labor to issue rules setting such standards. Only then do meaningful standards governing the behavior of employers actually exist. In effect, within the framework provided by Congress, OSHA both makes and implements policy on industrial health and safety.

A few policy decisions are essentially self-executing, such as the Nixon administration's decision to formally recognize the government of the People's Republic of China (which, in more doctrinaire years was called Communist China), presidential decisions to veto legislation passed by Congress, and the National Park Service's decision not to fight naturally caused fires in the national parks. Relatively few such decisions that entail clear-cut, one-time actions are made, however. Consequently, those concerned with the study of public policy can ill afford to neglect the implementation stage of the policy process. Much that occurs in the course of implementation may at first glance appear to be complex, tedious, or mundane, yet the consequences for the substance of policy and its impact on society may be quite profound. Moreover, closer examination will reveal that intensely strong political struggles attend the implementation of many policies, such as those relating to environmental protection, equal employment opportunity, and the management of public lands and forests.

The study of policy implementation was popularized for political scientists by the Jeffrey L. Pressman and Aaron Wildavsky study in the early 1970s of the failure of a federal jobs-creation program in Oakland, California.[1] Since then political scientists have expended much effort in seeking to develop systematic theories of policy implementation that rigorously explain why some policies are more successfully implemented than others.

Although they have yet to strike paydirt, they have helped to increase our understanding of the process of policy implementation.[2]

Although I draw generally on that body of research, in this chapter I shall pursue a more traditional approach to policy implementation. Following a discussion of some of the players in the policy implementation process, we shall examine administrative organization, politics, and policy making; the techniques of control that agencies may be authorized to use; and the problem of securing compliance with public policies. In total, this should provide the reader with a good working knowledge of the major institutional aspects of policy implementation, and some of its political features.

WHO IMPLEMENTS POLICY?

In the United States, as in other modern political systems, public policy is implemented primarily by a complex system of administrative agencies. These agencies perform most of the day-to-day work of government and thus affect citizens more directly in their actions than do any other governmental units. Nonetheless, it would not be necessary for policy analysts to be much concerned with public administration (that is, all those structures and processes involved in the implementation of public policy) were it not for the fact that agencies often have much discretion (that is, the opportunity to make choices among alternatives) in carrying out the policies under their jurisdiction. They do not automatically apply whatever the legislature or other policy adopters decide, although at one time it was widely assumed that they did.

A classic feature of the traditional literature of public administration was the notion that politics and administration were separate and distinct spheres of activity. Politics, Professor Frank Goodnow wrote in 1900, was concerned with the formulation of the will of the state; it was concerned with value judgments, and with determining what government should or should not do, and it was to be handled by the "political" branches of government, that is, the legislature and executive.[3] Administration, on the other hand, was concerned with the implementation of the will of the state, with carrying into effect, more or less automatically, the decisions of the political branches. Administration was concerned with questions of fact, with what *is* rather than what *should* be, and consequently could focus on the most efficient means (or "one best way") of implementing policy. Were this indeed the case, policy analysts could end their inquiry with the adoption of policy. However, with the possible exception of a few archaic or poorly informed souls, no one today accepts this politics-administration dichotomy.

Administrative agencies often operate under broad and ambiguous statutory mandates that leave them with much discretion to decide what should or should not be done. Thus, the Interstate Commerce Commission (ICC) is directed to fix "just and reasonable" railroad rates; the Federal Communications Commission, to license television broadcasters for the "public convenience and necessity"; the Forest Service, to follow a "multiple use" policy in the management of national forests that balances the interests of lumber companies, sportsmen, livestock grazers, and other users; the Consumer Product Safety Commission, to ban products that present an "unreasonable hazard"; and the Environmental Protection Agency (EPA), to ensure that the "best practicable" devices are used for the control of water pollutants. Such statutory mandates are in effect directives to the agencies involved to go out and make some policy.

Those who participate in the legislative process frequently are unable or unwilling to arrive at precise settlements of the conflicting interests on many issues. Only by leaving some matters somewhat nebulous and unsettled can agreement on legislation be reached. Lack of time, interest, information, and expertness as well as the need for flexibility in implementation may also help explain the delegation of broad authority to agencies. The product of these factors is often a statute couched in general language, such as that noted above, which shifts to agencies the tasks of filling in the details, making policy more precise and concrete, and trying to make more definitive adjustments among conflicting interests. Under these conditions, the administrative process becomes an extension of the legislative process, and administrators find themselves immersed in politics.

Although legislatures have delegated much policy-making authority to administrative agencies, especially in the twentieth century, it should not be assumed that legislatures cannot act in rather precise fashion. An illustration is Social Security legislation, which sets forth in rather definite terms the standards of eligibility, the levels of benefits, the amount of additional earnings permitted, and other considerations for old age and survivor's benefits. Most administrative decisions on these benefits simply involve applying the legislatively set standards to the facts of the case at hand. Under such circumstances, administrative decision making becomes largely routine and is therefore unlikely to produce controversy. In comparison, the disability standard under the Social Security program has produced considerable controversy. Disability is defined as the inability to engage in any substantial gainful activity by reason of a medically determinable physical or mental impairment expected to result in death or to be at least of twelve-month's duration. This definition of disability leaves much room for interpretation, conjecture, and disagreement.[4]

While administrative agencies are the primary implementors of public policy, many other actors may also be involved, and they should not be neglected in our study of policymaking. Those that will be examined here include the legislature, the courts, pressure groups, and community organizations. They may either be directly involved in policy implementation or act to influence administrative agencies, or both.

The Legislature

Legislative bodies display much interest in the implementation of policies and use a variety of means to influence administrative action. Here I will note some of the devices used by Congress.

One such device is the specificity of legislation. The more detailed is the legislation passed by Congress, the less discretion agencies have. Specific limitations on the use of funds may be written into statutes; or deadlines may be specified for the taking of some actions, as has been done in some environmental protection laws; or specific standards may be set, as in minimum-wage legislation. The committee reports that accompany many bills often contain suggestions or statements concerning how legislation should be implemented or indicating what projects money should go for. These reports do not have the force of law but are ignored by administrators only at their own peril.

Senatorial approval is required for many top-level executive appointments, and this may be used as a lever to influence policy. Commitments on policy matters may be extracted by Senators from nominees during hearings on their appointments. Or a nominee for a position may be rejected because of policy views or actions. In 1985, for example, the Senate rejected the nomination of William Bradford Reynolds for the position of associate attorney general, the number-three position in the Department of Justice. In the view of a majority of the Senate and of pro–civil rights groups Reynolds, as assistant attorney general for civil rights, had been unsympathetic and restrictive in his enforcement of civil rights policies. They did not want him in a higher-level, more influential Justice position.

The legislative veto, an arrangement under which either congressional approval has to be secured before an administrative action could be taken or a particular action can be subsequently rejected by Congress or its committees, originated in 1932. President Herbert Hoover wanted authority to reorganize the national administrative system but Congress was reluctant to grant it. A deal was made. The president was authorized to reorganize the system but Congress gave itself the right to disapprove his actions if they were deemed objectionable. Since then, and especially in the 1960s and 1970s, provisions for legislative veto arrangements have been included in over two hundred laws. The legislative veto gives administrative agencies the desired flexibility in the implementation of legislation while permitting Congress, if it so chooses, to exercise control over what is done. It also enables Congress to become involved in the details of administration.[5]

As was noted in Chapter 5, the legislative veto was declared unconstitutional in 1983 by the Supreme Court. Nonetheless, between then and 1989 over a hundred new legislative-veto provisions were included in laws. Others have been put in place by informal agreements between Congress and the executive. For instance, an agreement on aid to the Nicaraguan "Contras" (rebels) negotiated by Bush administration officials and congressional leaders gave each of four congressional committees a veto over the program. Otherwise, Congress might not have passed legislation authorizing the program. The legislative veto persists because both the executive and legislative branches find that it usefully serves their interests.

Finally, much of the time of many members of Congress and their staffs, and some of the time of all members, is devoted to "casework." Typically, casework involves handling problems that constituents are having with administrative agencies, such as delayed Social Security or veterans' benefits, difficulty in getting action on a license request, and uncertainty as to how to apply for a grant. The constituents, of course, want their representatives to secure favorable action for them. Members of Congress engage in casework because it is thought helpful to their chances of reelection. Casework also helps "humanize" administration by making it more responsive to individual needs and problems.

The Courts

Some laws are enforced primarily through judicial action. Laws dealing with crimes are the most obvious example. Some economic regulatory statutes, such as the Sherman Act, are enforced through lawsuits brought in the federal district courts, many of which are eventually appealed to the Supreme Court. Because of this and the generality of the act's language, the meaning of antitrust policy depends greatly upon judicial interpretation and application of the statute. In the nineteenth century, it was quite common for legislatures to enact laws requiring or prohibiting some action and then to leave it to the citizens to protect their rights under the law through proceedings brought in the courts. Generally, administrative regulation, in which primary responsibility is assigned to an agency for the enforcement of a statute, is now much more commonplace than judicial regulation in the American political system.

In some instances, the courts may be directly involved in the administration of policy. Naturalization proceedings for aliens are really administrative in form, but they are handled by the federal district courts.

Bankruptcy proceedings are another illustration. A complex system of trustees, receivers, appraisers, accountants, auctioneers, and others is supervised by federal bankruptcy courts. In all, it is "a large scale example of routine administrative machinery."[6] Many divorce and domestic relations cases handled by state courts also appear essentially administrative, involving matters of guidance and management rather than disputed law or facts.

The courts' most important influence on administration, however, is through their interpretation of statutes and administrative rules and regulations, and their review of administrative decisions in cases brought before them. Courts can facilitate, hinder, or largely nullify the implementation of particular policies through their decisions. The story of how the Supreme Court destroyed the effectiveness of early national railroad regulation under the Interstate Commerce Act of 1887 by unfavorable rulings on the ICC's authority to regulate rates is well-recorded history. In recent years the Supreme Court's rulings have been generally supportive of equal opportunity and affirmative action programs (more so than the Reagan administration sometimes preferred).

Pressure Groups

Because of the discretion often vested in agencies by legislation, once an act is adopted, the group struggle shifts from the legislative to the administrative arena. Given the operating discretion of many agencies, a group that can successfully influence agency action may have a substantial effect on the course and impact of public policies. Sometimes relationships between a group and an agency may become so close as to lead to the allegation that the group has "captured" the agency. In the past, for example, it was frequently stated that the ICC was the "captive" of the railroads,[7] and it is not uncommon now to hear comments to the effect that the Federal Maritime Commission is unduly influenced by the shipping companies. Also, groups may complain to Congress or the executive if they believe a statute is not being implemented in accordance with the intent of Congress.

Groups may become directly involved in administration, as when representation of particular interests is specified on the boards of plural-headed agencies. A common illustration is state occupational licensing boards, whose governing statutes frequently provide that some or all of the board members must come from the licensed profession. Occupational licensing (and regulatory) programs are usually controlled by the dominant elements within the licensed groups. Consequently, such programs usually do more to protect the interests of the licensed group than those of the general public.

Advisory bodies, such as the Advisory Committee on Vocational Education, the Advisory Committee on Hog Cholera Eradication, and the Advisory Committee on Reactor Safeguards, are another means by which groups may become participants in policy administration. Currently there are around a thousand advisory groups serving national administrative agencies.[8] Some simply provide needed advice to agencies and their officials, as their name implies; others become more directly involved in program administration. Membership in advisory bodies may give group representatives privileged or special access to governmental agencies. Thus many large defense contractors are represented on advisory committees for the Department of Defense. When advisory groups have a role in agency decision making, they add legitimacy to the policies that they have helped to develop.[9]

Some advisory committees may have direct control over program administration. For instance, each of the eleven institutes within the National Institutes of Health (NIH) has a twelve-member advisory council. Committee members must be leaders in science, medicine, and public affairs, including six who are specialists in the field covered by the particular institute (e.g., cancer, aging, or allergy and infectious diseases). Research grants to medical schools, universities, and others, which total around $6 billion annually, can be made only with the approval of each institute's advisory council.

Community Organizations

At the local level, community or other organizations have occasionally been used in the administration of national policies. Examples include farmer committees under the price-support and soil conservation programs of the Department of Agriculture; advisory boards for the Bureau of Land Management; and representatives of the poor for Community Action agencies. Participatory democracy of this sort may give those involved considerable influence over the application of programs at the grass-roots level and also build program support. Local draft boards ("little groups of neighbors" as they were sometimes called), had an important role during the Vietnam War years in determining, when only a portion of eligible males were required to meet military needs, who got drafted and who did not.[10] Many of the losers in the draft wound up in Vietnam. The compulsory draft and draft boards were later eliminated, although eligible males are still required to register.

In sum, a variety of participants may have a hand in the administration of a given policy. In addition to those discussed above, political party officials, the communications media (as by reporting, publicizing, or criticizing some agency actions), and executive staff agencies may also become involved. Certainly this is true of the Office of Management and Budget (OMB), whose concerns extend much beyond funding. Since 1981, for instance, the OMB has had authority to supervise the issuance of economic rules and regulations by executive branch agencies. (More will be said on this in Chapter 7.) The number and variety of implementation participants will vary from one policy area to another, depending upon a policy's salience and its breadth of impact.

ADMINISTRATIVE ORGANIZATION

One could say that one administrative agency looks pretty much like another or, in another usage, if you have seen one agency, you have seen them all. To take such a position, however, is to make a serious mistake. Agencies in fact do differ greatly in such respects as structure, operating styles, political support, expertness, and policy orientation. Those seeking to influence the nature of public policy often show much concern over the particular agency or type of agency that will administer a given policy. Conflict over questions of administrative organization can be every bit as sharp as conflict over substantive policies. The formation of administrative organizations is a political as well as a technical task.

Most public policies are not self-executing; hence, if they are to be carried into effect, responsibility for their implementation must be assigned either to an existing agency or to a new agency established for this purpose. The creation of new agencies is usually handled by the legislature. At the national level, however, some have been created by the executive under the administrative reorganization authority, which permits the president to propose reorganization plans that go into effect automatically unless disapproved by either house of Congress. The EPA, for example, was created by a Nixon administration reorganization proposal in 1970 and now handles pollution-control enforcement activities formerly spread among a number of agencies. The effect has been to give a sharper focus to the administration of antipollution policies. A few other agencies, such as ACTION, which administers some volunteer-service programs, and the Social and Rehabilitation Service, have been set up on the basis of broad substantive authority delegated by Congress to the executive.

The discussion in this section will be focused on the policy implications of administrative organization. A number of propositions will be presented and illustrated to indicate how organizational considerations affect policy, and, thus, why they should receive the attention of policy analysts.

1. When a new program is adopted, the contending interests may seek

to have its administration awarded to an agency they think will be more favorable to their interests. A major consideration during the enactment of the Occupational Safety and Health Act, the first major general industrial-safety bill passed by Congress, was who should administer it. Organized labor and most liberal Democrats favored locating all standard-setting and enforcement activity in the Department of Labor, which they regarded as sympathetic toward labor. Many Republicans, the Nixon administration, and business groups wanted an independent board (or boards) to make and enforce standards, to avoid Labor Department control of the program. The result was a compromise. The Department of Labor was given authority to set standards, to enforce them, and to assess penalties. Within the department these tasks are handled by OSHA. An independent, three-member, quasi-judicial Occupational Safety and Health Review Commission was created to hear appeals from Labor Department actions. A National Institute for Occupational Safety and Health was established within the Department of Health, Education, and Welfare (now Health and Human Services) to conduct research and to create an information base for health standards. Both organized labor and business expressed satisfaction with this administration arrangement. OSHA has, however, become a highly controversial agency because of some of its rule-making and enforcement actions. Some of the penalties it has imposed have been reduced on appeal by the review commission.

In 1953, an independent Small Business Administration was set up to handle assistance programs for small business, following the dismantling of the Reconstruction Finance Corporation by the Eisenhower administration. Some argued that control of such programs rested properly with the Department of Commerce, but small-business interests and their congressional supporters argued that the Department of Commerce was too heavily oriented toward big business to satisfactorily administer, from their point of view, small-business programs. The Office of Economic Opportunity was likewise given primary control of administering the War on Poverty partly because it was thought that old-line agencies like the Departments of Labor and Health, Education, and Welfare would not be sufficiently sympathetic and vigorous. "The best way to kill a new idea," President Johnson remarked at one point, "is to put it in an old-line agency."[11]

2. Administrative organization may also be used to emphasize the need for or to facilitate action on particular policy problems. The Kennedy administration established the Arms Control and Disarmament Agency to handle the topics in its title and to symbolize the abandonment of the visionary goal of total disarmament.[12] The agency, however, has never been the central player in developing arms-control policy because of competition from the Departments of State and Defense as well as national security advisors to the President.

To coordinate national drug policy, Congress in 1989 established the

Office of National Drug Control Policy in the Executive Office of the President. Various duties were assigned to the agency, including the development of an annual national drug-control strategy. Early in his administration, President Bush appointed William Bennett, a formerly controversial secretary of education, to lead the drug agency. Bennett quickly became designated as the "Drug Czar," although he did not have directive power over agencies enforcing the laws against drug trafficking.[13] The effectiveness of the new agency, whatever its symbolic value, is problematical.

Another good example is the struggle over the formation of an Agency for Consumer Advocacy. A bill passed by the House of Representatives in 1971 but defeated by a filibuster in the Senate would have created an independent, nonregulatory agency to represent consumer interests in actions before other agencies and the courts. Other unsuccessful efforts were launched in 1973 and 1975. The prospects for the creation of the agency appeared brighter in 1977 when it received the support of the Carter administration. Its supporters believed that such an agency would provide more effective representation of consumer interests and, consequently, foster policy actions by agencies and courts more favorable toward consumers. Conservatives and business groups opposed the proposal as giving too much power to the proposed agency, notwithstanding the fact that it would have no regulatory or enforcement powers. They, of course, did not openly oppose the protection of the consumer, as this is not a politically popular thing to do. They succeeded in defeating the legislation providing for the establishment of the agency in 1978. The issue dropped off the political agenda.

3. The internal structure of an agency may be fashioned to help secure desired action. Take the case of the National Institutes of Health which were set up within the Department of Health, Education, and Welfare in the 1950s. It would have been quite logical to have named the various institutes according to the kind of research they would support, such as pathology, microbiology, biochemistry, and genetics. This is the way university research centers are usually organized. Instead, among the institutes established were the National Cancer Institute, the National Heart and Lung Institute, and the National Institute of Arthritis and Metabolic Diseases. This action was based on the reasoning that, while it might be easy for members of Congress to vote against an appropriation for microbiology, they would be highly reluctant to vote against funds for cancer or heart research. This strategy has proved effective, for Congress consistently provides more funds for the NIH than are requested by the executive budget officials.

In another example, in 1985 Congress adopted legislation reorganizing the Department of Defense because of its concern that the parochial perspective of the armed services impeded interservice coordination and prevented the president from getting coherent military advice. Consequently, the chairman of the Joint Chiefs of Staff was named as the principal military advisor to the president, whereas previously this title was held collectively by the Joint Chiefs. The chairman was also given control over the Joint Staff. Another important set of changes gave the seven commanders-in-chief, who had the responsibility for directing multiservice operations in various geographic areas, more authority over their units. The intent was to lessen the control of the individual services over units assigned to the area commanders-in-chief. In all, the 1985 law was designed to strengthen the "joint" side of the Pentagon.[14]

4. Congress has established independent regulatory commissions, such as the ICC, the Federal Reserve Board, and the Commodity Futures Trading Commission, in order to reduce presidential control of some regulatory programs. The members of these plural-headed agencies, appointed by the president for fixed, staggered terms of office with Senate approval, can be removed only for such stated causes as inefficiency and malfeasance in office. There are now a dozen regulatory commissions in the national administrative system.

Progressive Era political theory held that the independent commission device was a means by which regulation could be "taken out of politics" and handled on a scientific basis. Other factors have since become more important in congressional decisions to set up commissions, namely, institutional rivalry between the president and Congress, partisan differences between the two branches, and a desire to disrupt clientele ties between executive departmental bureaus and interest groups.[15] It is not fully clear, however, why Congress sometimes sets up independent regulatory commissions and at other times relies on bureaus in executive departments to implement regulatory programs.

5. Once a group has developed a satisfactory if not ideal relationship with an agency or a program, it will resist changes in its organizational location that might disrupt the relationship or weaken the program. Thus, the railroads have steadfastly resisted locating the ICC in an executive department such as Transportation.

Under the Carter administration's plan for the new Department of Education, the Indian education program was to be transferred to it from the Bureau of Indian Affairs (BIA) in the Department of the Interior. Various Indian groups, although not fully satisfied with the operation of BIA, feared that the transfer would contribute to the breakup of the BIA. There was also concern that Indian education might become a minor program in the new department. They were successful in blocking the transfer.[16]

Such opposition to program relocation does not always succeed, however. Scientific and higher education organizations opposed the proposal to shift most funding for science education from the National Science Foundation (NSF) to the Department of Education. They were worried that their interests, well represented in the NSF, would be "swamped" in the new department by its many programs. They did not prevail.[17]

6. As a corollary to the fifth point, congressional committees typically oppose shifts that will remove an agency or program from the committees' jurisdiction and thus reduce their power. The Agriculture Committees have fended off efforts to move the multibillion-dollar food stamp program, which is clearly a welfare program, from the Department of Agriculture to the Department of Health and Human Services. Control of the program is important because of the money involved. It is also quite useful to the Agriculture Committee for bargaining and coalition building with urban interests in support of general farm legislation.[18] Such committee and subcommittee preferences for continued influence over "their" agencies thus lends rigidity to national administrative organization.

7. Those who support an existing program may seek to have it moved to another department or agency to avoid hostile or unfavorable handling of it. Conversely, opponents of a current program may seek to lessen its impact, or even kill it, by getting it reassigned to a hostile agency. A classic illustration of the first possibility involves the Forest Service, which was transferred early in this century from the Department of the Interior to the Department of Agriculture at the behest of conservationists. According to Gifford Pinchot, "The national forest idea ran counter to the whole tradition of the Interior Department. Bred into its marrow, bone, and fiber, was the idea of disposing of the public lands to private owners."[19] In Chapter 3 we also saw how the supporters of mine safety regulation have tried to get better enforcement by moving the program to a new agency in the Department of Interior and then to another new agency in the Department of Labor.

Viewed as a course of action, the substance of policy is affected by how it is administered. How it is administered, in turn, is thought to depend upon what agency administers it. Determination of what agency should administer a program, or where the agency should be located, is more than a technical matter. It is a political issue as well.

ADMINISTRATIVE POLITICS

A statute confers upon an agency only the legal authority to take action on some topic. How effectively the agency carries out its legal mandate and what it actually does and does not accomplish will be substantially affected by the amount of cooperation and political support it gets, and, conversely, the political opposition it runs into. To put it differently, an agency exists and acts in a political milieu that affects how it exercises its discretion and carries out its programs.

The environments of some agencies are more political, more volatile, and more tumultuous than those of other agencies. The Bureau of Engraving and the Geological Survey, for example, lead much more serene political lives than do the Federal Reserve Board and the Consumer Product Safety Commission. But whatever the particular case, the environment in which an agency exists may contain many forces that may, at one time or another, impinge on it and help give direction to its actions in multitudinous ways.[20] These forces may arise out of the following sources:

The "basic rules of the game." These include the relevant laws, rules, and regulations, accepted modes of procedure, and concepts of fair play that help form and guide official behavior and to which officials are expected to conform. Public opinion and group pressures may focus adversely on officials who violate the "rules of the game," such as by appearing or proposing not to follow a given statutory provision or by enticing persons to violate a law so that they can be prosecuted. Officials who are too zealous in the enforcement of laws, who cite companies for too many minor violations of health or safety standards, may be viewed as unreasonable. Adverse executive or legislative action may stem from such criticism.

The chief executive. Most administrative agencies are located within the presidential chain of command or are otherwise subject to presidential control and direction in such matters as personnel appointments, budget recommendations, expenditure controls, and policy directives. The presidential chain of command includes agencies and officials in the Executive Office of the President and top-level political appointees (e.g., secretaries and assistant secretaries) in the departments and agencies. Control and direction are more likely to emanate from those who work for the president than from the president himself. Whether those who act for the president always conform to his preferences is arguable.

The congressional system of supervision. Included here are the standing committees and subcommittees, their chairs, committee staffs, and influential members of Congress. Congressional concern and influence is fragmented and sporadic rather than monolithic and continuous. It flows from parts of Congress, rarely from Congress as a whole, and focuses mostly on particular issues or controversies. Professional staff members handle much of the day-to-day congressional communication with agencies.

The courts. Agencies may be strongly affected by the judiciary's use of its powers of judicial review and statutory interpretation. Agencies may have their statutory authority expanded or contracted by judicial interpretation, or decisons may be overruled because improper procedures were employed in making them. OSHA and the Federal Trade Commission (FTC), for example, have often had their actions challenged in the courts. Other agencies, such as the Federal Reserve Board and the Bureau of the Mint, may have little contact with the courts because their operations do not create issues of the sort normally handled by the courts.

Other administrative agencies. Agencies with competing or overlapping jurisdictions may affect one another's operations. In the drug law-enforcement area, the Drug Enforcement Administration, the U.S. Coast Guard, the Customs Service, and other agencies engage in "turf" battles, and compete for recognition and credit in making "drug busts," sometimes appearing to lose sight of their main task. Water agencies such as the Army Corp of Engineers and the Bureau of Reclamation have also been rivals for the right to control and construct particular water projects. Occasionally an agency may aspire to take over a program of another agency, and succeed. Thus the Department of Labor acquired the Job Corps program, which was initially run by the Office of Economic Opportunity. Agency "imperialism," however, is not as rampant as some commentators imply.[21] Some agencies may indeed develop cooperative relationships, as have the FTC and the Antitrust Division of the Department of Justice in the area of antitrust enforcement. An agency may even refuse to take a program from another agency. Stuart Udall, who was Secretary of the Interior during the Johnson administration, relates that he offered to give the Bureau of Indian Affairs Indian-education program to the Department of Health, Education, and Welfare so that its secretary John Gardner would have his own school system to run. Gardner refused the offer.

Other governments. State, municipal, and county governments, school districts, or associations of state and local officials (such as the National League of Cities) may attempt to influence national agency decisions. Associations of state highway officials, for example, are much interested in the activities of the Federal Highway Administration. The EPA encounters quite a lot of pressure, criticism, and resistance from state and local governments and agencies in the development and implementation of pollution-control standards. The effectiveness of many national programs depends upon how they are implemented at the state and local level, which provides such governments with some leverage.

Interest groups. The group context differs considerably from one agency to another. Some agencies, such as the Forest Service and the Food and Drug Administration (FDA), will attract the attention of many groups, some supportive and others hostile. Buffeted by opposition, such agencies may move more cautiously than an agency that deals primarily with a single group, such as the Department of Veterans Affairs. No matter what the decision of the FDA is on an important issue, some groups will likely be sufficiently offended by it as to launch a judicial or legislative challenge. Other agencies, such as the Bureau of Engraving and the Railroad Retirement Board, experience few if any group pressures.

Agencies often actively seek group support (or consent) to increase the size, ease, or effectiveness of their operations. Advisory groups may be created, presentations made at group meetings by agency officials, and program modifications initiated in the quest for support.

Political parties. The role of the party organizations has declined in recent decades with the extension of the merit system of hiring to most agency personnel. Appointments to top-level agency positions, however, may be influenced by considerations of party welfare and policy orientation. Only a majority of the members of independent regulatory commissions can be members of the same political party, which means that party affiliation is an explicit consideration in these appointments. Some agency actions may be influenced by an urge to enhance party success at the polls, as when the Reagan administration expanded the availability of agricultural loans in the months prior to the 1986 congressional elections.

Communications media. In addition to their use as forums for pressure groups, political parties, and others trying to influence agency action, the mass communications media have an independent role. The media may play an important part in shaping public opinion toward an agency by revealing and publicizing its actions, favorably or unfavorably. For decades the Federal Bureau of Investigation was quite well treated by the press, although its problems in recent years have caused some decline in its support. In contrast, the life of OSHA has been made more difficult by the battering it has received in the media.

There are also specialized media, mostly journals, newspapers, and newsletters, that inform their clients and other interested persons about the operations of particular agencies or programs. These are increasingly more important for many agencies than are the more general media. This would be true of the Agricultural Marketing Service and the Fish and Wildlife Service.

Each of the forces discussed above is multiple rather than monolithic in nature. Conflicting viewpoints may be held by the members of the same category as well as those in different categories. Thus a number of political forces may impinge on an agency, pushing and pulling against each other with varying intensity, and growing and ebbing over time. Agencies of course are not simply "sitting ducks" but rather will try to shape, influence, and mollify the forces in their environment. Pressure relationships between an agency and those who seek to influence it are therefore usually reciprocal.

The field of forces surrounding an agency will be drawn from the above categories and will form the *constituency* of the agency, that is, "any group, body, or interest to which [an administrator] looks for aid or guidance, or which seeks to establish itself as so important [in his judgment] that he 'had better' take account of its preferences even if he finds himself averse to those preferences."[22] Note that this is a broader concept than that of clientele, which consists of those reasonably distinct individuals and groups directly served or regulated by an agency. The constituency of an agency is dynamic rather than static. Some constituents will be concerned with the agency only as particular issues arise or are settled; others will be more or less continually involved and will compose the stable core of the agency's constituency. For example, the stable core of the Food Safety and Inspection Service (FSIS) in the Department of Agriculture includes commercial meat and poultry processing companies, the congressional Agriculture Committees, and the relevant appropriations subcommittees. The chief executive, the Food and Drug Administration, the communications media, and consumer groups are intermittently involved with the FSIS. All other things being equal, those constituents that continually interact with an agency will likely have the most success in influencing agency action.

The nature of an agency's constituency will affect its power and capacity to make policy decisions and carry those decisions into effect. The relationship of an agency to one part of its constituency will depend on the kinds of relationships it has with other parts. For example, an agency with strong presidential support tends to be less responsive to pressure groups than an agency without such support. On the other hand, strong congressional and group support may lessen presidential influence, as in the case of the Army Corp of Engineers. An agency encountering criticism from state and local government officials may find its congressional support waning also. In general, it can be said that agency policy making and implementation activities will reflect the interests supported by the dominant elements within its constituency, whether they are hostile or supportive.

An agency's clientele is an important part of its constituency. Some agencies benefit from having large active clienteles, such as the Social Security Administration and the Department of Agriculture. But size alone is not enough. Consumers are a vast group, but because they are poorly organized and lack self-consciousness as a group, they provide little support to consumer agencies such as the FDA. If the FDA has been unduly responsive to food and drug manufacturers, it is partly because of lack of consumer support and partly because the agency both needs their cooperation and encounters organized pressure from them. Some agencies have underprivileged or disadvantaged clienteles, such as the Legal Services Corporation, most welfare agencies, and the Federal Bureau of Prisons. OEO was hindered in its efforts to administer the War on Poverty by the fact that its clientele, the poor and especially the black poor, did not constitute a good source of political support.

Agencies that provide services to their clientele, rather than regulate them, usually draw more support from them. Most people prefer receiving benefits to being restricted or controlled. An agency with a foreign clientele, such as the Agency for International Development, can draw little political support from its clientele. The lack of an internal clientele has clearly been to the disadvantage of the foreign-aid program.

An examination of an agency's constituency and clientele can provide considerable insight into, and explanation of, why an agency acts as it does. It should not, however, be assumed that an agency is an inert force at the mercy of its constituency or the dominant elements therein. Agencies, because of their expertise, organizational spirit, or administrative statecraft, can exert independent control over events and help determine the scope of their power.[23]

Any bureaucratic agency has some expertise in the performance of its assigned tasks, whether those involve garbage collection or foreign policy. All bureaucratic skills, however, do not receive equal deference from society. Agencies whose expertise is derived from the natural and physical (i.e., "hard") sciences will receive more deference than those drawing from the social sciences, which are less highly regarded in society. Compare, for example, the situations of the National Aeronautics and Space Administration and the National Cancer Institute with the Census Bureau and the Family Support Administration (Department of Health and Human Services). Considerable deference is shown to the military as "specialists in violence," and Congress often defers to the judgment of the Department of Defense and the Joint Chiefs of Staff in military and defense policy. Professional diplomats, on the other hand, no longer receive the deference in foreign policy that they once did. Power based on expertise may thus vary considerably from one time to another as conditions and attitudes change.

Some agencies are more able than others to generate interest in, and enthusiasm and commitment for, their programs from both their own members and the public. This has been designated as *organizational esprit*. Its existence depends upon an agency's capacity to develop "an appropriate ideology or sense of mission, both as a method of binding outsiders to the agency and as a technique for intensifying its employees' loyalty to its purposes."[24] The Marine Corps, Peace Corps, Forest Service, and EPA, for example, are agencies served with considerable fervor and commitment by their members. Other agencies have displayed considerable zeal in their early years, only to ease into bureaucratic routines and stodginess as the years slip by. This has happened in some of the national independent regulatory commissions.

Leadership, or what Professor Francis E. Rourke calls "administrative statecraft,"[25] can also contribute to an agency's power and effectiveness. Although agency leadership, like all organizational leadership, is situational, being shaped significantly by factors in the environment other than the leaders themselves, can still have a significant impact on agency operation and success. Some agency leaders will be more effective than others in dealing with outside interest groups, cultivating congressional committees, opening the organization to new ideas, and communicating a sense of purpose to agency personnel. The revitalization of the EPA in the mid-1980s, following its decline in the early years of the Reagan administration, was aided by the leadership of William Ruckelshaus and Lee Thomas as successive administrators. James A. Baker, III was a capable and vigorous secretary of the Treasury during Reagan's second term. Under Baker's skilled leadership the department played a major role in both domestic and international economic policy development. President Reagan generally deferred to Baker's leadership, as on the decision in 1985 to weaken the dollar to encourage exports, reduce imports, and lessen the balance of payments deficit.

ADMINISTRATIVE POLICYMAKING

Although administrative agencies are often deeply involved in policy formation at the legislative stage, attention here will be on how agencies shape policy through the implementation of legislation. Two facets of agency action will be examined: characteristics of agency decision making and the ways in which agencies develop policy. It is well to keep in mind here the distinction between decisions and policy.

Decision Making

In agency decision making, *hierarchy* is of central importance. Although in legislatures, all members have an equal vote, within agencies those at upper levels have more authority over final decisions than those at lower levels. To be sure, factors such as the decentralization of authority, the responsiveness of subunits to outside forces (such as pressure groups), and the participation of professionals in administrative activity work against hierarchical authority, but the importance of hierarchy should nonetheless not be underestimated. Complexity, size, and the desire for economical operation and more control over the bureaucratic apparatus all contribute to the development of hierarchical authority. As for its consequences for decision making, it is a means by which discrete decisions can be coordinated with one another and conflicts among officials at lower levels of the process can be resolved. Hierarchy also means that those at the upper levels have a larger voice in agency decisions because of their high status, even though lower-level officials may have more substantive expertness. A separation of power and knowledge may thus threaten the rationality of administrative decisions.[26] Hierarchy can also adversely affect the free flow of ideas and information in an organization, because subordinates, for example, may hesitate to advance proposals they think may run counter to "official" policy or antagonize their superiors.

Secrecy also plays a role in administrative decision making. In comparison with that of legislatures, administrative decision making is a relatively invisible part of government. Agencies may hold public hearings, issue press releases, and the like, but they exercise considerable control over what information becomes available on their internal deliberations and decisions, and consequently much of what they do is little noticed by the public or reported by the media. This secrecy, or invisibility, can contribute to the effectiveness of decisions by providing an environment for presentation and discussion of policy proposals that might otherwise be avoided as publicly unpopular. Deliberations by Kennedy administration officials during the 1962 Cuban missile crisis were more effective because of their private nature.[27] Secrecy may also facilitate the bargaining and compromise often necessary to reach decisions and take action, because officials will find it easier to move away from privately stated than publicly stated positions. On the other hand, the private nature of administrative deliberation may mean that some pertinent facts are not considered and that significant interests are not consulted. While secrecy contributed to the effectiveness of the Cuban missile crisis decisions, it had the opposite effect with regard to the Bay of Pigs invasion the previous year.

Secrecy is, on the whole, more common to administrative deliberations in the area of foreign and defense policy than in domestic matters.[28] In the latter area, secrecy has been reduced by legislation intended to open the administrative process to greater public participation and scrutiny. The Freedom of Information Act provides a procedure for extracting documents and records from agencies, while the Government in the Sunshine Act requires most plural-headed agencies to open their decision-making sessions to the public.

Administrative agencies constitute "a governmental habitat in which expertise finds a wealth of opportunity to exert itself and to influence policy."[29] Agencies in their decision making are clearly affected by *political considerations* and also by the wish to protect their own power. Thus the Department of Commerce is unlikely to make policy decisions that sharply conflict with important business interests. Nor is the Tennessee Valley Authority likely to ignore important interests within its region. Agencies nonetheless do provide a context within which experts and professionals, official and private, can work on policy problems.

Scientific and technical considerations and *professional advice* play an important part in most administrative decision making. Whether it is the Federal Aviation Agency considering the adoption of a rule on aircraft safety, the FDA acting on the safety of medical devices, or the secretary of defense confronting a major choice on weapons systems, each needs good information on the technical feasibility of proposed alternatives. Decisions that are made without adequate consideration of their technical aspects or that run counter to strong professional advice may turn out to be faulty on both technical and political grounds.

Professional and scientific advice may not always be sound, however. In 1976, following the identification of a few cases of influenza at Fort Dix, New Jersey, public health officials became concerned that the nation was confronted with the possibility of a swine flu epidemic, similar to one that had killed 500,000 people in 1918. Acting on their advice, the Ford administration decided to initiate a nationwide immunization campaign. The epidemic never developed, however, and the entire venture became a policy fiasco.[30]

Finally, administrative decision making is very frequently characterized by *bargaining*. Experts and facts are important in administrative decision making, as has been noted, but so also are accommodation and compromise. Some agencies may be less involved in bargaining than others. The National Institute of Standards and Technology and the Patent Office come to mind as two agencies whose decisions seem primarily expert decisions based on factual records. Economic regulatory agencies, such as the ICC and the EPA, often find it necessary to bargain with those whom they regulate. In setting emission standards, the EPA has had to bargain with both polluters and state and local officials in order to reach tolerable decisions and secure compliance. Another notable example of bargaining involves the consent decrees used by the Antitrust Division of the Department of Justice to close most civil antitrust cases. Negotiated in privacy—it should be observed—by representatives of the division and of the alleged offender, the consent decree provides that the division will drop its formal proceedings in turn for the alleged offender's agreement to stop certain practices, such as price fixing or the proposed acquisition of a competitor. Negotiations with foreign countries for tariff reductions are another good illustration of bargaining, in this instance with foreign administrators.[31]

Policy Development

Turning now to the second concern of this section, administrative decisions may be productive of policy (recall how it was defined in Chapter 1) in several ways: through rule making, adjudication, law enforcement, and program operations.

RULE MAKING.   A *rule* may be defined as an agency statement of general applicability and future effect that concerns the rights of private parties and has the force and effect of law. Some rules fill in the details of general statutory provisions; others define the meaning of words such as *small business* or *discriminate* that appear in statutes; still others state how an agency will act in certain matters, as in the location of highways. Many national administrative agencies have been delegated rule-making (or legislative) authority by Congress. Thus the Securities and Exchange Commission is authorized to make certain rules governing the stock exchanges "as it seems necessary in the public interest or for the protection of investors," and OSHA is empowered to make rules setting health and safety standards for working conditions that employers must meet.

For toxic substances, OSHA is directed by statute to set the standard "which most adequately assures, to the extent feasible, on the basis of the best available evidence, that no worker suffers material impairment of health," even when exposed to a toxic substance over the course of a working career. The conditions embedded in this delegation reflect compromises made on the agency's authority during the legislative process and leave it vague in meaning.

Most agency rule-making proceedings take the form of informal notice and comment rule making. The Administrative Procedure Act (Section 553) sets forth several procedural requirements that govern informal rule making:

1. A notice of a proposed rule making (NPRM) must be published in the *Federal Register* that specifies the legal authority for the rule, the content of the rule, and the time, place, and nature of the public rule-making proceeding.
2. Opportunity must be provided for interested persons to participate in the rule making, either through oral or written comments.
3. A concise statement of the rule's basis and purpose must be included in the final rule.
4. The final rule must be published at least thirty days before it becomes effective.

These requirements are intended to give those interested in or affected by a rule an opportunity to participate and have an impact on its content. In some instances, some agencies are required by statutes to follow more detailed and stringent procedures in rule-making actions.

In exercising their rule-making authority, agencies may have a great deal of discretion or leeway in shaping the substance of rules because, as has been noted, the legislation delegating authority to agencies is often quite general or vague in nature. Customarily, though, agencies can exercise their authority only in specified areas. Thus the Federal Communications Commission is restricted to the communications industry, the Food Safety and Inspection Service to meat and poultry processors, and the Comptroller of the Currency to banking. Few agencies have as expansive jurisdiction as the Consumer Product Safety Commission, whose legal domain includes several thousand consumer products.

It should not be assumed, however, that only economic regulatory agencies have rule-making authority. Various agencies in the Departments of Agriculture, Health and Human Services, and Housing and Urban Development also possess extensive *rule-making* authority. Many of their programs involve the expenditures of large sums of money, and they make rules governing the use and disposition of these funds. Each operates a variety of research, benefit, and grant-in-aid programs.

Collectively, the volume of rules issued each year by national administrative agencies and reported in the *Federal Register* is much greater than the legislation enacted by Congress and recorded in the *United States Statutes-at-Large.*[32]

ADJUDICATION.   Agencies can make policy when they apply existing laws or rules to particular situations by case-to-case decision making. In so doing, they act in much the same manner as courts, just as they act in legislative fashion when engaged in rule-making. In the past, the Federal Trade Commission has made policy by applying the legislative prohibition of unfair methods of competition to specific cases. Over time, these cases marked out public policy and indicated the kinds of practices banned by the general prohibition. Again, an agency may make policy when it gives a particular interpretation to a statutory provision in the course of applying it in a case. Thus, the National Labor Relations Board (NLRB), which administers labor-management relations legislation, makes statutory interpretations in deciding unfair-practice cases that then serve to inform its action in future cases. In such instances NLRB opinions become policy statements of much interest to those concerned with policy in this area.

Agencies not infrequently choose to make policy through adjudication, even though they have rule-making authority. (They may be authorized, but not required to make rules.) An agency may find it no easier than a legislature to agree on what form a general policy should take, especially in a novel or highly controversial situation. Those affected by agency action may be left in the dark as to what policy is supposed to be when it is made on a case-by-case basis. Agencies have indeed often been criticized for relying too much on adjudication and too little on rule making in the development of policy.

Much of the adjudication engaged in by administrative agencies is rather routine, such as the hundreds of thousands of decisions made annually by the Department of Veterans Affairs and the Social Security Administration on applications for benefits. Still, within the framework of statutory language, seemingly routine decisions may shift the direction or affect the impact of policy. Noteworthy in this regard is the operation of the Internal Revenue Service (IRS), which routinely closes most cases of disputed income-tax returns by informal adjudication (and bargaining). IRS statistics for fiscal year 1972, which were obtained under a Freedom of Information Act proceeding, for example, showed that in cases that did not end up in the courts—and most do not—the agency settled for 67 percent of the amounts owed in the $1 to $999 range, while settling for an average of 34 percent when $1 million or more was allegedly owed. Moreover, settlements varied widely from district to district, ranging from 12 percent of the amount alleged by the IRS in the St. Paul district to 76 percent in Pittsburgh.[33] Obviously such actions significantly affect policy content and impact.

LAW ENFORCEMENT.   Agencies may also make policy through their various law-enforcement actions. A statute may be enforced vigorously or even rigidly, in a lax manner, or not at all; it may be applied in some situations and not in others, or to some persons or companies and not to others. Everyone is familiar with the discretion possessed by the police officer on the beat or, what is more likely, in the patrol car. A ticket may be issued to a speeder, or only a warning may be issued. If no drivers are ticketed unless they exceed posted speed limits by a certain rate, this amounts to an amendment of public policy. Even when statutory provisions are quite precise, thus seeming to eliminate discretion in their interpretation, enforcement officers still have some discretion with respect to whether they will be enforced.

The Hepburn Act of 1906, which dealt primarily with railroads, also authorized the ICC to regulate the rates charged by oil pipeline companies. Except for requiring the filing of rates, however, the ICC took no action by itself on the subject until 1934. If did not actually complete a pipeline rate proceeding until 1948, and even then no effective action resulted. The ICC continued to do little to carry out this authorization,[34] essentially substituting a policy of minimal regulation for the legislatively declared policy of regulation. The ICC's reluctance to carry out congressional intent illustrates an aspect of the administrative process that needs more systematic attention from policy analysts. (Authority over pipelines now rests with the Federal Energy Regulatory Commission.) Policy may be shaped by administrative inaction or apathy as well as by agency action and zeal. Inaction often affects only the inarticulate general public and consequently may pass unnoticed.

Agency enforcement activity depends not only on the attitudes and motives of agency officials, and external pressures, but also on the enforcement techniques available to the agency. Opponents unable to block the legislative enactment of a law may seek to blunt its impact by handicapping its enforcement. Take the case of the equal-employment opportunity provisions of the Civil Rights Act of 1964, which prohibit firms or unions representing twenty-five or more employees from discriminating against individuals because of their race, color, religion, national origin, or sex. Along with the rest of the act, these provisions were adopted over strong opposition. The Equal Employment Opportunity Commission (EEOC) was established to enforce the law through investigations, conferences, and conciliation, which means essentially voluntary action. If this failed, the EEOC could recommend civil action in the federal courts, which would require the cooperation of the Department of Justice. Moreover, the law provided that the EEOC could not act on complaints from states in which there was an antidiscrimination law and an agency to enforce it, unless the state agency was unable to complete action within sixty days. Complaints had to be filed "in writing under oath," which is not a customary requirement for a law violation complaint. This stipulation undoubtedly had a chilling effect on many southern blacks as well as others. Whatever the intent behind these provisions, they clearly limited the effectiveness of the law by making the successful completion of cases a slow, tedious process.

After 1964, the EEOC and many supporters of stronger enforcement advocated giving the agency authority to issue cease-and-desist orders[35] in discrimination cases and then on its own initiative to seek their enforcement in the federal courts. Opposition to this change was particularly strong from conservatives and southerners. In 1972, the EEOC was finally empowered to initiate court action on its own but not to issue cease-and-desist orders when conciliation of complaints was not successful. Though perhaps not as much as hoped, this new authority did help strengthen the enforcement and effectiveness of the anti–job discrimination policy.

PROGRAM OPERATIONS.   Many agencies handle the conduct of loan, grant, benefit, insurance, and service policies and programs or engage in the management of public properties, such as forests, parks, and hydroelectric plants. Although these activities are not usually thought of as being law enforcement in nature because they are not designed *directly* to regulate or shape people's behavior they are often of much importance to many people. How such programs are administered helps to determine policy both directly and indirectly. Some examples will clarify what is involved here.

Fire was once anathema to both the U.S. Forest Service and the National Park Service (NPS) in their management of forest and park lands.[36] In 1971, however, on the basis of scientific findings concerning the role of fire in the natural regeneration of forests, the NPS decided that it would allow most naturally caused fires in national parks to burn themselves out. Such fires were a part of the normal life cycle of forests. (The Forest Service continued to fight all fires.) The NPS policy on fires came under severe challenge in the summer of 1988, when the buildup of flammable materials plus an exceptionally dry summer contributed to severe forest fires in Yellowstone National Park. A substantial portion of the park land was burned and many public officials called for changes in the NPS policy. Assessments of the impact of the fire revealed that it had not been as disastrous as originally thought. The natural, or "let it burn," regulation was not repealed but, on the other hand, all park fires were fought in 1989. In all, policy was left unsettled.[37]

Another example involves the Federal Housing Administration (FHA) of the Department of Housing and Urban Development, which since the 1930s has administered a mortgage insurance program under which the risks of nonpayment and foreclosure are assumed by the government rather than by private lenders. Until 1967, a regulation provided that housing loans, to be FHA-insured, had to meet a standard of "economic soundness." Consequently, many low-income people in slum or deteriorating areas could not obtain FHA-insured loans because of the "excessive risk" involved. When loans were available, the interest costs were high relative to the incomes of the poor. Because of these operating requirements, the mortgage insurance was much more beneficial for high and middle income persons than for the poor. Only a tiny fraction of FHA-insured home loans went to the poor.[38]

Legislation was enacted in 1968 by Congress to reorder FHA priorities and to make public policy in this area more responsive to the needs of low-income people. This has lessened but not eliminated discrimination against low-income borrowers. Also, over the years the FHA has become less important because of the development of private loan guarantee companies that offer more flexible insurance rates to borrowers.

To take another case, the Elementary and Secondary Education Act (ESEA) of 1965, under its Title I, provided federal financial aid for the education of disadvantaged children in urban and rural poor areas. In the view of the social reform advocates among its supporters, this policy was intended to help eliminate poverty by improving the educational facilities and opportunities that state and local governments made available to children of low-income families. As initially administered by the Office of Education (now the Department of Education), however, it was unclear to what extent the funds were actually expended upon poor children, and whether they bought services beyond the level of those provided for other children in the aided districts. Many cases of the misuse of funds were also reported.[39]

A number of factors contributed to this situation. Although the ESEA clearly specified disadvantaged children as its focus, its legislative history provided "the semblance if not the reality of general aid." This ambiguity, together with the fact that reformers supporting the legislation did not much concern themselves with the process of implementation, meant that officials in the Office of Education were given leeway to interpret the legislation in accord with traditional modes of operation. The traditional task of the Office of Education had long been to provide assistance and advice to state and local school agencies. It was not inclined to regulate or police their activities and consequently did not act with much vigor to ensure that funds were expended as intended. Further, state and local agencies had historically dominated the field of public education, and they had strong political support in this regard. This made it difficult for national officials, even were they so inclined, to impose directives that did not mesh with local priorities.

By the end of the 1970s, however, administration of the ESEA's Title I had changed markedly. New staff members in the Office of Education had succeeded in securing much tighter supervision of spending under the program. Interest groups, such as the National Welfare Rights Organization and the National Advisory Council for Education of Disadvantaged Children, helped keep the program focused on the disadvantaged. Offices concerned with compensatory education were established in most state departments of education, and they had a stake in ensuring that funds were used for the disadvantaged. As a consequence of such developments, the effort to target Title I funds on the disadvantaged become much more successful. Various studies indicated that Title I funds had increased the educational performance of the affected students.

The change in administration of the Title I program brought it more closely into line with the expectations of its originators, that is, to provide benefits to the disadvantaged. In 1981 it was maintained as a separate program, although over twenty other education programs were consolidated in an education block grant by the Education Consolidation and Improvement Act, a Reagan administration initiative.

TECHNIQUES OF CONTROL

All public policies, whether labeled promotional, regulatory, prohibitive, redistributive, or whatever, contain an element of control. That is, by one means or another, they are designed to cause people to do things, refrain from doing things, or continue doing things that they otherwise would not do. This is true whether reference is to a tax credit to encourage industrial plant modernization, the provision of information and other assistance to encourage international trade, or a prohibition of some activity such as restraint of trade with penalties for violators.

An important component of public policies is the control techniques by which they are to be implemented. Decisions on these matters, like those on the substance of policy itself, can be highly controversial. The control techniques authorized may have much importance for the substance and impact of policy, for policy as an "operational reality." Those who oppose a policy, for example, may attempt to lessen or even nullify its impact by restricting the administering agency's powers of enforcement or implementation. Two examples will illustrate this point. The first state minimum-wage law was enacted in 1912 in Massachusetts over strong opposition from manufacturers. The only means of enforcement provided was the publication in newspapers of the names of employers who did not meet the standard. The law, as one might guess, was not overly effective. In 1976, after much controversy, including a Senate filibuster by opponents, legislation was passed requiring that the Antitrust Division of the Department of Justice be notified in advance of proposed large corporate mergers. Proponents believed that this would increase the effectiveness of antitrust enforcement activity. Opponents, drawn mostly from conservative and business ranks, apparently did also. If not, why the controversy?

In short, for a policy to be effective, more is needed than substantive authority and the appropriation of funds to pay the financial costs of implementation. Adequate techniques of control and policy implementation must also be provided. In this section a variety of techniques will be examined. Our list is not exhaustive, however.

Noncoercive Forms of Action

Many of the methods used to implement policies to bring about compliance are noncoercive in nature. By "noncoercive" is meant that they do not involve the use of legal sanctions or penalties, rewards, or deprivations. The effectiveness of these forms depends largely upon the voluntary collaboration or acceptance by the affected parties, although social and economic pressures arising out of society may lend an element of compulsion to them. The following are examples of noncoercive forms of action.

Declarations of policy by themselves may cause people to comply, "to go along." This would seem to be the case especially if the declarations are made by respected or high-status officials. Presidential appeals to labor and management to avoid making inflationary wage contracts or price increases, for example, may have a restraining effect in and of themselves.

Voluntary standards may be established by official action. The National Bureau of Standards has developed commercial standards, such as uniform weights, measures, and grades of products and materials, that are not mandatory in nature. They are widely adhered to because their use facilitates or promotes business and economic activity. While the use of most of the standard grades, such as prime, choice, and good, for beef established by the United States Department of Agriculture for agricultural commodities is permissive (some are mandatory for interstate commerce), they are widely followed in practice.

Mediation and conciliation are noncoercive measures often used in an effort to settle labor-management disputes, as by the Federal Mediation and Conciliation Service. The mediator works to bring the parties together, to clarify the facts of the disputes and the points at issue, and to offer advice and suggestions to promote settlement. The mediator has, however, no formal powers of decision or sanction. Many labor-management disputes are successfully resolved by these procedures.

The use of publicity to bring the social and economic effects of adverse public opinion to bear on violators may induce compliance with policy. Much stress was placed on "pitiless publicity" during the Progressive Era as a means of preventing monopoly. Although labor and business organizations today exhibit much concern about their public image, it is impossible to measure the effectiveness of publicity as a control device. Still, the revelation of "poor" working conditions or "undesirable" business practices by congressional or agency investigations may produce some correction or improvement.

Educational and demonstration programs are widely used by agencies in securing compliance with policy. Much effort is expended to inform people of their rights under Social Security and veterans' benefits programs, for example. Employers are informed through publications and conferences of the meaning and requirements of wage and hours legislation. The demonstration technique is especially used in the field of agriculture. Preferred practices in soil conservation and crop production are shown and explained to farmers with the hope that their demonstrated superiority will lead to their acceptance and use.

Inspection

Inspection is the examination of some matter (such as premises, products, or records) to determine whether it conforms to officially prescribed standards. The inspection may be either continuous, as in the inspection of meat in packing plants, or periodic, as in the inspection of banks. Whichever form it takes, inspection is intended to reveal compliance or noncompliance by all those involved in a particular matter, with the objective of preventing or correcting undesirable or dangerous conditions. Typically an effort is first made to persuade violators to conform with the law, with the imposition of sanctions or penalties as a last recourse. Indeed, the ultimate purpose of inspection is to aid in obtaining the cooperation of the regulated.

Inspection is the most commonly used form of regulatory action. Examples of its use at the national level include the inspection of locomotives and railroad safety devices by the Federal Railroad Administration, sanitary conditions in food and drug manufacturing establishments by the FDA, income-tax returns by the IRS, and national banks by the Comptroller of the Currency.

Licensing

Licensing, or enabling action, as it is sometimes called, involves government authorization to engage in a particular business or profession or to do something otherwise forbidden. Licensing is an extensively used form of action known by a variety of names. Licenses are required to engage in many professions and occupations and to do such things as operate motor vehicles and radio stations. In addition, the term certificate of public convenience and necessity is used in the public utility field. "Permits" may be necessary to drill oil wells; the corporate charter constitutes authorization to use a particular form of business organization; and franchises are granted to utilities to use city streets.

Licensing is a form of advance check in which a person who wishes to engage in a particular activity must demonstrate the possession of certain qualifications or the meeting of certain standards. The burden of proof in securing a license rests with the applicant rather than the granting official. The use of licensing ordinarily goes beyond the initial authorization or denial to do something. It may also include: "(1) imposition of conditions as part of the authorization; (2) modification of the terms or conditions at the discretion of the granting authority; (3) renewal or denial of the authorization at periodic intervals; (4) revocation of the authorization."[40] When these are involved, licensing becomes a form of continuing control. Radio and television broadcasters, for example, must periodically renew their broadcasting licenses with the FCC and may have them revoked under certain circumstances.

Loans, Subsidies, and Benefits

Loans, subsidies, and benefits are means by which public economic policies are advanced through aid, in the form of money or other resources, to private economic units. Cash operating subsidies are granted to some commuter airlines to maintain an adequate system of air transport. Construction and operating subsidies are used to promote the domestic shipbuilding industry and the American merchant marine. Commodity loans and payments are made to farmers to support farm prices and income. Small businesses are assisted by loans from the Small Business Administration. Also related is the guarantee of loans by the government for the purpose of expanding the volume of private lending, as in the case of the guarantee of home mortgages by the FHA.

In addition to their broad control, loans, subsidies, and benefit programs may include an explicit regulatory feature. For example, under the agricultural price-support programs, commodity loans and payments are available only to those who comply with production and marketing controls. Farmers Home Administration loans for the purchase of farms are made under conditions intended to ensure good farm management. In effect, the government is using the loan and benefit operations to purchase consent to particular policies. The effectiveness of such operations depends considerably upon the need or desire for the assistance offered.

Contracts

Many governmental programs are carried out through contracts with private companies. The defense, atomic energy, and space programs are well-known examples. Many private companies want to do business with the government, and some, such as in the aerospace industry, depend heavily upon governmental contracts for their very existence. The power to grant or deny contracts contains an obvious element of control.

Contracts are sometimes used as the basis for specific economic controls. Under the Walsh-Healey Act of 1936, for example, companies wishing to supply goods or services to the national government must comply with statutory standards on wages, hours, and conditions of work. Again, presidential executive orders prohibit discrimination in employment by federal contractors. Some companies have been denied contracts because they violated such requirements.

General Expenditures

Apart from their use in connection with the loan, subsidy, and benefit operations, governmental expenditures for the purchase of goods and services can be used to attain policy goals. Administrative agencies often have considerable discretion in spending funds appropriated by Congress. The expenditures of funds for goods and services can be used to foster domestic or local industries, or to increase the level of economic activity in depressed areas. Competition may be promoted by purchasing from smaller rather than larger businesses so as to strengthen the economic position of the former. The rate and timing of expenditures may be geared to counteract inflationary or deflationary trends in the economy.

Market and Proprietary Operations

When government enters the market to buy, sell, or provide goods and services, its actions often have control effects. Thus the purchase and sale of government securities in the market (that is, open-market operations) is a potent tool used by the Federal Reserve Board to expand or contract the money supply in the economy. The prices of some agricultural commodities, such as milk, have been supported by direct purchases in the market by the Department of Agriculture. The Johnson administration sold some of the government's previously acquired stockpiles of aluminum and copper in its efforts to prevent price increases in those industries in the mid-1960s.

Government enterprises also may have a control effect, as when they compete with private enterprises. Thus the sale of electric power at "reasonable" rates by the Tennessee Valley Authority led to rate reductions by private companies operating in the region. This is sometimes referred to as "yardstick regulation" in that the reasonableness of private utility rates can be measured by the public rates. Governmental competition has not been used extensively as a control device, although it remains as a possibility.

Taxation

The power to tax has occasionally been used for regulatory purposes. A 10 percent annual tax on state bank notes levied by Congress in 1865 drove them out of existence. For several decades high taxes on colored oleomargarines were levied to discourage its use in preference to butter. The Carter administration proposed increasing the federal tax on gasoline as a means of discouraging its consumption and promoting energy conservation. Congress refused to act on the recommendation, however, because of strong public opposition.

In recent years, some have advocated the use of taxation in a more positive fashion. Thus it has been contended that environmental pollution could be better reduced through use of a tax on effluents rather than the present system of standards setting and enforcement.[41] The tax would provide an economic incentive to reduce discharges while permitting firms to determine the most efficient manner to do this. Resistance to the use of taxation in this fashion has been based on various premises: taxes should be used only to raise revenue; the present pattern of regulation is adequate; and the tax device would be difficult in practice to administer. As a consequence, no use has been made of taxation as a more positive regulatory technique.

Exemptions from existing taxes have now become a widely used promotional device and are often referred to as "tax expenditures." A variety of deductions, exclusions from income, preferential rates, and the like permit individuals and corporations who engage in favored activities, such as capital investment, the purchase of homes, or charitable giving, to retain funds that would otherwise be paid in taxes. The effect is the same as if the government had made a direct payment to the favored party, but it is a little less open and obvious. The use of tax expenditures has become widespread and, in 1988, it was estimated that on a combined basis they amounted to $79.8 billion for corporations and $281.2 billion for individuals.[42] This technique capitalizes on the general aversion to paying taxes, which seems characteristic of Americans. It also makes the subsidization of private activity less obvious.

Directive Power

Many agencies have authority, on the basis of adjudicatory proceedings, to issue orders or directives applicable to private parties. (In the preceding section, the general nature of administrative adjudication and its use in policy development was discussed.) Agencies may issue orders to settle disputes between private parties, as when a shipper claims to have been charged an unreasonable rate by a railroad; to resolve complaints, as when a company is charged with false or misleading advertising; and to approve or deny applications, as for a license for a nuclear power project or a Social Security benefit. Congressional standards governing administrative adjudication are usually more specific for benefit programs, such as Social Security and veterans' benefits, than for regulatory programs. This may result from the fact that political conflict is often less intense over benefit legislation than regulatory legislation.[43] Congress is consequently less inclined to pass the buck to agencies through general legislation.

Informal Procedures

Much of the work of agencies in settling questions involving private rights, privileges, and interests is accomplished through the use of informal procedures, that is, without the use of formal action and adversary hearings. For example, most disputes arising out of income-tax returns are settled by consultation and correspondence between the IRS and the private parties involved. Claims for benefits under the Social Security program are mostly settled by administrative officials on the basis of work records, personal interviews, and eligibility rules. A large portion of the unfair labor practice complaint cases initiated with the NLRB are also informally disposed of through conferences between agency field examiners and the parties in dispute.

Informal procedures have been referred to as "the lifeblood of the administrative process." Certainly they are an important facet of policy implementation. Many decisions affecting private rights and interests are reached through such means as negotiations, bargaining and compromise, consultation, conference, correspondence, reference to technical data, and examination of material. Extensive use is made of such methods because of such factors as the large number of cases coming before agencies, the need or desire for quick action, the wish of agencies to avoid becoming embroiled in formal proceedings, and the desire of private parties to avoid the courthouse and unfavorable publicity.

Services

Many public policies, mostly of the distributive variety, involve the provision of services such as information, advice, legal counsel, medical treatment, and psychiatric services. Thus, the Small Business Administration, in addition to making loans, administers a variety of informational and technical services for the operators of small businesses. The National Weather Service's forecasts are of use to groups such as farmers, commercial fishermen, and airline companies, as well as to weekend weather-watchers generally. The Department of Veterans Affairs provides many medical, psychiatric, and counseling services to veterans, often at no cost. Service programs variously provide benefits to recipients or users, help to enhance the personal or material well-being of many people, and support the more efficient operations of markets (as in the instances of job training and foreign trade data).

Sanctions

Sanctions are the means—penalties and rewards—that agencies use to encourage or compel compliance with their decisions.[44] Sanctions put some "sting" into administrative action. In some instances, sanctions are built into control techniques. Thus, when an agency decides to grant or deny a conditional benefit, the sanction rests in this action. Other external sanctions that may be applied by agencies include the threat of prosecution, monetary penalties, favorable or unfavorable publicity, modification or revocation of licenses, seizure or destruction of goods, the award of damages, and the issuance of injunctions. Agencies may also seek to impose criminal penalties (fines and jail sentences), but this requires action through the courts. Further, those who deal with agencies often seek to maintain their goodwill and hence are often reluctant to challenge agency actions.

There appears to be general agreement that policies should be implemented in such manner as to cause the least necessary material and psychological disturbance to the affected persons. Given this, the most technically or economically efficient method of enforcement may not be the most acceptable politically. This consideration will affect both the legislature in authorizing control techniques for an agency and the agency in the use of the techniques and sanctions that it possesses. Another consideration in the choice of control techniques stems from the fact that the general objective of public policy is to control behavior (or secure compliance) and not to punish violators, except as a last resort. Consequently, there will usually be a preference for less harsh or coercive techniques. Some sanctions may be viewed as so harsh that they are rarely used, as was long the case with jail sentences for business executives who violate the antitrust laws. Government tends to follow a rule of parsimony in the employment of legal restraint and compulsion in policy implementation.

A Controversy: Standards or Incentives?

Traditionally, many economic regulatory programs have relied heavily upon such administrative practices as standard setting, inspection to determine compliance, and the imposition of sanctions upon violators. Following the lead of economist Charles Schultze, however, many now designate and stigmatize this pattern of regulation as "command and control" regulation. (In reality, of course, there is a great deal of education, persuasion, negotiation, bargaining, and compromise in the regulatory process.) Opponents object to the "command and control" approach because they say it dictates behavior, discourages private initiative and innovation in attaining policy goals, and causes waste or misuse of societal resources. In its stead they prefer the use of economic incentives, whether in the form of rewards or penalties, which in their view utilize individual interest to achieve public purposes. The incentive system, it is said, "lets individuals make their own decisions, thus enhancing freedom and voluntarism, and yet (under the right circumstances) achieves desired goals at the lowest possible cost to society."[45]

Environmental pollution control will be used as an illustration of the incentive system because it is here that the incentive approach has been most widely proposed. It would work like this: It would first be determined how much reduction in a given pollutant would be necessary to meet a policy goal. A tax or fee would then be imposed on each unit (perhaps a pound) of a pollutant (perhaps sulfur oxide) discharged sufficient to achieve the goal. Those discharging the pollutant would then have a choice of paying the tax or lowering their discharges. Ideally, they would choose the latter alternative and reduce their discharges, by whatever means chosen, to the extent that is was economically practicable, or to the extent that it cost less to reduce pollution than to pay the tax. Economists Allen Kneese and Charles Schultze have provided an explanation of the consequences of a particular level of taxes:

> firms with low costs of control would remove a larger percentage [of a pollutant] than would firms with higher costs—precisely the situation needed to achieve a least-cost approach to reducing pollution for the economy as a whole. Firms would tend to choose the least expensive methods of control, whether treatment of wastes, modification in production processes, or substitution of raw materials that had less serious polluting consequences. Further, the kinds of products whose manufacture entailed a lot of pollution would become more expensive and would carry higher prices than those that generated less, so consumers would be induced to buy more of the latter.[46]

The incentive system, in the eyes of its supporters, would be easy to administer. Once the appropriate level of taxes to achieve a policy goal was determined, it would then be a simple matter to monitor discharges and collect the taxes due. Large bureaucracies would be unnecessary, and political struggles would be avoided. Governmental coercion to cause compliance with standards would give way to choice based on self-interest.

In practice, however, the incentive system would be unlikely to do away with the need for either politics or administrative agencies. Determining how much reduction of pollution was necessary (or conversely, how clean the air should be) and what level of taxes would be needed to achieve this goal would be open to much disagreement, conflict, and struggle; in short, such decisions would be highly political. Businesses would want to hold down the taxes, environmentalists would opt for higher taxes, small businesses would likely seek preferential treatment, and so on. Administrative structures would be needed to develop studies and information for making these decisions. Moreover, once goals and taxes were set, an agency would be needed to monitor the discharge of pollutants and to collect the taxes due. The more complex and finely calibrated the structure of pollution taxes, the more complex the monitoring process would have to be. As Professor Deborah A. Stone remarks, "Where a standard and penalty system might levy a single fee for all discharges in excess of the standard, an incentive system would vary the taxes according to the amount of the discharges, and thus its information needs are greater than those of a standard system."[47]

Nor would the incentive system eliminate government coercion, because it represents a control system imposed by government on economic behavior. Companies do have a choice between cleaning up or paying up, or some combination of the two. However, their real preference might be to do nothing; they are left to select from among governmentally mandated alternatives.

A couple of other objections to the incentive system need to be noted. One is that it leaves decisions on how much to pollute to the judgment of private parties, based on self-interest, and fails to stigmatize pollution as morally wrong.[48] A second objection is based on equity grounds. Some, because of the stronger economic position, will be better able to pay the emission taxes and avoid restriction. In other words, the law will bear down more heavily on some than on others.

The incentive system has not actually been used for regulatory programs for pollution control or other purposes. Should it be used, one can conjecture that the incentive system might be as effective, or even more so, than standard setting and enforcement. Its use, however, would not obviate the need for political decision-making processes, administrative agencies, and governmental control as conditions for effective regulatory activity. In short, there is nothing about the incentive system that makes it inherently better than standard setting.

COMPLIANCE

All public policies are intended to influence or control human behavior in some way and to induce people to act in accordance with governmentally prescribed rules or goals, whether reference is to policy or such diverse matters as patents and copyrights, open housing, interest rates, night-time burglary, agricultural production, or military recruitment. If compliance with policy is not achieved, if people continue to act in undesired ways, if they do not take desired actions, or if they cease doing what is desired, to that extent policy becomes ineffective or, at the extreme, a nullity. (Foreign policy also depends for its effectiveness on compliance by the affected foreign countries and their officials.) To make consideration of this problem more manageable, we will focus primarily but not exclusively on compliance with domestic economic policies.

Except perhaps for crime policies, social scientists have not given much attention to the problem of compliance.[49] This may be partly due to our traditional legalistic approach to government, with its assumption that people have an absolute duty to obey the law. Too, those concerned with securing action on public problems often lose interest therein or shift their attention elsewhere once they secure the enactment of legislation. Such was the case with the Elementary and Secondary Education Act of 1965 referred to above. Political scientists have certainly been far more interested in the legislative and executive formation and adaptation of policy than in its administration, which is where compliance comes in. A complete study of policy making must be concerned not only with the events leading up to a policy decision but also with what is done to implement it and, ultimately, whether people comply with it.

In this section, some of the factors affecting compliance and noncompliance with policy will be examined, along with the role of administrative agencies in securing compliance.[50] Because of a scarcity of empirical data, the discussion must be somewhat speculative.

Causes of Compliance

Substantial respect for authority exists in our society, including authority as expressed in the decisions of governmental agencies. Statements to the effect that Americans are a lawless people appear as exaggerations and should not be permitted to obscure this fact. Respect for and deference to authority are built into our psychological makeup by the process of socialization. Most of us are taught from birth to respect the authority of parents, knowledge, status, the law, and governmental officials, especially if these forms of authority are considered to be reasonable. Consequently, we grow up generally believing it to be morally right and proper to obey the law. Disobedience of the law may produce feelings of guilt or shame. Prior conditioning and force of habit thus contribute to policy.

Compliance with policy may also be based on some form of reasoned, conscious acceptance. Even some whose immediate self-interest conflicts with a particular policy may be convinced that it is reasonable, necessary, or just. Most people undoubtedly would rather not pay taxes, and many do try to avoid or evade payment. But when people believe that tax laws are reasonable and just, or perhaps that taxation is necessary to provide needed governmental services, such beliefs will in all likelihood contribute to compliance with tax policy. Are not factors such as this and the one discussed in the preceding paragraph contributory to the high degree of compliance with the national income tax in the United States?

Another possible cause of compliance is the belief that a governmental decision or policy should be obeyed because it is legitimate, in the sense that it is constitutional, or was made by officials with proper authority to act, or that correct procedures were followed. People would probably be less inclined to accept judicial decisions as legitimate if the courts utilized decision procedures akin to those of legislatures. Courts gain legitimacy and acceptance for their decisions by acting as courts are supposed to act. For example, some people in the South were willing to comply with the Supreme Court's 1954 school desegregation decision because they viewed it as legitimate, as within the Court's competence, even though they disagreed with its substance.

Self-interest is often an important factor in compliance. Individuals and groups may directly benefit from their acceptance of policy norms and standards. Thus farmers have complied with production limitations in the form of acreage allotments and marketing quotas in order to qualify for price supports and benefit payments. Securities regulation is accepted by responsible members of the securities business as a way of protecting themselves and the reputation of their business against unethical practices by some dealers. Businesses engage in industrial-plant modernization in order to receive investment tax credits. Milk price–control laws have long been sought and complied with by dairy interests as a way of improving their economic well-being. Compliance thus results because private interests and policy prescriptions are harmonious, a fact sometimes ignored. Or, to put it differently, compliance may yield positive rewards. This situation, we should note, is not likely to occur outside the economic policy area.

For any given piece of legislation, such as a minimum-wage law or a Sunday closing law, there will not be simply supporters and opponents. Rather many points of view will exist, ranging from strong support through indifference to intense opposition. A considerable proportion of the population will often be indifferent or neutral toward the legislation in question, if indeed they feel affected by it at all. This group, given the general predisposition toward obedience, would seem especially subject to the authority of the law. Here in effect the law becomes a "self-fulfilling prophecy"; by its very existence it operates to create a climate of opinion conducive to compliance.

The possibility of punishment in the form of fines, jail sentences, and other penalties also may contribute to compliance. "Classical deterrence theory assumes that individuals respond to the severity, certainty, and celerity (speed) of punishment," state political scientists Anne Schneider and Helen Ingram, "and in this respect it implies that individuals are utility maximizers."[51] The threat or imposition of sanctions alone, however, is not always sufficient, even given overestimations of the likelihood of their use. "The strong disposition in this country to believe that any behavior can be controlled by threatening punishment has filled American statute books with hundreds of unenforced and unenforceable laws."[52] The experience with national prohibition, World War II price and rationing controls, many

Sunday "blue laws," highway speed limits, and penalties for marijuana use show that the threat of punishment is not always sufficient to induce general compliance with policies.

Although many people may comply with policies because they fear punishment, the main function of sanctions is to reinforce and supplement other causes of compliance. To a great extent, policies depend for their effectiveness upon voluntary or noncoerced compliance, because those concerned with enforcement cannot effectively handle and apply sanctions in large numbers of cases. The IRS, for example, would find itself at an impasse if several millions of people decided not to file returns. If those who would normally comply with policies see others benefiting from noncompliance, they too may become violators. Here the application of sanctions to some violators may be an effective promoter of compliance. Thus the IRS does prosecute flagrant and prominent tax evaders to prove by example that punishment awaits the tax evader.

In many instances, sanctions are effective more because people desire to avoid being stigmatized as lawbreakers than because they fear the penalties involved. In criminal proceedings for antitrust violations, for example, the fines levied have usually been quite nominal, given the economic resources of the violators. Not until 1961 did a businessman actually spend time in jail for an antitrust violation, although this punishment had been possible since the adoption of the Sherman Act in 1890. The real deterrent in these cases is probably the adverse publicity that flows from the proceedings. In recent years, Antitrust Division officials have been advocating more severe penalties for antitrust violators, especially jail sentences, to encourage compliance. Legislators and judges, however, are often reluctant to create or impose jail sentences and other severe penalties on business people because of their social status and because of the often diffuse and complex impact of law violations such as embezzlement or the misuse of "inside information" in stock deals. In other situations, sanctions may be more severe and certain and have a more powerful deterrent effect.

Finally, acceptance of most policies seems to increase with the length of time they are in effect. As time passes—and it always does—a once controversial policy becomes more familiar, a part of the accepted state of things, one of the conditions of doing business. Further, increasing numbers of persons come under the policy who have had no experience with the prepolicy situation. Because "freedom is (in part) a state of mind, such men feel the restrictions to rest more lightly upon them."[53] Although at one time the Wagner Act of 1935 was found highly objectionable by business interests, and the Taft-Hartley Act of 1947 was vigorously opposed by labor unions, today these statutes have lost much of their controversial quality. They have become a fixed part of the environment of labor-management relations, and businesses and labor unions have "learned to live with them."

Predictably, environmental pollution control policies will seem less restrictive or intrusive in a decade from now than they do at present.

Causes of Noncompliance

It will be readily apparent even to the most casual observer that all persons affected by public policies do not comply with them. Statistical information on reported violations is readily obtainable, as in the Federal Bureau of Investigation's Uniform Crime Reports. In addition, a lot of violations go undetected or unreported. Why do some people, or in some situations many people, deviate from officially prescribed norms of behavior? As the obverse of compliance, noncompliance may result when laws conflict too sharply with the prevailing values, mores, and beliefs of the people generally or of particular groups. The extensive violations of national prohibition and wartime price and rationing controls can be attributed in considerable measure to this cause as may much of the noncompliance in the South with the 1954 school desegregation decision and related policy. In such instances, the general predisposition to obey the law is outweighed by strong attachment to particular values and established practices.

It is not very useful, however, to ascribe noncompliance to a broad conflict between law and morality. Those who proclaim that "you can't legislate morality" not only oversimplify the situation but also ignore the fact that morality *is* frequently legislated with considerable success. Failure to comply results when a particular law or set of laws conflicts with particular values or beliefs in a particular time and situation. This law-value conflict must be stated in fairly precise terms if it is to have operational value in explaining noncompliance.

Thus there has been quite a bit of noncompliance with the Supreme Court's 1962 decision in *Engel* v. *Vitale* that the use of officially required prayers, even those that were nondenominational, in the public schools violated the First and Fourteenth Amendments' prohibition of the establishment of religion.[54] All efforts to legally circumvent this decision have failed.[55] The Supreme Court stirred the fire again in 1989 when, in a Georgia case, it let stand an appeals court ruling that banned religious invocations at public high-school football games.[56] In a very different area of human activity, opinion surveys have indicated that tax evasion is most common among persons who do not believe that the federal tax system is fair in its impact.[57]

The concept of selective disobedience of the law is closely related to law-value conflict.[58] Some laws are thought to be less binding than others on the individual. Those who strongly support and obey what are ordinarily labeled criminal laws, for example, sometimes have a more relaxed or permissive attitude toward economic regulatory legislation and laws concerning the conduct of public officials. Here one can aptly reflect on the behavior of Vice President Spiro T. Agnew, a staunch advocate of "law and order," who resigned his position after pleading no contest (following plea bargaining) to a charge of federal income-tax evasion. Many business people likewise apparently believe that laws relating to banking operations, insider stock trading, trade practices, and environmental pollution are not as mandatory for individuals as laws prohibiting robbery, burglary, and embezzlement. This may be partly because legislation controlling economic activity developed later than criminal laws and has not yet gained the same moral force. Moreover, economic legislation runs counter to the ideological belief in nonintervention by government in the economy held by many people in business. They then regard it as "bad law." Also, the same degree of social stigma usually is not attached to violations of economic policies as to criminal law offenses. Sociologist Marshall B. Clinard notes, "this selection of obedience to law rests upon the principle that what the person may be doing is illegal, perhaps even unethical, but certainly not criminal."[59]

One's associates and group memberships may also contribute to noncompliance (or, under other conditions, we should note, to compliance). Association with persons who hold ideas disrespectful of law and government, who justify or rationalize law violation, or who violate the law may cause an individual to acquire deviant norms and values that dispose the person to noncompliance. In a study of labor relations policy, Professor Robert E. Lane found that the rate of law violations varied with the community in which the firms studied were located. It was "fairly conclusive" that one reason for these differential patterns was the "difference in attitude toward the law, the government, and the morality of illegality. Plant managers stated they followed community patterns of behavior in their labor relations activities."[60] Similarly, attorneys for some of the defendant executives in the great price-fixing conspiracy in the electrical industry in the late 1950s attempted to explain and justify their actions, in the hope of lessening their punishment, as being in accord with the "corporate way of life."[61]

The desire to "make a fast buck," or something akin thereto, is often stated as a cause of noncompliance. This would certainly seem to be the case in many instances of fraud and misrepresentation, such as short-weighting and passing one product off for another in retail sales, the promotion of shady land sales and investment schemes, and price-fixing agreements. (Price-fixing is both the most obvious and the most common violation of the Sherman Antitrust Act.) It is really not possible, however, to determine how widespread greed is as a motive for noncompliance. By itself it often seems inadequate as an explanation. If two companies have equal opportunities to profit by violating the law, and one violates the law while the other does not, what is the explanation? One explanation may be that companies that are less profitable or in danger of failure are more likely to violate in an effort to survive than are more financially secure firms.[62] One should be careful, however, in attributing noncompliance to pecuniary motives. Many violations of labor-management relations policy stem from a desire to protect the prerogatives of management, while noncompliance with industrial health and safety standards may rest on the conviction that they are unnecessary or unworkable.

Noncompliance may also result from such factors as ambiguities in the law, a lack of clarity, conflicting policy standards, or the failure to adequately transmit policies to those affected by them. Income-tax violations often stem from the ambiguity or complexity of provisions of the Internal Revenue Code, which someone once described as a "sustained essay in obscurity." In other instances, persons or companies may believe that a given practice is not prohibited by existing law, only to find upon prosecution that it is. Such a situation may arise because the frames of reference of business people and public officials are different, thus each interpreting the law differently. Violations may also result from difficulties in complying with the law, even when its meaning is understood. For example, insufficient time may be allowed for filing complicated forms or for making required changes in existing patterns of action, such as in the installation of pollution-control devices. Sheer ignorance of the existence of laws or rules regulating conduct also cannot be discounted as a cause of noncompliance. While ignorance of the law may be no excuse, it often does account for violations. In sum, noncompliance may stem from structural defects in the law and its administration, and from ignorance and lack of understanding of the law, as well as from behavior that is more consciously or deliberately deviant.

Administration and Compliance

The burden of securing compliance with public policies rests primarily with administrative agencies; the court plays a lesser role. The broad purpose of administrative enforcement activities, such as conferences, persuasion, inspection, and prosecution, is to obtain compliance with policies rather than merely to punish violators.

Concious human behavior involves making choices among alternatives, deciding to do some things and not to do others. For purposes of discussion, we can assume that there are essentially three ways in which administrative agencies, or other governmental bodies concerned with implementing public policy, can influence people to act in the desired ways—to select behavioral alternatives that result in policy compliance. First, to achieve a desired result agencies can strive to shape, alter, or utilize the values people employ in making choices. Educational and persuasional activities are illustrative of this type of activity. Second, agencies can seek to limit the acceptable choices available to people, as by attaching penalties to undesired alternatives and rewards or benefits to desired alternatives. Third, agencies can try to interpret and administer policies in ways designed to facilitate compliance with their requirements. Thus time limits for compliance may be extended to give businesses more opportunity to meet pollution standards. More than one of these alternatives are normally used in seeking compliance with a given policy.

Administrative agencies engage in a wide range of educational and persuasional activities intended to convince those directly affected, and the public generally, that given public policies are reasonable, necessary, socially beneficial, or legitimate, in addition to informing them of the existence and meaning of those policies. The effectiveness of public policies depends considerably on the ability of agencies to promote understanding and consent, thereby reducing violations and minimizing the actual use of sanctions. This is in keeping with our earlier comment on the importance of voluntary compliance. When changes are made in the coverage and level of the federal minimum-wage law, for example, the Department of Labor seeks to acquaint the public, and especially employers and employees, of their nature and implications by the distribution of explanatory bulletins, reference guides, and posters, announcements through the news media, meetings with affected groups, appearances at conventions, direct mailings, telephone calls, and the like. After the changes become effective, press releases and mailed materials are used to provide information on enforcement activities and legal interpretations of the law. The Federal Deposit Insurance Corporation likewise relies heavily on advice and warnings to banks, based on inspections, to get them to bring their operations into accord with banking regulations. Formal proceedings are initated only when persuasion appears ineffective.

Agencies may also use propaganda appeals in support of compliance. (Propaganda is used here not in a pejorative sense but rather to denote efforts to gain acceptance of policies by identifying them with widely held values and beliefs.) Appeals to patriotism were used to win support and acceptance of the military draft. Agricultural programs have been depicted as necessary to ensure equality for agriculture and to help preserve the family farm as a way of life. Antitrust programs have been described as necessary to maintain our system of free competitive enterprise. The Forest Service utilizes Smokey the Bear to tell us that "only you can prevent forest fires." Propaganda appeals are more emotional than rational in thrust. They can be viewed as attempts either to reduce the moral costs of adapting to a policy or to make compliance desirable by attaching positive values to policies.[63]

In the course of administering policies, agencies may make modifications in the policies or adopt practices that will contribute to compliance. Revealed inequities in the law may be reduced or eliminated, conflicts in policy standards may be resolved, or simplified procedures for compliance may be developed, such as simplified federal income-tax forms for lower-income earners. Administrative personnel may develop knowledge and skill in enforcing policy that enables them to reduce misunderstanding and antagonism. Consultation and advice may be used to help those affected by laws come into compliance without the issuance of citations. Laws may be interpreted or applied to make them more compatible with the interests of those affected. For instance, until 1970 the administration of oil-import controls policy by the Oil Import Administration "was almost wholly in the interests of the petroleum industry."[64] They had little cause for complaint. Many of the health and safety "consensus" standards initially issued by OSHA were later rescinded because of widespread complaints that they were outdated, trivial, or had little usefulness in protecting against health and safety hazards. OSHA hoped to reduce the antagonism of the business community toward itelf by their elimination.

Sanctions will be resorted to by agencies when the various sociological and psychological factors supporting obedience and the other methods available fail to produce compliance. Sanctions are penalties or deprivations imposed on those who violate policy norms and are intended to make undesired behavior patterns unattractive. They directly punish violators and serve to deter others who might not comply if they saw violators go unpunished.

Sanctions may be imposed by either administrative agencies or the courts. Common forms of judicial sanctions are fines, jail sentences, award of damages, and injunctions. However, in most areas of public policy (crime policy is a major exception), administrative sanctions are used much more frequently because of their greater immediacy, variety, and flexibility. Among the sanctions that agencies may impose are threat of prosecution; imposition of fines or pecuniary penalties that have the effect of fines, as by OSHA; unfavorable publicity; revocation, annulment, modification, suspension, or refusal to renew licenses; summary seizure and destruction of goods; award of damages; issuance of cease-and-desist orders; and denial of services or benefits. To be most effective, the severity of sanctions must be geared to the violations against which they are directed. If they are too severe, the agency may be reluctant to use them; if they are too mild, they may have inadequate deterrent effects, as seems to be the case with most fines for antitrust violations. The Office of Education was thus handicapped in its early administration of Title I of the Elementary and Secondary Education Act because the only sanction it had for state and local violations was to cut off funds. Because of the adverse reaction this would have caused, the agency was politically reluctant to impose the penalty and indeed did not.

Agencies clearly need appropriate and effective sanctions to help ensure policy compliance.

Agencies may also seek to induce compliance by conferring positive benefits on compliers and thereby bring self-interest into support for compliance. This method can be referred to as the *purchase of consent*. Benefits may take such forms as favorable publicity and recognition for nondiscrimination in hiring, price-support payments for compliance with agricultural production limitations, tax credits for industrial plant modernization, and federal grants-in-aid for the support of state programs of medical aid to the indigent that meet federal standards. It is often difficult, however, to distinguish rewards from sanctions. Does an individual comply with a policy provision to secure a benefit or to avoid losing it? Whatever the motives of persons seeking benefits, the government does use rewards extensively to gain compliance with policy. They are undoubtedly much more acceptable politically in many situations than would be a clear-cut prohibition or requirement of some action with penalties for noncompliance. Imagine the reaction if, rather than using tax credits, businesses were required to modernize their plants or else be subject to fines and other penalties. Subsidy payments clearly have also made compliance with production controls more palatable to farmers.

Clearly, then, compliance—or noncompliance—with public policy may stem from a variety of factors. It is a complex topic that needs greater attention by policy analysts because of its importance for the actual content and impact of public policy.

Notes

1. Jeffrey L. Pressman and Aaron Wildavsky, *Implementation* (Berkeley: University of California Press, 1973).
2. Some good illustrations of implementation research are Eugene Bardack, *The Implementation Game: What Happens After a Bill Becomes Law?* (Cambridge, Mass.: MIT Press, 1977); Daniel A. Mazmanian and Paul A. Sabatier, *Implementation and Public Policy* (Chicago: Scott Foresman, 1983); and Malcolm L. Goggin, *Policy Design and the Politics of Implementation* (Knoxville: University of Tennessee Press, 1987).
3. Frank J. Goodnow, *Politics and Administration* (New York: Russell and Russell, 1900).
4. Martha Derthick, *Policymaking for Social Security* (Washington, D.C.: Brookings Institution, 1979), chap. 15.
5. *The New York Times*, March 31, 1989, p. 8.
6. David T. Stanley and Marjorie Girth, *Bankruptcy: Problems Process Reform* (Washington, D.C.: Brookings Institution, 1971), p. 172.

7. See Samuel P. Huntington, "The Marasmus of the ICC," *Yale Law Journal*, LXI (1952), pp. 470–509.
8. This discussion draws on Harold Seidman and Robert Gilmour, *Politics, Position, and Power*, 4th ed. (New York: Oxford University Press, 1986), pp. 276, 293–300. See also General Accounting Office, *Federal Advisory Committee Act* (Washington, D.C.: General Accounting Office, October, 1988).
9. Kay Lehman Scholzman and John T. Tierney, *Organized Interests and American Democracy* (New York: Harper & Row, 1986), p. 334.
10. James W. Davis, Jr., and Kenneth M. Dolbeare, *Little Groups of Neighbors: The Selective Service System* (Chicago: Markham, 1968).
11. Rowland Evans and Robert Novak, *Lyndon B. Johnson: The Exercise of Power* (New York: New American Library, 1966), p. 430.
12. *The New York Times*, November 27, 1986, p. 4.
13. *Congressional Quarterly Weekly Report*, Vol. 46 (October 29, 1988), pp. 3145–3146; *Newsweek*, Vol. 113 (April 10, 1989), pp. 20–24.
14. *Congressional Quarterly Weekly Report*, Vol. 44 (September 20, 1986), pp. 2207–2208.
15. Patty D. Renfrow, "The Politics of Organizational Structure." Unpublished paper presented at the annual meeting of the American Political Science Administration (September 1–4, 1983).
16. *Congressional Quarterly Weekly Report*, Vol. 40 (September 16, 1978), pp. 2485–2486; and Vol. 40 (October 7, 1978), pp. 2752–2753. For a full-scale treatment of the establishment of the Department of Education, see Beryl A. Radin and Willis D. Hawley, *The Politics of Federal Reorganization: Creating the U.S. Department of Education* (New York: Pergamon Press, 1988).
17. *Congressional Quarterly Weekly Report*, Vol. 40 (October 7, 1978), p. 2753.
18. John A. Ferejohn, "Logrolling in an Institutional Context: A Case Study of Food Stamps Legislation." Working Paper No. P-85-5, The Hoover Institution, Stanford University (October, 1985).
19. Quoted in V. O. Key, Jr., *Politics, Parties, and Pressure Groups*, 4th ed. (New York: Crowell, 1958), p. 743.
20. This discussion draws on my *Politics and the Economy* (Boston: Little, Brown, 1966), pp. 86–90.
21. Cf. Matthew Holden, Jr., " 'Imperialism' in Bureaucracy," *American Political Science Review*, LX (December, 1966), pp. 943–951.
22. *Ibid.*, p. 944.
23. This discussion, and that in the first part of the next section, draws on Francis E. Rourke, *Bureaucracy, Politics and Public Policy*, 3rd ed. (Boston: Little, Brown, 1984), chaps. 4 and 5.
24. *Ibid.*, pp. 106–107.
25. *Ibid.*, p. 108.
26. On the separation of the ability to decide from the authority to decide in organization, see Victor Thompson, *Modern Organizations* (New York: Knopf, 1961).
27. Theodore C. Sorensen, *Kennedy* (New York: Harper & Row, 1965), chap. 25. On secrecy in administration generally, see Harold L. Wilensky, *Organizational Intelligence* (New York: Basic Books, 1967), chaps. 3 and 7; and Sym-

posium on "The Freedom of Information Act," *Public Administration Review*, Vol. XXXIX (July–August 1979), pp. 310–332.

28. See James A. Nathan and James K. Oliver, *Foreign Policy Making and the American Political System*, 2d ed. (Boston: Little, Brown, 1987).

29. Rourke, *op. cit.*, p. 108.

30. This story is told well by Richard E. Neustadt and Harvey V. Finebert, *The Swine Flu Affair* (Washington, D.C.: Department of Health, Education, and Welfare, 1978).

31. Stefanie Ann Lenway, *The Politics of U.S. International Trade* (Marshfield, Mass.: Pitman, 1985).

32. The number of pages published annually in the *Federal Register* has sometimes been used as a simplistic measure of the volume of federal regulation. The rules themselves, however, are only a small portion of the *Register's* total pages.

33. *The Wall Street Journal*, February 5, 1973, p. 1.

34. Kenneth Culp Davis, *Administrative Law Treatise* (St. Paul, Minn.: West, 1958), Vol. 1, pp. 263–265.

35. A cease-and-desist order is an agency's civil directive to stop engaging in a practice held to be in violation of the law. Agencies such as the Federal Trade Commission and the NLRB are authorized to issue such orders.

36. Ashley Schiff, *Fire and Water: Scientific Heresy in the Forest Service* (Cambridge, Mass.: Harvard University Press, 1962).

37. Thomas Hackett, "A Reporter at Large (Yellowstone)," *The New Yorker*, LXV (October 2, 1989), pp. 50–73.

38. Harold Wolman, *Politics of Federal Housing* (New York: Dodd, Mead, 1971), pp. 26–28.

39. This account draws on Michael Kirst and Richard Jong, "The Utility of a Longitudinal Approach in Assessing Implementation: A Thirteen-Year View of Title I, ESEA," in Walter Williams et al., *Studying Implementation* (Chatham, N.J.: Chatham House, 1982), chap. 6; and June A. O'Neil and Margaret C. Simms, "Education," in John L. Palmer and Isabel C. Sawhill (eds.), *The Reagan Record* (Washington, D.C.: Urban Institute, 1982), chap. 11.

40. Emmette A. Redford, *The Administration of National Economic Control* (New York: Macmillan, 1952), p. 104.

41. Charles Schultze, *The Public Use of Private Interest* (Washington, D.C.: Brookings Institution, 1977).

42. Joseph A. Pechman, *Federal Tax Policy*, 5th ed. (Washington, D.C.: Brookings Institution, 1987), pp. 355–362.

43. Peter Woll, *American Bureaucracy*, 2d ed. (New York: Norton, 1977), p. 95.

44. Redford, *op. cit.*, pp. 164–177.

45. This discussion draws on Deborah A. Stone, *Policy Paradox and Political Reason* (Glenview, Ill.: Scott, Foresman, 1988), p. 225; and Schultze, *op. cit.*

46. Allen Kneese and Charles Schultze, *Pollution Prices and Public Policy* (Washington, D.C.: Brookings Institution, 1975), p. 89.

47. Stone, *op. cit.*, p. 228.

48. Michael D. Reagan, *Regulation: The Politics of Policy* (Boston: Little, Brown,

1987), p. 142. See also Steven Kelman, *What Price Incentives? Economists and the Environment* (Boston: Auburn House, 1981), pp. 27–28.

49. A notable recent exception is Kenneth J. Meier and David R. Morgan, "Citizen Compliance with Public Policy: The National Maximum Speed Law," *Western Political Quarterly*, XXXV (June, 1982), pp. 258–273.

50. This discussion draws heavily on my "Public Economic Policy and the Problem of Compliance: Notes for Research," *Houston Law Review*, IV (Spring–Summer, 1966), pp. 62–72.

51. Anne Schneider and Helen Ingram, "Behavioral Theories in Policy Designs." Unpublished paper presented at the Midwest Political Science Association Meeting (1989).

52. Herbert A. Simon, Donald Smithburg, and Victor Thompson, *Public Administration* (New York: Knopf, 1950), p. 479.

53. Robert Lane, *The Regulation of Businessmen* (New Haven: Yale University Press, 1954), pp. 69–70.

54. 370 U.S. 421 (1962).

55. See John A. Murley, "School Prayer: Free Exercise of Religion or Establishment of Religion," in Raymond Tatalovich and Byron W. Daynes (eds.), *Social Regulatory Policy* (Boulder: Westview Press, 1989), chap. 1.

56. *Houston Post*, May 31, 1989, pp. 1, 6.

57. Timothy B. Clark, "Honesty May Become the Best Tax Policy If Tax Compliance Bill Becomes Law," *The National Journal*, Vol. 14 (July 24, 1982), pp. 1292–1296.

58. Marshall B. Clinard, *Sociology of Deviant Behavior* (New York: Holt, Rinehart and Winston, 1957), pp. 168–171.

59. *Ibid.*

60. Robert E. Lane, "Why Business Men Violate the Law," *Journal of Criminal Law, Criminology, and Police Science*, XLIV (1953), pp. 151, 154–160.

61. John G. Fuller, *The Gentlemen Conspirators: The Story of the Price-Fixers in the Electrical Industry* (New York: Grove Press, 1962), pp. 88, 109–110.

62. Lane, *op. cit.*, chap. 5.

63. Simon, Smithburg, and Thompson, *op. cit.*, p. 457.

64. Roger G. Noll, *Reforming Regulation* (Washington, D.C.: Brookings Institution, 1971), p. 65.

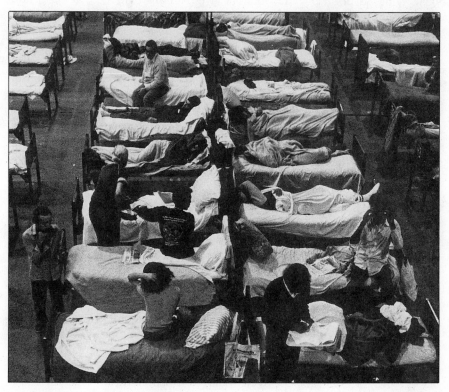

7

POLICY IMPACT, EVALUATION, AND CHANGE

A Red Cross shelter for the homeless in New York City: For some policy makers, such an outcome demands new and more effective policies.

The final stage of the policy process, viewed as a sequential pattern of activities, is the evaluation of policy. Generally speaking, policy evaluation is concerned with the estimation, assessment, or appraisal of policy, including its content, implementation, and effects. As a functional activity, evaluation can and does occur throughout the policy process and not simply as its last stage. For instance, an attempt is usually made to determine, that is, estimate, the consequences of various policy alternatives for dealing with a problem prior to the adoption of one of them. In this chapter, the focus will be primarily but not exclusively on policy evaluation connected with efforts to implement or carry out policies. As we shall see, evaluational activity may restart the policy process (problem, formulation, and so on) in order to continue, modify, or terminate existing policy.

Policy evaluation, as a functional activity, is as old as policy itself. Policy makers and administrators have always made judgments concerning the worth or effects of particular policies, programs, and projects. Many of these judgments have been of the impressionistic or "seat of the pants" variety, based often on anecdotal or fragmentary evidence, at best, and strongly influenced by ideological, partisan self-interest and other valuational criteria. Thus, a welfare program may be regarded as "socialistic" and hence undesirable by some, regardless of its actual impact, or a tax cut may be considered necessary and desirable because it enhances the electoral chances of the evaluators' political party. Unemployment compensation may likewise be deemed "bad" because the evaluator "knows a lot of people" who improperly receive benefits. Most of us are quite familiar with this kind of policy evaluation and have undoubtedly done, and enjoyed doing, a bit of it ourselves. Much conflict may result from this sort of evaluation, however, because different evaluators, employing different value criteria, reach different conclusions concerning the merits of the same policy.

Another common variety of policy evaluation centers on the operation of particular policies or programs. Questions asked may include: Is the program honestly run? What are its financial costs? Who receives benefits (payments or services) and in what amounts? Is there unnecessary overlap or duplication with other programs? Were legal standards and procedures followed? This kind of evaluation may tell us something about the honesty or efficiency in the conduct of a program, but, like the first kind of evaluation, it will probably yield little if anything in the way of hard information on the societal effects of a program. A welfare program, for example, may be ideologically and politically satisfying to a given evaluator as well as being honestly and prudently conducted. Assuming we are in agreement with this evaluation, it will in all likelihood tell us little about the impact of the welfare program on the poor or its social cost-benefit ratio, or whether it is achieving its officially stated objectives.

A third type of policy evaluation, which is comparatively new in usage, and which has been receiving increasing attention within the national government in recent years, is the systematic, objective evaluation of programs to measure their societal impact and the extent to which they are achieving their stated objectives. We shall refer to this as *systematic evaluation*, for want of a better term. The Departments of Labor and of Health and Human Services have assistant secretaries whose responsibilities include program evaluation. Bureaus within these and other departments often include policy and program evaluation staffs. More attention appears to be given to the evaluation of social welfare programs than of most other areas of governmental activity. This probably arises from their proliferation in recent decades, their substantial costs, and the controversies that surround them.

Systematic evaluation directs attention to the effects a policy has on the public need or problem to which it is directed. It permits at least tentative, informed responses to such questions as: Is this policy achieving its objectives? What are its costs and benefits? Who are its beneficiaries? What happened as a consequence of the policy that would not have happened in its absence? Consequently, systematic evaluation gives policy makers and the general public, if they are interested, some notion of the actual impact of policy and provides policy discussions with some grounding in reality. Evaluation findings can be used to modify current policies and programs and to help design others for the future.

Of course, evaluation can also be used for less laudable purposes. As Professor Carol Weiss has noted, "Program decision-makers may turn to evaluation to delay a decision; to justify and legitimate a decision already made; to extricate themselves from controversy about future directions by passing the buck; to vindicate the program in the eyes of its constituents, its funders, or the public; to satisfy conditions of a government or foundation grant through the ritual of evaluation."[1] In short, evaluators may be motivated by self-service as well as public service and by a desire to use analysis as ammunition for partisan political purposes. Thus, the various analytical studies used by members of Congress in the 1977–78 debate over natural gas pricing were based on assumptions that predetermined their conclusions. Members tended to rely on the studies that supported their particular preferences.[2]

POLICY IMPACT

An important distinction must be made between policy outputs and policy outcomes. *Policy outputs* are the things actually done by agencies in pursuance of policy decisions and statements. The concept of outputs focuses one's attention on such matters as amounts of taxes collected, miles of highways built, welfare benefits paid, price-fixing agreements prosecuted, traffic fines collected, or foreign-aid projects undertaken. Outputs usually can be readily counted, totaled, and statistically analyzed. An examination of outputs may indicate, or seem to, that a lot is being done to implement a policy. Such activity, however, sometimes amounts to what Professor William T. Gormley, Jr., calls "beancounting." Agencies, under pressure from legislators, interest groups, and others to demonstrate results, "may focus on outputs, not outcomes, in order to generate statistics that create the illusion of progress."[3]

Policy outcomes, in contrast, are the consequences, for society, intended and unintended, that stem from governmental action or inaction. Social welfare policies can be used to illustrate this concept. It is fairly easy to measure welfare policy outputs such as amounts of benefits paid, average level of benefits, and number of people assisted. But what are the outcomes, or societal consequences, of these actions? Do they increase personal security and contentment? Do they reduce individual initiative? In the case of Aid to Families with Dependent Children (AFDC), does it have the effect of encouraging promiscuity and illegitimacy, as some allege? Do welfare programs help keep the poor quiescent, as others contend?[4] Questions such as these, which are tough to answer, direct our attention to the societal impacts of policies. Among other things, as policy students, we want to know whether policies are accomplishing their purposes, whether society is changing policy actions as a consequence, and whether it is changing as intended or in other ways. Policy impacts are an amalgam of outputs and outcomes.

The impact of a policy has several dimensions, all of which must be taken into account in the course of evaluation:[5]

1. Policies have impacts on the public problem at which they are directed and the people involved. Those whom the policy is intended to affect must be defined, whether they are the poor, small business people, disadvantaged school children, petroleum producers, or whatever. The intended effect of the policy must then be determined. If, for example, it is an anti-poverty program, is its purpose to raise the income of the poor, to increase their opportunities for employment, or to change their attitudes and behavior? If some combination of such purposes is intended, analysis becomes more complicated because priorities must be assigned to the various intended effects.

Further, it must be noted that a policy may have either intended or unintended consequences, or even both. A welfare program, for example, may improve the income situation of the benefited groups, as intended, but what impact does it have on their initiative to seek employment? Does it decrease this, as some have contended? A public housing program may improve the housing situation of urban blacks, but it may also contribute to racial segregation in housing. An agricultural price-support program, intended to improve farmers' incomes, may lead to overproduction of the supported commodities, or to higher food prices for consumers, or to increased land values.

A good illustration of a policy with unintended consequences is the 1970 legislation prohibiting the broadcasting of cigarette advertising on radio and television.[6] This ad ban represented a legislative victory for the antismoking forces. However, the ban also eliminated the need for broadcasters, under the Federal Communications Commission's fairness doctrine, to donate air time to antismoking groups on the controversial issue of smoking. Research has indicated that the antismoking messages prepared by these groups had a substantial deterrent effect upon cigarette consumption. The antismoking ad campaign, however, was substantially dependent upon donated time. As a consequence, after the cigarette ad ban went into effect, most of the antismoking ads were also eliminated. The short-term effect was clearly a significant increase in smoking, which was obviously not what the proponents of the ban had intended. Although the long-run effects are less clear, "the weight of the evidence seems to favor the conclusion that the ad ban was myopic policy."[7]

2. Policies may have effects on situations or groups other than those at which they are directed. These are variously called third-party effects, spillover effects, or externalities.[8] The testing of nuclear explosives in the atmosphere, for example, would provide useful data for weapons development, but it would also generate radiation hazards for the present and future generations. An urban renewal project may cause much inconvenience, dislocation, and social disruption for a neighborhood, but these results are difficult if not impossible to measure. How does one place a value on them?

These two examples represent negative externalities, but externalities may also be positive. Public education programs not only educate students, they also provide employers with a more capable work force and the community with better informed citizens. Those who contend that only those who have children in public schools should contribute toward their support ignore such positive externalities. Many of the outcomes of public policies can be most meaningfully understood as externalities.

3. Policies have impacts on future as well as current conditions, and in some instances most of their benefits or some of their costs may occur in the far future. For example, was the Head Start program—a preschool education program for the poor—supposed to improve the cognitive abilities of participating children in the short run or their long-range development and earning capacity? Did the regulation of the field price of natural gas, a policy initiated in the 1950s, really contribute to a shortage of gas in the 1970s, as some contended (notably those in the petroleum industry, who had long opposed the policy)?

The future effects of some policies may be very diffuse. Assuming that patent and copyright policies do indeed stimulate invention and creativity, and that these in turn enhance economic growth and societal development, how do we measure their benefits, either qualitatively or quantitatively?

Again, how does one appraise the impact of high interest rates generated by the Federal Reserve Board on "inflationary psychology?"

4. The costs of policies are another element for evaluation. It is usually fairly easy to calculate the direct dollar costs for the government of a particular policy or program, whether this is stated as the actual number of dollars spent on the program, its share of total governmental expenditures, or the proportion of the gross national product devoted to it. Budgetary documents will yield such figures. In some instances, however, a governmental expenditure may serve multiple purposes, such as operation of the space shuttle program and the development of new technology. Allocation of costs then becomes more difficult.

Other direct costs of policies may be more difficult to discover or calculate, such as the expenditures for pollution-control devices by private industries that are necessitated by an air-pollution control policy. Moreover, would some companies have installed such devices in the absence of the policy? If so, should the costs be attributed to the policy? In the absence of governmental subsidies, the costs of complying with regulatory policies fall primarily on the regulated, who have an incentive to inflate claimed costs in order to make the policies appear more costly. Ultimately, of course, such costs may be passed on to consumers in the form of higher prices for goods and services.

5. Of course, it is also difficult to measure the indirect benefits of public policies for the community. Assuming that patent and copyright policies do indeed stimulate inventive and creative activity, and that these contribute to economic growth and social development, how may we assess their benefits quantitatively? The Social Security program may contribute to social stability and political contentment as well as the retirement incomes of recipients, but the problem of measurement is again apparent.

The evaluation of policy becomes even more complex when we give explicit consideration to the fact that the effects of policy may be symbolic (or intangible) as well as material (or tangible). Symbolic outputs, in the view of political scientists Gabriel A. Almond and G. Bingham Powell, "include affirmations of values by elites; displays of flags, troops, and military ceremony; visits by royalty or high officials; and statements of policy or intent by political leaders" and "are highly dependent on tapping popular beliefs, attitudes, and aspirations for their effectiveness."[9] Symbolic policy outputs produce no real changes in societal conditions. No one eats better, for example, because of a Memorial Day parade or a speech by a high public official on the virtues of free enterprise, however ideologically or emotionally satisfying such actions may be for many people. More to the point, however, is the fact that policy actions ostensibly directed toward meeting material wants or needs may turn out in practice to be more symbolic than material in their impact.

This is well illustrated by the Fair Housing Act of 1968. Enacted by Congress in part because of pressure created by the assassination of Dr.

Martin Luther King, Jr., the law prohibited discrimination in the rental or sale of housing on the basis of race, color, religion, sex, or national origin. However, the Department of Housing and Urban Development (HUD), which was assigned primary responsibility for its enforcement, could only seek to mediate disputes between a person who thought he or she had been discriminated against and the rentor or seller. The Justice Department in turn could act only if it found a "pattern of practice" of discrimination. As a consequence of these weak enforcement provisions, the Fair Housing Act in practice did not live up to its promise. The act, which one member of Congress called a "toothless tiger," was of little use in preventing housing discrimination.

The Congress in 1988 reached a compromise agreement on legislation to strengthen enforcement of the Fair Housing Act. Now a person who believes he or she has been discriminated against can file a complaint with HUD, which, if it cannot settle the dispute, can issue a charge of housing discrimination. At this point either party to the dispute can choose to have it decided by either a federal district court or an administrative hearing. If either party chooses to go to the federal court, that choice prevails. It was expected that this procedure would put some real "teeth" into the enforcement of the act and give it material rather than symbolic effect.

Other public policies that appear to promise more symbolically than their implementation actually yields in material benefits include antitrust activity, public-utility rate regulation, and equal employment opportunity. Even though the actual impact of a policy may be considerably less than is intended or desired, it nonetheless may have significant consequences for society. An antipoverty program that falls short of the mark may nonetheless assure people that the government is concerned about poverty. Equal employment opportunity legislation assures people that their government, officially at least, does not condone discrimination in hiring on the basis of race, sex, and nationality. Apart from effects such policies have on societal conditions, they may contribute to social order, support for government, and personal self-esteem, which are not inconsequential considerations.

The analysis of public policy is usually focused upon what governments actually do, why, and with what material effects. We should not, however, neglect the symbolic aspects of government, despite their intangible and nebulous nature. The rhetoric of government—what governments say, or appear to say—is clearly a necessary and proper concern for the policy analyst.

PROBLEMS IN POLICY EVALUATION

The most useful form of policy evaluation for policy makers and administrators, as well as for policy critics who wish to have a factual basis for their positions, is a systematic evaluation that tries to determine cause-and-effect relationships and rigorously measure the impact of policy. It is of course often impossible to measure quantitatively the impact of public policies, especially social policies, with any real precision. In this context, then, to "measure rigorously" is to seek to assess as carefully and objectively as possible the impact of policy.

Determining whether a policy or program is doing what it is supposed to do, or doing something else, is not an easy, straightforward task, as some appear to assume. Snap judgments are easy to make but lacking in definitiveness. A number of conditions create obstacles or problems for the effective accomplishment of policy evaluation. These include uncertainty over policy goals, difficulty in determining causality, diffuse policy impacts, and others that will be reviewed in this section.

Uncertainty over Policy Goals

When the goals of a policy are unclear, diffuse, or diverse, as they frequently are, determining the extent to which they have been attained becomes a difficult and frustrating task.[10] This situation is often a product of the policy adoption process. Because support of a majority coalition is needed to secure adoption of a policy, it is often necessary to appeal to persons and groups possessing differing interests and diverse values. Commitments to the preferred policy goals of these various groups may be included in legislation in order to secure their votes. The Model Cities Act of 1966 reflects this process. Its goals included, among others, the rebuilding of slum and blighted areas; the improvement of housing, income and cultural opportunities; the reduction of crime and delinquency; a lessened dependency on welfare; and the maintenance of historic landmarks. No priorities were assigned to the various goals, nor were their dimensions well-specified. Model cities evaluation research had to try to come to grips with these diverse goals. It may thus be no easy task to determine what the real goals of a program are. Officials in different positions in the policy system, such as legislators and administrators, or national and state officials, may define them differently, act accordingly, and reach differing conclusions concerning the accomplishments of the program.

Difficulty in Determining Causality

Systematic evaluation requires that societal changes must be demonstrably caused by policy actions. The mere fact that when action A is taken condition B develops does not necessarily mean that a cause-and-effect relationship exists. Other actions (or variables) may have been the actual causes of condition B. Many common colds are "cured," not by ingestion of medicines, the application of ointments, and the use of nasal sprays, but by that natural recuperative power of the human body.

Consider the following example. Many states require periodic automobile safety inspections in an attempt to reduce highway traffic accidents and fatalities. Research indicates that states with mandatory inspection laws do tend to have fewer traffic fatalities than do other states. However, other factors, such as population density, weather conditions, and percentage of young drivers, might in fact explain the difference. Only if such conditions are controlled in the analysis and if differences remain between states with and without inspections, can it be accurately stated that a policy of periodic automobile inspections reduces traffic deaths. In actuality, such laws do seem to have a modest beneficial effect.[11]

To illustrate the problem of determining causality further, let us take the case of crime-control policies. The purpose, or at least one of the purposes, of these policies is the deterrence of crime. Deterrence may be defined as the prevention of an action that can be said to have had a "realistic potential of actualization,"[12] that is, one that really could have happened. (This assumption is required to avoid the kind of analysis that holds, for example, that the consumption of alcoholic beverages prevents stomach worms, since no one has ever been afflicted with them after starting to drink.) The problem here is that not doing something is a sort of nonevent, or intangible act. Does the fact that a person does not commit burglary mean that he or she has been effectively deterred by policy from so acting? The answer, of course, first depends upon whether he or she was inclined to engage in burglary. If so, then was the person deterred by the possibility of detection and punishment, by other factors such as family influence, or by the lack of opportunity? As this should indicate, the determination of causality between actions, especially in complex social and economic matters, is a difficult task.

Diffuse Policy Impacts

Policy actions may affect groups other than those at whom they are specifically directed. A welfare program, for example, may affect not only the poor but also others such as taxpayers, public officials, and low-income people who are not receiving welfare benefits. The effects on these groups may be either symbolic or material. Taxpayers may grumble that their "hard-earned dollars are going to support those too lazy to work." Some low-income working people may decide to go on welfare rather than continue working at unpleasant jobs for low wages. So far as the poor who receive material benefits are concerned, what effects do benefits have on their initiative and self-reliance, on family solidarity, and on the maintenance of social order? We should bear in mind that policies may have unstated goals. Thus, an antipoverty program may be covertly intended to help defuse the demands of black activists; or, to take another case, a beef import control program may be intended to appease cattlemen politically, while not really doing much to limit foreign competition.

The effects of some programs may be very broad and long-range in nature. Antitrust policy is an example. Originally intended to help maintain competition and prevent monopoly in the economy, how does one now evaluate its effectiveness? We can look at ongoing enforcement activity and find that particular mergers have been prevented and price-fixing conspiracies broken up, but this will not tell us much about competition and monopoly in the economy generally. It would be nice to be able to determine that the economy is *n* percent more competitive than it would have been in the absence of antitrust policy. Given the generality of its goals and the difficulties of measuring competition and monopoly, this just is not possible. Interestingly enough, after a century of antitrust action, there are still no agreed-upon definitions of monopoly and competition to guide policy action and evaluation. It is no wonder that those assessing the effectiveness of antitrust policy sometimes come to sharply different conclusions.

Difficulties in Data Acquisition

As some previous comments have implied, a shortage of accurate and relevant statistical data and other information may handicap the policy evaluator. Thus econometric models may predict the effect of a tax cut on economic activity, but suitable data to indicate its actual impact on the economy are hard to come by. Again, think of the problems involved in securing the data needed to determine the effect on criminal law enforcement of a Supreme Court decision such as *Miranda* v. *Arizona*,[13] which held that a confession obtained when a suspect had not been informed of his or her rights when taken into custody was inherently invalid. The members of the President's Crime Commission in 1967 disagreed about its effect. The majority said it was too early to determine its impact. A minority, however, held that, if fully implemented, "it could mean the virtual elimination of pretrial interrogation of suspects. . . . Few can doubt the adverse effect of *Miranda* upon the law enforcement process."[14] An absence of data does not necessarily hinder all evaluators.

The use of "*Miranda* cards" to inform suspects of their rights has become standard practice. A consensus now exists among criminal justice scholars and law enforcement officers to the effect that this reform has had *little* adverse effect on law enforcement. Various field and quantitative studies support this view. Moreover, it is suggested that the *Miranda* rule has helped improve professionalism among the police.[15]

For many social and economic programs, a question that typically arises is, "Did those who participated in programs subsequently fare better than comparable persons who did not?" Providing an answer preferably involves an evaluation design utilizing a control group. The task of devising a control (or comparison) group for a manpower program is summed up in the following passage:

> A strict comparison group in the laboratory sense of the physical sciences is virtually impossible, primarily because the behavior patterns of people are affected by so many external social, economic, and political factors. In fact, sometimes the legislation itself prevents a proper comparison group from being established. For example, the Work Incentive Program legislation of 1967 required that *all* fathers must be enrolled in the WIN program within 30 days after receipt of aid for their children. Therefore, a comparison group of fathers with comparable attributes to those fathers enrolled in the program could not be established. Even if all the external factors of the economy could be controlled, it would still be impossible to replicate the social and political environment affecting any experimental or demonstration program. Thus, it is easy for a decision-maker to discount the results of almost any evaluation study on the basis that it lacks the precision control group.[16]

Because of difficulties such as those noted in the quotation, experimental designs often cannot be used. (This is apart from their often high dollar costs.) Second-best alternatives must then be utilized, such as a quasi-experimental design using a nonequivalent control group,[17] which will provide useful but less than conclusive data on program accomplishments.

Another kind of data problem can be illustrated by cost-benefit analysis, which has been used to evaluate regulatory policies and water projects.[18] A formal, quantitative evaluation technique, cost-benefit analysis requires identification of the various costs and benefits of a policy (proposed or actual) and their translation into dollar values for comparison. This is relatively easy to do for some costs, such as the direct administrative costs, and some benefits, such as the reclamation of land, when market prices can be used.

In many instances, however, it will be very difficult to identify the benefits of a policy, let alone place dollar values on them. They may be indirect, as when lower unemployment in a community because of a job training program reduces the need for welfare services. They may even appear in future generations, as when the risks of mutagenic and teratogenic effects of radiation are reduced by health and safety rules. Some benefits, even when identified, defy valuation. How does one put a price tag on benefits for which there are no market prices, such as prolongation of life, the existence of clean air, the preservation of scenic vistas, a more equitable distribution of income, or fairness in agency proceedings?

Some of the problems encountered in appraising the benefits of improved water quality standards are explained in the following statement by an official of the Environmental Protection Agency (EPA):

> Take one of our water pollution effluent guidelines. . . . It will be set at, say, 10 micrograms per gram of water. So you have an immediate measurement possible—the number of tons of pollution you will avoid putting in the water and a percentage reduction from the previous level.
>
> But that's not very meaningful, in terms of measuring benefits. So you try to convert that into the standard's effect on water quality. Using models of a stream's rate of flow, you can tell when you have done enough to make the ambient water quality good, but, of course, the quality will vary from the Mississippi to some small river. It costs a bundle to develop models, and often we just don't have data on individual streams.
>
> But if you can reach the judgment that a stream's water quality now will be improved enough to sustain fish life and to permit industrial use of the water without further treatment, so that a brewery might possibly locate there, you have now characterized the uses of the water and you have started to characterize the actual benefits.
>
> If you want to quantify the benefits, you must assign a dollar value to swimming or fishing. You must estimate the number of recreational visits there will be and how much they are worth. You must calculate the number of adverse health effects avoided and assign a dollar value to them.
>
> Each step is very uncertain. The water quality models are uncertain. The projections of how many fishing trips and illnesses there will be are uncertain. The range of error is larger and larger. Is it really worth the large expense entailed going to the end of the chain? . . .[19]

Clearly, cost-benefit analysis is not the precise evaluation instrument that some of its more enthusiastic proponents consider it to be, especially when it is used prospectively rather than retrospectively. The assumptions on which its "facts" (or numbers) are based often make them quite tenuous or dubious.

Official Resistance

The evaluation of policy, whether it be called policy analysis, the measurement of policy impact, or something else, involves the making of judgments on the merits of policy. This is true even if the evaluator is a university researcher who thinks that he or she is objectively pursuing knowledge. Agency and program officials are going to be concerned about the possible political consequences of evaluation. If the results do not come out "right" from their perspective and if the results come to the attention of decision makers, their program, influence, or careers may be in jeopardy. Consequently, program officials may discourage or disparage evaluation studies, refuse access to data, or keep records that are incomplete. Within agencies, evaluation studies are likely to be most strongly supported by higher-level officials, who must make decisions concerning the allocation of resources among programs and the continuation of given programs. They may, however, be reluctant to require evaluations, especially if their results may have a divisive effect within the agencies. Finally, we should note that organizations tend to resist change, while evaluation implies change. Organizational inertia may thus be an obstacle to evaluation, along with more overt forms of resistance.

A Limited Time Perspective

Public officials and others often expect quick results from governmental programs, even social and educational programs whose effects may take time to appear. As a consequence, short-run evaluations of programs may be unfavorable. Take as an illustration the New Deal's resettlement program, which provided land ownership opportunities for thousands of black sharecroppers in the South during the late 1930s and early 1940s. It was judged as a failure and just another New Deal boondoggle, by contemporary critics. However, a recent evaluation of the program by policy analyst Lester Salamon concluded that it had significant, positive, long-term effects, although not as an agricultural policy.[20] It did, however, at modest cost transform "a group of landless black tenants into a permanent landed middle class that ultimately emerged in the 1960s as the backbone of the civil-rights movement in the rural South." If the time dimension is ignored in evaluation studies, the results may be flawed and neglect important impacts. The pressure for rapid feedback concerning a policy can then create a dilemma for the evaluator.

Evaluation Lacks Impact

Once completed, an evaluation of a program may be ignored or attacked as inconclusive or unsound on various grounds. For example, it may be alleged that the evaluation was poorly designed, the data used were inadequate, or the findings are inconclusive. However, those who have a strong interest in a program, whether as administrators or beneficiaries, are unlikely to lose their affection for it merely because an evaluation study concluded that its costs are greater than its benefits. Moreover, there is also the possibility that the evaluation may be wrong.

I am unable to think of a governmental program that has been terminated solely as a consequence of an unfavorable systematic evaluation. Of course, evaluations frequently lead to incremental changes or improvements in the design and administration of programs. That is the intent of many of the program evaluations done by the General Accounting Office, for instance, which, perhaps is all that should be asked or expected of most evaluations.

POLICY EVALUATION PROCESSES

Within the national government, policy evaluation is carried on in a variety of ways by a variety of actors. Sometimes it is highly systematic; other times it is rather haphazard or sporadic. In some instances policy evaluation has become institutionalized; in others it is quite informal and unstructured. A few forms of official policy evaluation, including congressional oversight, studies by the General Accounting Office (GAO), the work of presidential commissions, and agency action, will be examined briefly.

There is, of course, much policy evaluation carried on outside government. The communications media, university scholars, private research organizations such as the Brookings Institution, the Urban Institute, and the American Enterprise Institute, pressure groups, and public-interest organizations such as Common Cause and Ralph Nader and his "raiders" all make evaluations of policies that have greater or lesser effects on public officials. They also provide the larger public with information, publicize policy action or inaction, sometimes serve as advocates of unpopular causes, and often effectively represent the unrepresented, such as the aged confined to negligently run nursing homes or exploited migrant workers. Limitations of space do not permit discussion of the activities of such groups here, but this should not be taken to mean that they are not important in the policy evaluation process.

Congressional Oversight

One of the primary functions of Congress, although it is not specified in the Constitution, is the scrutiny and evaluation of the application, administration, and execution of laws or policy. Some, agreeing with John Stuart Mill, think that this is the most important function performed by a legislature. Oversight, however, is not a separable, distinct activity; rather, it is a part of almost everything that members of Congress do, including gathering information, legislating, authorizing appropriations, and helping constituents. It may be intended either to control the actions of agencies, as when they sometimes are required to clear actions in advance with particular committees, or to evaluate agency actions, as when individual members or committees seek to determine whether administrators are complying with program objectives established by Congress. It is the evaluative aspect of oversight that is pertinent here.

Oversight may be exercised through a number of techniques, including: (1) casework, that is, intercession with agencies as a consequence of constituent demands and requests; (2) committee hearings and investigations; (3) the appropriations process; (4) approval of presidential appointments; and (5) committee staff studies. In the course of these activities and others, members of Congress reach conclusions regarding the efficiency, effectiveness, and impact of particular policies and programs—conclusions that can have profound consequences for the policy process. Congressional oversight is in essence more fragmented and disjointed than continuous and systematic. Bits and pieces of information, impressionistic judgments, and the members' intuition and values are blended to yield evaluation of policies and those who administer them. On the whole, however, members of Congress are more likely to be concerned with policy initiation and adoption rather than with evaluation.

General Accounting Office

The GAO, which is usually regarded as an arm of Congress, has broad statutory authority to audit the operations and financial activities of federal agencies, to evaluate their programs, and to report its findings to Congress.[21] The agency has become increasingly involved with the evaluation of programs since the early 1970s and now gives only a minor portion of its attention to financial auditing.

The Legislative Reorganization Act of 1970, which revamped the congressional committee system, also directed the GAO to "review and analyze the results of government programs and activities carried on under existing law, including the making of cost-benefit studies," and to make personnel available to assist congressional committees in handling similar activities. A subsequent statute authorized GAO to establish an Office of Program Review and Evaluation. Because of its expanded evaluation activities, the agency hires many more people trained in the social sciences than once it did.

Evaluation activities may be undertaken by GAO on its own initiative, on the basis of directives in legislation, at the request of congressional committees, or sometimes at the behest of individual members of Congress. In the course of a year, GAO will produce several hundred evaluation studies varying in length from several pages to a few hundred pages. Three important studies in 1988 bore the following titles, which indicate both their subject and thrust: *"Foreign Aid: Better Management of Commodity Import Programs Could Improve Development Impact,"* "Environmental Protection Agency: *Human Health and the Environment through Improved Management,"* and *"Medicare and* Medicaid: *Updated Effects of Rent Legislation on Program and Beneficiary Costs."* The studies are delivered to Congress for use in its oversight and decision-making activities. Their impact depends either on subsequent congressional action or voluntary agency action, perhaps taken in anticipation of or to forestall action by Congress.

Presidential Commissions

Earlier we examined the role of Presidential commissions in the formulation of policy. Now we will see that they can also be used as an instrument of policy evaluation. Whether set up specifically to evaluate policy or governmental management in some area or for other purposes such as fact finding, making policy recommendations, or simply creating the appearance of presidential concern, most commissions involve themselves in policy evaluation to some degree.

In November 1986 it was disclosed that the United States government, under the leadership of National Security Council (NSC) officials, had sold arms to the Iranian government and diverted some of the profits to the Nicaraguan rebels. This set off a major political controversy. To inquire into this matter and to make recommendations for correction, President Reagan appointed the President's Special Review Board. Better known as the Tower Commission, it was composed of former Senator John Tower (D, Texas) as chair, Edmund Muskie, former Democratic senator from Maine and secretary of state, and Brent Scowcroft, former national security advisor to President Gerald Ford.

In its report issued in early 1987, the Tower Commission was sharply critical of President Reagan and his administration for their conduct of the Iran-Contra matter. The NSC was depicted as carrying on operations outside its advisory realm, deceiving Congress, paying little heed to the law, and avoiding any effective oversight. The President himself was viewed as uninformed, detached, and not in control of NSC action that ran counter to his administration's own policy of no arms sales to the Iranians. The commission's report made specific recommendations for bringing the NSC system under more effective presidential control and direction.[22]

A more "traditional" presidential commission was the Commission on Aviation Safety, established in 1986 to appraise the adequacy of governmental efforts to ensure safety in commercial airline operations. It concluded that the Federal Aviation Agency (FAA), which has primary responsibility for air safety, was hampered by its location in and subordination to the Department of Transportation. The commission, to the distress of the secretary of transportation, recommended that the FAA be converted into an independent agency and given more operating freedom.

It appears that the policy evaluations and recommendations made by presidential commissions often do not have much immediate impact on policy making. For whatever impact they *do* have, the important variables are probably not the quality and soundness of their findings. Charles Jones concludes that an evaluation commission is likely to have the greatest effect when its report coincides with other supporting events and is in accord with the president's policy preferences, when it includes some members who hold important governmental positions and are committed to its recommendations, and when commission staff personnel return to governmental positions in which they can influence acceptance of its recommendations.[23] These conditions, however, are often not present.

Administrative Agencies

Much program and policy evaluation is engaged in by the administering agencies, either on their own initiative or at the direction of Congress or the executive. Agencies usually want to get some notion of how their programs are working and what can be done to improve them. Educational program evaluations are often labeled as formative and summative. *Formative evaluations* are designed to assist officials in making mid-course corrections or adjustments in programs to improve their operation. *Summative evaluations* are broader and more thorough in scope and are used to inform upper-level policy makers on the overall effects of important policies and programs. They may lead to major program changes. There is not much reason to expect, however, that such evaluations will cause agency officials to recommend the termination of favored policies or programs.

In the 1960s and 1970s efforts were made by the Johnson, Nixon, and Carter administrations to build policy analysis and evaluation into the national budgetary process. The Johnson administration instituted the Planning-Programming-Budgeting System (PPBS), which required agencies to search for the most effective and efficient (least-cost) means to achieve their goals. The Nixon administration replaced it with Management by Objectives (MBO), a more modest effort requiring agencies to specify goals and measure progress in achieving them. MBO had evaporated by the time the Carter administration came to town and put

Zero-Base Budgeting (ZBB) into place. This required agencies to specify different levels of funding and accomplishment for programs, including the "zero" base (defined not as nothing but rather as the funding level below which the program would have no real worth). By so doing they would assess the worth of programs and indicate where spending would do the most good. ZBB did not survive the Carter administration.

These efforts at reform failed for a number of reasons. They conflicted with existing budgetary practices and habits, they were difficult and time-consuming to use, they were viewed as efforts to shift power to higher executive levels, and they lacked continuing presidential interest and support. They were not, however, without impact, for they left behind in the agencies a residue of interest and support for more systematic analysis and evaluation of agency activities.

It has now become fairly common for agencies to be specifically directed by Congress to undertake program and policy evaluations. In fact, many agencies have separate units to handle the task of evaluation. Some executive departments have assistant secretaries whose responsibilities encompass planning, analysis, and evaluation. There may not, however, be much interchange between evaluation staffs and operating officials. Evaluation reports will often be of secondary or even less interest to officials pressed for time and harried by the tasks of directing the day-to-day operations of their agencies.

An illustrative case involves the Department of Energy, created by Congress in 1977 by the Department of Energy Organization Act. Title X of the statute directed the department to submit a comprehensive review of each of its programs to Congress within a few years. The information to be provided for each program was spelled out in detail, including but not limited to the following requirements:

An identification of the objectives intended for the program and the problem or need which the program was intended to address. . . .

An assessment of alternative methods of achieving the purposes of the program. . . .

An assessment of the degree to which the original objectives of the program have been achieved, expressed in terms of the performance, impact, or accomplishments of the program and of the problem or need which it was intended to address, and employing the procedures or methods of analysis appropriate to the type or character of the program. . . .

A statement of the number and types of beneficiaries or persons served by the program. . . .

An assessment of the effect of the program on the national economy, including but not limited to, the effects on competition, economic stability, employment, unemployment, productivity, and price inflation, including costs to consumers and to businesses. . . .

An assessment of the degree to which the overall administration of the program, as expressed in the rules, regulations, orders, standards, criteria, and decisions of the officers executing the program, are believed to meet the objectives of Congress in establishing the program. . . .

This evaluation requirement placed substantial burdens on the department. One should reflect for a moment on the sorts of data needed for the evaluation. Can some of the questions implied in the requirement, such as the economic effects of a program, really be answered?

POLICY EVALUATION: THE MISUSE OF COST-BENEFIT ANALYSIS

As we have seen, cost-benefit analysis requires that all of the costs and benefits of a policy, present and future, be specified and assigned dollar values. Two additional features of cost-benefit analysis are added here. One is the discount rate, which is used to equate the value of present and future costs and benefits to permit their comparison. The basic assumption underlying the discount rate is that a dollar today is worth more than a dollar next year or next decade. A discount rate can be based on such criteria as the rate of inflation or the opportunity costs of capital, that is, the rate of return that money would earn if devoted to private investment rather than public purposes. There is no scientific way to set a discount rate, despite its importance. A low discount rate preserves the value of future benefits, whereas a high discount rate sharply reduces them. During the Reagan years the Office of Management and Budget (OMB) favored a discount rate of 10 percent. If used, this would have meant that the value of future benefits, such as lives prolonged two or three decades hence, had very low value.

Second, when all of the calculations are complete, costs and benefits are compared. If the value of benefits exceeds costs, if the ratio is more than 1.0, the activity under evaluation can be considered desirable in that it contributes to the economic welfare of society. Conversely, if costs exceed benefits in value, the activity lessens the well-being of society and, on the basis of efficiency, should be avoided or abandoned. If several items or alternatives are being compared, then the one with the greatest net benefits (above a 1.0 ratio) is preferred.[24]

Cost-benefit analysis has been used as a tool in governmental decision making for several decades. The Flood Control Act of 1936, for example, specified that flood-control projects could be undertaken by the Army Corps of Engineers only "if the benefits to whomsoever they may accrue are in excess of the estimated costs." This standard must also be used for water projects handled by the Soil Conservation Service and has been voluntarily employed by the Bureau of Reclamation. In the 1960s cost-benefit analysis was first used in evaluating defense programs and then domestic programs as part of PPBS.

In the 1970s Presidents Ford and Carter directed executive branch regulatory agencies to prepare "inflation impact statements" and "regulatory analyses," respectively, in the course of developing some proposed regulations. These statements involved analyses of their expected economic consequences. The Carter administration made it clear, however, that while regulatory agencies should consider the burdens and gains of proposed regulations, a cost-benefit test was not to be used in appraising them.

One of the goals of the Reagan administration when it took office was a substantial reduction in governmental regulation of private economic activity. People who were critics of the programs under their jurisdiction were appointed to regulatory positions. A second action involved the issuance of Executive Order 12291 in February 1981,[25] which drew heavily upon the experience of the Carter administration. The order required that proposed major regulations issued by executive branch agencies (the independent regulatory commissions were exempt) must be accompanied by regulatory impact analyses that assessed the potential benefits, costs, and net benefits of the regulations, including effects that could not be quantified in monetary terms, unless such calculations were prohibited by law. Some statutes ban the use of cost-benefit analysis for the programs they establish.

Major regulations were defined as those likely to have an annual impact on the economy of $100 million or more, to lead to major cost or price increases, or to have "significant adverse effects on competition, employment, investment, productivity, invocation, or the ability of U.S.-based enterprises to compete with foreign-based enterprises in domestic or export markets." The OMB was authorized to make the final determination of what was a major rule, to supervise the evaluation process, and to delay the issuance of proposed or final rules if it found the regulatory analyses were unsatisfactory.

Rules could be issued only if their estimated benefits exceeded their estimated costs. If a choice was available, the less costly alternative was to be used. The burden of proof that this standard was met rested with the agency. An action by the OMB holding up a rule could be appealed to the President's Task Force on Regulatory Relief, which was staffed by the OMB and comprised of several executive officials. (The word *relief* in the task force's title indicates its orientation.) Although the task force was phased out in 1983, all of this was intended to insure, among other things, that "Regulatory Action shall not be undertaken unless the potential benefits to society for the regulation outweigh the potential costs to society." Thus cost-benefit analysis was to be more than an analytical technique; it became a decision rule with a conservative bias.

In the first two years (1981–82) of the review program established by Executive Order 12291, 5,436 proposed and final rules were submitted by the agencies to OMB for review. Most were approved without change.[26] Only 89 of the rules were classified as being "major" and thus requiring regulatory impact analyses. Some major rules were not analyzed, however, as a consequence of the OMB's use of its authority under the executive order to exempt rules from cost-benefit analysis that "relax or defer regulatory requirements, or which delegate regulatory authority to the states." During the 1985–86 period, 4,216 proposed and final rules, including 131 major rules, were sent to the OMB. Again most were approved without change. Whatever the specific explanation—OMB review, the appointment of agency officials less inclined to be vigorous regulators, or other factors—the data indicate a significant decline in rule-making activity.

The Reagan regulatory analysis program generated a lot of controversy. Critics contended that it was used improperly to reduce the amount of regulation and to delay the issuance of rules rather than to improve the quality of regulations by encouraging better analysis. The OMB was also accused of improperly interfering in the regulatory process by usurping authority vested in the regulatory agencies. Such accusations were denied by the administration. In practice, though, administration officials did demonstrate much more concern about the costs than the benefits of regulation in their efforts to reduce the burden of regulatory costs on businesses.

Properly used, cost-benefit analysis can be used to help increase the rationality of the decision-making process by aiding in the identification and appraisal of alternatives, and by developing information and insights that will assist persons in making well-considered decisions. A systematic appraisal of the likely costs and benefits of a proposed action, and upon whom they will fall, is certainly useful, regardless of whether they are all converted into dollar figures. Cost-benefit analysis, however, is open to manipulation in support of particular preferences. In the instance of Executive Order 12291, given the antiregulation orientation of those administering the program, their emphasis upon the costs of regulation, and their insufficient attention to its benefits, cost-benefit analysis became a form of partisan political analysis in the guise of regulatory rationality.[27]

Policy evaluation, as the discussion to this point should indicate, is more than a technical or objective analytical process; it is also a political process. In the next section, a case study of the Head Start program will illustrate how political factors can affect the conduct and impact of the evaluation of social program evaluation. The case also demonstrates that such evaluations, even when intended to be neutral or objective in form, become political when they affect the allocation of resources.

THE POLITICS OF EVALUATION: THE CASE OF HEAD START

In January 1965, President Lyndon Johnson announced that a preschool program named Head Start would be initiated as part of the Community Action Program (CAP) authorized by the Economic Opportunity Act of 1964. Head Start was intended to help overcome the effects of poverty on the educational achievement of poor children. The program included early classroom education, nutritional benefits, parent counseling, and health services.

Initially, $17 million in CAP funds were earmarked for the summer of 1965 to enable 100,000 children to participate in Head Start. The announcement of the program, however, produced requests for a much larger volume of funds from many localities. Officials of the Office of Economic Opportunity (OEO), who had jurisdiction over the program, decided to meet this demand. Ultimately, $103 million was committed to provide places for 560,000 children. To say the least, the Head Start program was highly popular, undoubtedly because it directed attention to poor preschool children, who readily aroused the public's sympathy, and to the goal of equal opportunity.

Late in the summer of 1965, Head Start was made a permanent part of the antipoverty program. According to President Johnson, Head Start had been "battle-tested" and "proven worthy." It was expanded to include a full-year program. In fiscal year 1968, $330 million were allocated to provide places for 473,000 children in summer programs and another 218,000 for full-year programs, making Head Start the largest single component of the CAP. Essentially, Head Start was a multifaceted program for meeting the needs of poor children. More than a traditional nursery school or kindergarten program, it was designed also to provide poor children with physical and mental health services and meals to improve their diet. Further, an effort was made to involve members of the local community in the program.

With this as a background, let us turn to evaluation of the program.[28] The OEO was among the leaders in efforts to evaluate social programs. Within the agency the task of evaluating the overall effectiveness of its programs was assigned to the Office of Research, Plans, Programs and Evaluations (RPP&E). Some early efforts had been made to evaluate the effectiveness of Head Start, mostly by Head Start officials and involving particular projects, but, as of the middle of 1967, no good evidence existed regarding overall program effectiveness. This was becoming a matter of concern to OEO officials, the Bureau of the Budget, and some members of Congress. Consequently, the Evaluation Division of RPP&E, as part of a series of national evaluations of OEO programs, proposed an *ex post facto* study design for Head Start in which former Head Start children currently in the first, second, and third grades of school would be given a series of cognitive and affective tests. Their test scores would then be compared with those of a control group. The Evaluation Division believed such a design would yield results more quickly than a longitudinal study that, although more desirable, would take longer to complete. (A longitudinal study examines the impact over time of a program on a given group.)

Within OEO, Head Start officials opposed the proposed study on various grounds, including its design, the test instruments to be used, and the focus on only the educational aspect of the program to the neglect of its health, nutrition, and community involvement goals. RPP&E evaluators acknowledged the multiplicity of Head Start goals but contended that cognitive improvement was its primary goal. They agreed with Head Start officials that there were risks, such as possible misleading negative results, in making a limited study, but insisted that the need for evaluative data necessitated taking the risks. Following much internal debate, the OEO Director decided the study should be made, and in June 1968, a contract was entered into with the Westinghouse Learning Corporation and Ohio University. The study was conducted in relative quiet, but hints of its negative findings began to surface as it neared completion.

Early in 1969, a White House staff official became aware of the Westinghouse study and requested information on it because the president was preparing an address on the Economic Opportunity Act that would include a discussion of Head Start. OEO officials reported the preliminary negative findings of the study. In his message to Congress on economic opportunity on February 19, 1969, President Nixon referred to the study, noting that "the preliminary reports . . . confirm what many have feared: the long term effect of Head Start appears to be extremely weak." He went on to say that "this must not discourage us" and spoke well of the program. Nonetheless, his speech raised substantial doubts about Head Start in the public arena.

The president's speech touched off considerable pressure for the release of the study's findings. OEO officials were reluctant to do so because what had been delivered to them by Westinghouse was the preliminary draft of the final report. It was to be used to decide such matters as what additional statistical tests were needed and what data required reanalysis. From Congress, where hearings were being held on OEO legislation, claims were made that the study was being held back to protect Head Start and that the report was going to be rewritten. The pressure on the White House became sufficiently great that it directed OEO to make the study public by April 14. A major conclusion of the report was that the full-year Head Start program produced a statistically significant but absolutely slight improvement in participant children.

The release of the report set off a flood of criticism from Head Start proponents, including many academicians, concerning the methodological and conceptual validity of the report. A sympathetic article in the *New York Times* bore the headline "HEAD START REPORT HELD 'FULL OF

HOLES.' " Much of the ensuing controversy focused on the statistical methods of the report and involved a considerable range of claims, charges, rebuttals, and denials. The proponents of Head Start seemed to fear that their program was being victimized by devious design. This fear had several dimensions. One was that persons within OEO who favored Community Action over Head Start wanted a study that would indicate Head Start's deficiencies. Another was that the administration was going to use the findings to justify a major cutback in Head Start. Finally, there was the fear that "enemies of the program" in Congress would use the negative results as the basis for attacking it. Although there now appears not to have been much factual basis for these fears, they were real to the proponents of Head Start and contributed to the intensity of their attack on the evaluation study.

The methodological issues in the controversy over the study focused on such standard items as the sample size, the validity of the control group, and the appropriateness of the tests given the children. An examination of these issues would be too lengthy and too technical to include here. However, an assessment of the study by economist Walter Williams summarizes the methodological issues.

> In terms of its methodological and conceptual base, the study is a *relatively* good one. This in no way denies that many of the criticisms made of the study are valid. However, for the most part, they are the kinds of criticisms that can be made of most pieces of social science research conducted outside the laboratory, in a real-world setting, with all of the logistical and measurement problems that such studies entail. And these methodological flaws open the door to the more political issues. Thus, one needs not only to examine the methodological substance of the criticisms which have been made of the study, but also to understand the social concern which lies behind them as well. Head Start has elicited national sympathy and has had the support and involvement of the educational profession. It is understandable that so many should rush to the defense of such a popular and humane program. But how many of the concerns over the size of the sample, control-group equivalency, and the appropriateness of co-variance analysis, for example, would have been registered if the study had found positive differences in favor of Head Start? . . .
>
> We imagine that this type of positive, but qualified assessment will fit any relatively good evaluation for some time to come. We have never seen a field evaluation of a social action program that could not be faulted legitimately by good methodologists, and we may never see one.[29]

Interestingly enough, the results of the Westinghouse study were as favorable to Head Start as were the earlier evaluations of particular projects made by Head Start officials. These, too, showed that the program had limited lasting effects on the children. What the Westinghouse study, and the controversy over it, did was to put these findings into the public arena and expand the scope of the conflict over them.

Despite the essentially negative evaluations of its impact, the Westinghouse report recommended that Head Start be preserved and improved, at least partly on the ground that "something must be tried here and now to help the many children of poverty who may never be helped again." Head Start was, and is, a politically popular program. Congress and the executive have generally been favorably disposed toward the program, and it has suffered little of the criticism directed at other aspects of the antipoverty program.

Ten years after the Westinghouse study was made public, the findings of another group of researchers on the long-term effects of Head Start were published by the Department of Health, Education and Welfare. On the basis of a series of longitudinal studies, it was concluded that Head Start had significant, long-lasting social and educational benefits for its participants. Thus children who had been in the program had much less need for remedial classes, were less likely to be retained in grade, and were half as likely to drop out of high school than were adolescents of comparable age who had not been in the program. As a consequence, Head Start was now hailed as a success by the communications media. Why the substantial difference in the findings of the two evaluations? The explanation rests primarily with the different methodological approaches. The Westinghouse study, using an experimental design, focused on short-run effects, especially as measured by intelligence test scores. The second study focused on long-range effects.

In 1981, Head Start was designated as part of President Reagan's "social safety net," which provided assistance to the truly needy, and thus was not tagged for reduced funding, as were several other programs for poor people. In 1988 approximately 450,000 children were in the Head Start program, which now operates year-round, at a cost of $1.2 billion. However, only about a quarter of the eligible children were actually enrolled.[30] In their support of the program, members of Congress and others have been influenced not only by Head Start's success as an educational and child care program but also by the belief that it could lead to reduced future expenditures for other programs, such as welfare, juvenile delinquency, and criminal justice. Many evaluative studies support the effectiveness of Head Start.

WHY PUBLIC POLICIES MAY NOT HAVE THEIR INTENDED IMPACT

Formal policy evaluations, less systematic studies, and actual experience often indicate that public policies either do not achieve their ostensible goals or do not have the impact on public problems that they were expected to have. Although reference is frequently made to something called "policy failure," it is unclear what exactly comprises failure. In actuality there are few public policies that have no impact on their targets. What we are dealing with then is not a situation of either-or but one of more or less. A variety of factors may impede or prevent the fullest possible attainment of policy goals. The following list is suggestive rather than complete.

First, inadequate resources may be provided for implementing a policy. The Johnson administration's War on Poverty, for example, was not wholly successful in part because, as many commentators have noted, only limited funds were allocated to what was billed as an "all-out war." Congress had less enthusiasm for the poverty program than did the executive. Public housing programs have likewise never produced the amount of housing projected in legislation because Congress has usually failed to appropriate the required amounts of funds.

Second, policies may be administered so as to lessen their potential impact. The Federal Maritime Commission, for example, has never been diligent in regulating the rates of ocean-shipping companies. Requests to raise rates are handled in a *pro forma* manner that imposes little or no restraint on the companies. Again, for much of its existence the Occupational Safety and Health Administration chose to focus its efforts on preventing industrial accidents rather than industrial illness, which is more difficult to handle. Consequently, few health standards have emanated from the agency.

Third, public problems are often caused by a multitude of factors, while policy may be directed at only one or a few of them. For instance, job-training programs may help those who are unemployed because they lack adequate job skills, but do little for those who have chronic ailments or inadequate motivation or suffer from racial or sex discrimination. Wage and price controls will have little success in counteracting inflation that stems from excess demand for goods and services as well as inflationary expectations.

Fourth, people may respond or adapt to public policies in a manner that negates some of their impact. The enforcement of highway speed limits may be frustrated by motorists' use of electronic devices such as "fuzz-busters." As another example, the effectiveness of agricultural production control programs has been lessened because they are based on acreage rather than quantity limitations. Acreage controls were effective when first used in the early 1930s because there had been little fluctuation in crop yields per acre for over a century, but the scientific revolution in agriculture after World War II changed this. Farmers are now able through the use of improved plant varieties and the greater application of chemical fertilizers and pesticides to increase crop yields. Consequently, a larger volume of commodities may be produced on fewer acres and "surpluses" will continue to persist.

Fifth, policies may have incompatible goals that bring them into conflict with one another. Thus under the price-support programs of the Department of Agriculture, the Agricultural Conservation and Stabilization Service is concerned with limiting the production of some commodities. However, the basic programmatic concern of the Agricultural Research Service involves increasing agricultural productivity. That is also the effect of the actions of the Bureau of Reclamation in the Department of the Interior when it provides farmers with low-cost water for irrigation. The tobacco price-support program is likewise viewed as inconsistent with the quest of the National Cancer Institute and the antismoking campaign of the Department of Health and Human Services, given the link between tobacco smoking and chewing and cancer. Special tax provisions to encourage economic development of charitable giving also reduce the revenue-raising ability of the income tax.

Sixth, the solutions for some problems may involve costs and consequences greater than people are willing to accept. Crime in the streets probably could be eradicated if we were willing to pay the costs in greatly enhanced police surveillance and individual repression through extensive use of lie detectors, curfews, and the like. The effect of this policy on individual freedom, however, would then become a public problem. The *total* elimination of environmental pollution is another example. An estimate in the 1970s put the cost of eliminating 85 to 90 percent of water pollution at $61 billion. Elimination of 100 percent of water pollution in the United States would have cost an additional $258 billion.[31] Because of inflation, these estimates would have to be increased substantially. Is total cleanup worth the additional cost? Although there is disagreement on this issue, the answer implicit in current practice is no.

Seventh, many public problems cannot be solved, or at least not completely. Given human nature and national interests, tension and strife among nations will undoubtedly continue to exist to some degree in the world, even in the presence of the Soviets' policy of *glasnost* and other ameliorative actions. Nations have many bases on which to disagree, such as religion, language, historical hatreds, and economic interests. Some children simply may not be able to learn much in the public schools, regardless of the amount spent on public education, the number of times the curriculum is revised, and the amount of testing of teachers for competency. Crime can be listed as an example here also, because it has been part of the human condition since Cain slew Abel.

Eighth, new problems may arise that distract attention and action from a given problem. For example, the "energy crisis" and concern with the costs of the regulation of economic activity as a cause of inflation for a time diverted attention from the environmental pollution problem, just as the War in Vietnam shifted attention away from the War on Poverty in the 1960s. When this happens, governmental action tends to be diverted from the older to the newer problems. In the American political system it is

difficult to secure the sustained, substantial effort necessary to deal effectively with many public problems.

Ninth, many national policies and programs in such areas as education, environmental protection, economic development, and social welfare
are actually implemented by state and local government agencies. This
complicates the implementation process by creating a lengthy chain of
national, state, and local officials concerned with making rules and taking
actions on policy problems. As a result, the effectiveness of programs may
suffer. National clean air policy, for example, has been reduced in impact
because state and local officials are sometimes uncertain of their responsibilities, in disagreement with national standards, or overly responsive to
the interests of polluters. Established by the Safe Streets Act of 1968, the
Law Enforcement Assistance Administration awarded nearly $8 billion in
grants-in-aid to state and local governments before its demise in 1981.
Intended to help state and local governments strengthen their crime-
fighting capabilities and make the streets safer, quite a bit of the money
went for unnecessary weaponry, anticrime gadgetry, and ineffective planning activity. Although not without its positive aspects, the LEAA program
fell far short of the original expectations for it.[32]

This discussion of obstacles to effective or successful policy action
should not be viewed as a counsel of despair. Many public policies and
programs accomplish a great deal. At the local level, for instance, garbage is
collected, fires are put out, traffic moves reasonably well (except during
rush hours), water flows from the tap, most children learn to read and
write, and parks and recreation facilities exist. If few public problems are
entirely resolved by governmental actions, many are at least partly solved
or ameliorated. Employment problems still exist, but not to the extent they
would were there no job-training, economic development, unemployment
compensation, and other employment-related programs. Consumers may
still be misled and defrauded, but not in the numbers they would be in the
absence of consumer protection programs. More wildlife survives than
would have without fish and game laws, national and state parks, and
wildlife refuges. Public-health policies have greatly reduced the incidence
of infectious diseases. And so it goes.

The goals of public policies are usually stated in absolute rather than
relative terms. Thus the streets are to be made safe for all law-abiding
people, or poverty is to be banished from America. Absolute statements,
because they are more appealing than conditional phrasing of goals, are
used to garner public and interest-group support for policies. The Clean
Water Act of 1972, for example, set a goal of "zero" discharge of pollutants
into the nation's streams by 1985. The goal has not been met, although most
streams are undoubtedly much cleaner than they would have been in the
absence of the act. Has the act then "failed," as some allege?

Given the intractability of most public problems, public policies can at best mitigate or reduce the target problems. The prevalence of heart disease can be lessened, for instance, or the amount of juvenile delinquency can be reduced. When, however, goals are stated in absolute terms, anything less than complete success tends to be construed as failure. This masks the real accomplishments of many public policies.

THE RESPONSE TO POLICY

In this chapter, quite a bit has been said about the systematic evaluation of policy. It has clearly become a more widespread and potentially significant part of the policy process. Up to the present time, however, as various observers have remarked, systematic evaluation does not appear to have had really significant effects upon policy decision making. As was seen in the case of Head Start, an essentially unfavorable early evaluation of its impact did not lead to its abandonment nor, we might add, to major change in its substantive form. This should not be taken to mean, however, that systematic evaluation is either useless or unlikely ever to have much impact on policy making. It is a relatively new activity and encounters many problems, as we have noted, but as time goes on, and as evaluation techniques and designs become more effective, its impact will undoubtedly increase. After all, few would contend that intelligence does not provide a more sound basis than intuition in determining public policy.

People and groups, citizens and officials alike, do of course make many judgments concerning the impact and desirability of existing policies and, on this basis, react to them with support, opposition, or indifference. There is much evaluatory activity of the first two kinds discussed at the beginning of this chapter. Political decision makers may frequently temper their evaluations of the substantive content or impact of policies with responsiveness to political factors such as partisan pressures, emotional appeals, or re-election considerations. Professor Ralph K. Huitt notes that "political feasibility" is a concern entering into the selection of policy priorities and programs designed to meet them by decision makers, who ask questions such as, "Will it 'go' on the Hill? Will the public buy it? Does it have political 'sex appeal'? What 'can't be done' is likely to get low priority."[33]

At this point the concept of feedback can be injected usefully into the discussion. This concept, which was briefly touched upon in the treatment of systems theory in Chapter 1, holds that past policy decisions and impacts can generate demands for change or support for them. Thus the enactment and administration of the National Environmental Policy Act of 1969 have given rise to various demands for its repeal, modification, and continuation. Its use to prevent the construction of the Alaskan oil pipeline finally resulted in legislation exempting the project from NEPA requirements. The Soil Conservation Act of 1935 and its administering agency, the Soil Conservation Service, gave rise to a pressure group, the National Association of Soil Conservation Districts, that has strongly supported their continuation. As a consequence of feedback to decision makers, a variety of actions subsequently can be taken concerning policy, including continuation; legislative amendment to strengthen or weaken the policy; adjustments in its administration, such as strong or lax enforcement of given provisions; increasing, decreasing, or restricting funds to support its administration; challenges to its meaning or constitutionality in the courts (this is more likely to be done by private interested parties than by officials); and repeal of the statute (or permitting it to expire if it has a time limit).

So far as major policies and programs are concerned, repeal or termination of them is unlikely to occur, even when much controversy, and even bitterness, attend their adoption. They soon come to be taken for granted as a part of the environment, and debate over their propriety, if not their details or impact, soon quiets down. This has been the case with the Social Security Act of 1935, the Taft-Hartley Act of 1947, the Civil Rights Act of 1964, and the Elementary and Secondary Education Act of 1965, to cite a few. Few statutes have stirred as much controversy as the Economic Opportunity Act, and yet, although it has been variously amended and control of the programs it created has been transferred from the now-defunct OEO to other agencies, the act remains in existence. As a general proposition, it can be suggested that the longer a policy, program, or agency remains in existence, the less likely it is to be terminated. Over time, accommodations are made and support is developed that enables it to survive. Exceptions include policies, programs, or agencies established to deal with emergency problems such as relief during the Depression of the 1930s (e.g., Works Progress Administration) and price controls and rationing as well as production allocation during World War II (e.g., Office of Price Administration and War Production Board).

The revision, or demands for revision, of existing policies will depend upon such factors as the extent to which they are held to "solve" the problem at which they are directed or their perceived impact, the skill with which they are administered, the defects or shortcomings that may be revealed during implementation, and the political power and awareness of concerned or affected groups. In addition, the manner in which the costs and benefits of a policy are distributed will have important consequences for its future.

The costs and benefits of public policies may be either broadly or narrowly distributed. In the case of Social Security, both benefits and costs are broadly distributed, whereas a statute regulating relationships between automobile manufacturers and dealers involves a narrow distribution of costs and benefits. Narrow costs–broad benefits and broad costs–

narrow benefits are other possible patterns. The costs and benefits of policies, it will be recalled, can be either material or symbolic. The proposition here advanced is that the response to *existing* policies, and demands for changes therein, will be affected by the way their benefits and costs are distributed.[34]

Broad Benefits and Broad Costs

Policies that involve a broad distribution of costs and benefits, such as Social Security, highway construction, police and fire protection, public education, and national defense, tend to become readily accepted, institutionalized, and beyond major challenge. Controversy may focus on such particular features as the location of highways, whether to provide sex education, or the acquisition of a weapons system, but the continuation of the programs as a whole is not seriously in question. It has been easy to propose and difficult to resist increases in the benefits of a program like Social Security because of the many specific beneficiaries. National defense also provides a collective good (all benefit from it, although the amount of benefit cannot be precisely measured or defined) related to the important value of national security and survival. (Note the defensive position you tend to find yourself in when you argue that something proposed is not really necessary for national defense.) Radical changes in most policies in this category are unlikely.

Some policies, however, that fall in this category may never really gain wide and continued acceptance, as occurred with the War on Poverty. It had many potential beneficiaries, but most of them were poor, and the poor in our society have long lacked substantial political power and consequently effective ability to secure and support policies benefiting them. Many changes have been made in the poverty programs since 1964, although most of them remain in existence. The OEO was finally abolished, however, because it had become such a strong negative symbol and focus of controversy.

Occasionally, the costs of a program may come to be seen by many as exceeding its benefits. This has been true in recent years with the public-assistance programs that provide aid to various needy groups, such as the working poor and families with dependent children. Controversy has been especially intense over Aid to Families with Dependent Children (AFDC). Much has been spoken and written about the "welfare mess," the "welfare crisis," and so on. Many proposals for change, including the elimination of the programs, have been made, and some have been adopted. A major change proposed by the Nixon administration, the Family Assistance Plan, failed of enactment in the early 1970s. After much furor, the public-assistance programs remain much the same as they were a few years ago, except that most are now totally funded by the national government. Only AFDC is now jointly funded by the national and state governments. The groups supporting public-assistance programs are sufficiently strong to maintain them, if not to bring about basic reform. The critics are sufficiently strong to prevent their major expansion, while perhaps securing some restrictive changes that somewhat reduce their scope or impact. Public education is another policy area in which this kind of conflict, promising much but delivering little, may develop.

Broad Benefits and Narrow Costs

Some policies seem to provide benefits for large numbers of people, while their costs fall primarily upon fairly distinct, identifiable groups in society. Illustrative are environmental pollution control, automobile safety, food and meat inspection, public utility regulation, and industrial and coal mine safety policies. Coal mine companies have felt that they are being asked to bear the burden of safety regulation and that many specific requirements are unnecessary. They have complained of the unfairness of the regulatory program and have sought both legislative and administrative amelioration of its impact upon them. Just so, many industries have protested having to meet the costs and inconveniences of pollution control programs. Of course, they may be able to pass the financial costs on to consumers as part of the final price of their product. Small business groups have been especially shrill in their criticism of the National Occupational Safety and Health Act, even though a great many small businesspeople have undoubtedly never seen an OSHA inspector.

The enactment of policies falling within this category is usually achieved through the actions of a loose coalition of interests, perhaps in response to a crisis of some sort. Once the legislation is enacted, the supporting coalition tends to lose interest in the matter, assuming that with the enactment the problem is adequately cared for. The groups that opposed the law and perceive themselves as bearing the brunt of it remain concerned and active, however, as in the cases of automobile manufacturers and safety legislation and, earlier, the railroads and rate regulation. Much more is heard from them by the enforcing agencies and the legislature concerning the undesirable effects of the legislation. The result may be administrative action and legislative changes tempering the original legislation.[35] Conversely, it may become very difficult for supporters of the original legislation to get together again to secure amendments to strengthen the law. For instance, a loophole was created in the antimerger provision for the Clayton Act of 1914 in the early 1920s by judicial interpretation. Not until the Celler Antimerger Act of 1950 were the supporters of antitrust able to secure corrective legislation. Again, automobile manufacturers have been unremitting in their opposition to emission control standards for cars since their adoption and have succeeded in delaying implementation of some EPA standards.

Narrow Benefits and Broad Costs

Some policies and programs benefit readily identifiable interest groups, while their costs do not appear to fall upon any particular groups. Veterans' benefits, agricultural subsidies, hospital construction grants, rivers and harbors projects, and special tax provisions (for example, the accelerated depreciation for machinery) fall within this category. The costs of these policies are usually in the form of higher taxes or prices that affect people generally. Those who benefit from these policies have a clear incentive to organize and act to maintain them. As James Q. Wilson notes, policies of this variety encourage the formation of pressure groups to support their continuation, often in close relationship with the administering agency.[36] Good examples are the National Rivers and Harbors Congress and the Army Corps of Engineers, the National Rural Electrification Cooperative Association and the Rural Electrification Administration, and veterans' groups and the Department of Veterans Affairs.

Those who are critical of such policies find it difficult to mobilize sufficient interest and political support to bring about changes. Presidents Johnson and Nixon both urged Congress to reduce greatly the funds for the Rural Environmental Assistance Program, which provides financial grants to farmers for soil-conserving activities, such as the application of limestone to the soil and the construction of erosion-control terraces, on the grounds that such costs can and should properly be borne by farmers. They did not have much success, because those who benefit from the program work actively for its continuation at present levels, and Congress has been responsive to them. The cost is paid by the fabled John Q. Taxpayer, who is little aware of either the program or the way in which it affects his tax bill. Sometimes, though, policies in this category may arouse sufficient opposition, both among citizens and officials, as to lead to their alteration. One example is the oil depletion allowance, which had become a symbol of privilege for the oil industry. In 1969 it was reduced from 27.5 percent to 22 percent. The energy crisis helped bring it under further attack, and in 1975 the depletion allowance was repealed for all but small producers. The deregulation movement, which began in the middle 1970s, similarly provided the political impetus needed to enact legislation in 1978 to eliminate economic regulation of commercial airlines by the Civil Aeronautics Board. CAB regulation had long been criticized on the ground that by restricting competition it imposed costs on many travelers in order to benefit a few airlines. The deregulation movement expanded the conflict over the program by focusing public attention on it and by increasing the forces in favor of change.

Narrow Benefits and Narrow Costs

Policies that provide benefits to a well-defined group but at the cost of another distinct group tend to produce continuing organized conflict among the groups and their partisans. In point here are the conflicts between organized labor and management over the Taft-Hartley Act and the Wagner Act, commercial banks and savings and loan associations over banking policies, and railroads and motor carriers over freight regulation by the Interstate Commerce Commission. Conflict repeatedly and continually develops over amendments to and interpretations of the original policy. Efforts may also be made to secure a repeal. Top-level appointments to the administering agency are another item of contention. The National Labor Relations Board, for example, has alternated between prolabor and promanagement treatments of the labor laws, as Democratic administrations have appointed prolabor people to the board and Republican administrations have reciprocated with promanagement people when the opportunity has arisen.[37] In situations where the costs and benefits of policy are concentrated on active, organized groups, major policy changes tend to result either from shifts in the balance of power among them, such as that leading to the Taft-Hartley Act, or from negotiated settlements, such as that between business and environment groups, that led to the extension of pesticide control legislation in the 1980s.

These four policy categories based on the allocation of costs and benefits are only approximate. All policies will not fit neatly and exclusively into one or another of them. Readers may want to refine and develop them further, which they are encouraged to do. The categories are put forward here as being useful in gaining insight into why the responses to policies vary and in estimating what the feedback responses will be to policy actions. Moreover, the categories should also be helpful in analyzing the struggles that attend the adoption of policy, because to some extent the kind of policy proposed will help shape the enactment process.

POLICY TERMINATION

The evaluation and appraisal of a policy, dissatisfaction with its costs and consequences, and the development and growth of political opposition may lead to its termination. Most of us can readily identify a number of governmental policies that we regard as unnecessary, wasteful, or inappropriate. Others, however, may not share our feelings and may regard these same policies as necessary and desirable, perhaps needing some change or improvement, but on the whole worth keeping. Perhaps they benefit directly from the policies, or maybe on the basis of their political ideology they consider them laudable. Just as policies arise out of conflict, so there will be conflict over their worth and retention.

If criticism of and opposition to a policy become sufficiently strong that the policy makers feel impelled to take action, alteration rather than termination of the policy is more likely. An effort may be made to strengthen it in order to make it more effective, or portions of it that appear especially ineffective or offensive may be pruned away. This is illustrated by the conversion of the Comprehensive Employment and Training Act of 1973 into the Job Partnership Training Act of 1982, as discussed at the opening of Chapter 1. Alternations were made in the administration of job training and the public-employment program was jettisoned.

Policy termination is difficult for a number of reasons. Policies come into being because they have political support and they may retain some or all of that support. Even though few in number, supporters of a policy or program may be strongly committed to it, and may intensely resist change and ignore contrary evidence. The U.S. Army, for example, did not eliminate the horse cavalry until World War II, even though the cavalry had been obsolete for years because of the development of weapons like the machine gun and rapid-fire artillery.[38] Some in the army could not comprehend an effective fighting force without the cavalry, reality to the contrary.

The critics and opponents of a policy may be less intense in their feelings, and they may be somewhat disorganized and diverse in their concerns as well. It may also be quite difficult to pull together a coalition of sufficient strength to repeal a policy. Some potential opponents of a policy, for instance, may be more interested in preserving their own favored policies, and thus an attitude of live-and-let-live may prevail. An intense minority can often prevail over an indifferent majority.

Within Congress, with its fragmentation and dispersion of power, those with jurisdiction over a policy are likely to be friends and supporters of a policy. They can then use their committee or subcommittee positions to protect the policy against attack, to fend off unwanted changes, and to block its termination, should that be proposed. Governmental structure favors those seeking to retain policies, just as it favors those opposing their enactment. There is perhaps a rough equity in this.

Termination, moreover, is a severe action with unpleasant and negative connotations.[39] There is in it an undertone of admission of failure. Unpleasant consequences may ensue when a policy is terminated: people may suffer income losses, prices for services or products may increase, or communities may decline. Ill will and other political costs may be entailed.

Most public officials thus prefer to be involved in the creation of new or better policies rather than the termination of the old.

Although these factors may make policy termination a controversial and difficult process, successful termination does occasionally happen. Some terminated policies (and their dates of demise) include the following:

Fair trade legislation (1975). This legislation, adopted during the 1930s, permitted the manufacturers of trademarked or brand-named products to set mandatory minimum resale prices for their products. Over the years fair trade had become a tired, worn-out policy whose time had passed. Little support for it remained, and it was easily repealed.

Commercial airline regulation (1978). Almost all economic (but not safety) regulation was eliminated by the Airline Deregulation Act of 1978, the first major victory of the deregulation movement that began in the 1970s. Many policy makers became convinced as a consequence of a multitude of policy studies, that market forces would more effectively regulate the airlines and protect users than regulation.

Regulation of petroleum prices (1980). This policy, which always had much opposition, came into being as a consequence of the energy crises of the 1970s. Hard to administer, it was intended to prevent domestic oil companies from unduly profiting from high world oil prices. Its elimination in preference for market prices was coupled with a windfall profits tax (see below).

Synthetic fuels research (1985). This policy was another product of the energy crises. A costly program to develop commercial synthetic fuel facilities, it had accomplished little by the time of its elimination, partly because of the length of time needed to get complex projects underway. By 1985 the energy crisis and memories of it had ebbed, and the Reagan administration wanted more reliance on the market.

Revenue sharing (1986). Adopted during the Nixon administration, revenue sharing channeled billions of dollars annually to state and local governments, with few strings attached, partly to encourage them to be more creative in dealing with public problems. Large federal budget deficits were the ultimate reason for its termination, although there was always considerable congressional opposition to revenue sharing.

Crude Oil Windfall Profits Tax Act (1986). Enacted in 1980, COWPTA was the price the petroleum industry reluctantly paid for oil price deregulation, which permitted oil prices to rise. From 30 to 70 percent of the windfall, the difference between the selling (or market) price of oil and a specified base price, was taxed away. A phase-out of the tax was to begin in January, 1988, if $227 billion in revenue had been collected, or one month after that amount had been collected, but in any event no later than January 1911.

The price of oil fell, however, in the mid-1980s, and the tax ceased to produce revenue. An industry-supported effort to repeal the act failed in 1986. Success finally came in 1988, when a repeal provision was included in the Omnibus Trade and Competitiveness Act to pick up or solidify votes for that legislation. Time and events had thus made the windfall tax symbolic.

As these examples indicate, a variety of factors may contribute to the termination of policies. Systematic evaluation played a major role only in the case of airline deregulation, in which evaluators (mostly economists) were able to gather substantial evidence on the defects of the existing policy and to make a persuasive case for market regulation as an effective and satisfactory substitute. Most commonly, however, systematic evaluation plays a lesser role in policy termination. Indeed, to emphasize a point made earlier, it is more likely to reinitiate the policy sequence. Problems may be identified, alternatives formulated, and so on, until the policy is modified in some way. The policy may also be so administered as to make it more acceptable. Whether legislative or administrative in origin, policy change is more likely than termination.

Notes

1. Carol Weiss, *Evaluating Action Programs: Readings in Social Action and Education* (Boston: Allyn and Bacon, 1972), p. 14.
2. This matter is ably discussed by Michael J. Malbin, *Unelected Representatives: Congressional Staff and the Future of Representative Government* (New York: Basic Books, 1979), chap. 9.
3. William T. Gormley, Jr., *Taming the Bureaucracy* (Princeton: Princeton University Press, 1989), p. 5.
4. See Piven, Frances Fox, and Richard A. Cloward, *Regulating the Poor* (New York: Pantheon, 1971).
5. Thomas R. Dye, *Understanding Public Policy*, 2d ed. (Englewood Cliffs, N.J.: Prentice-Hall, 1975), pp. 327–330.
6. Kenneth E. Warner, "Clearing the Airwaves: The Cigarette Ad Ban Revisited," *Policy Analysis* (Fall, 1979), pp. 235–250.
7. *Ibid.*
8. A useful discussion of externalities in public policy can be found in Larry L. Wade, *The Elements of Public Policy* (Columbus, Ohio: Merrill, 1972), chap. 3.
9. Gabriel A. Almond and G. Bingham Powell, *Comparative Politics: A Developmental Approach* (Boston: Little, Brown, 1966), p. 199.
10. Carol H. Weiss, "The Politics of Impact Measurement," *Policy Studies Journal*, I (Spring, 1973), pp. 180–181.
11. Edward R. Tufte, *Data Analysis for Politics and Policy* (Englewood Cliffs, N.J.: Prentice-Hall, 1974), chap. 1.
12. Solomon Kalirin and Steven G. Lubeck, "Problems in the Evaluation of Crime Control Policy." Unpublished paper presented at the annual meeting of the American Political Science Association (1973), p. 29.
13. 384 U.S. 436 (1966).

14. President's Commission on Law Enforcement and the Administration of Justice, *The Challenge of Crime in a Free Society* (Washington, D.C.: Government Printing Office, 1967), p. 305.
15. *Time*, Vol. 112 (July 18, 1988), p. 53.
16. Jeremy A. Lifsey, "Politics, Evaluations and Manpower Programs." Unpublished paper presented at the annual meeting of the American Political Science Association (1973).
17. See the discussion of policy evaluation techniques in Carol H. Weiss, *Evaluation Research: Methods of Assessing Program Effectiveness* (Englewood Cliffs, N.J.: Prentice-Hall, 1972).
18. Robert H. Haveman and Julius Margolis (eds.), *Public Expenditure and Policy Analysis*, 2d ed. (Chicago: Rand-McNally, 1977), contains several useful essays on cost-benefit analysis. On its use for regulatory policies, see House Committee on Interstate and Foreign Commerce, *Hearings on Use of Cost-Benefit Analysis by Regulatory Agencies*, 96th Cong., 1st Sess. (1979).
19. Quoted in Timothy B. Clark, "Do the Benefits Justify the Costs? Prove It, Says the Administration," *National Journal*, Vol. 13 (August 1, 1981), p. 1385.
20. Lester M. Salamon, "The Time Dimension in Policy Evaluation: The Case of the New Deal Land-Reform Experiments," *Public Policy*, XXVII (Spring, 1979), pp. 129–184.
21. This discussion draws on Elmer B. Staats, "General Accounting Office Support of Committee Oversight," in *Committee Organization in the House* (panel discussion before the House Select Committee on Committees), 93d Cong., 1st Sess. (1973), II, pp. 692–700. Staats was the head of the GAO. See also Frederick C. Mosher, *A Tale of Two Agencies* (Baton Rouge: Louisiana State University Press, 1984), chap. 5.
22. *The Tower Commission Report* (New York: Bantam Books, 1987).
23. Charles O. Jones, *An Introduction to the Study of Public Policy* (Belmont, Calif.: Wadsworth, 1970), p. 118. Insight into the operation of a commission set up to appraise legislation regulating the political activities of public employees can be gained from Charles O. Jones, "Reevaluating the Hatch Act: A Report on the Commission on Political Activity of Government Employees," *Public Administration Review*, XXIX (May–June, 1969), pp. 249–254.
24. For further discussion, see George W. Downs and Patrick D. Larkey, *The Search for Government Efficiency* (New York: Random House, 1986), chap. 4; and Edith Stokey and Richard Zeckhauser, *Primer for Policy Analysis* (New York: Norton, 1978), chap. 9.
25. *Federal Register*, Vol. 46 (February 19, 1981), pp. 13193–13198.
26. President's Task Force on Regulatory Relief, *Reagan Administration Regulatory Achievements* (Washington, D.C.: Government Printing Office, 1983), pp. 59–61.
27. On partisan political analysis, see Charles E. Lindblom, *The Policy Making Process*, 2d ed. (Englewood Cliffs, N.J.: Prentice-Hall, 1980), chap. 4.
28. This account draws upon Walter Williams, *Social Policy Research and Analysis* (New York: American Elsevier, 1971); and Walter Williams and John W. Evans, "The Politics of Evaluation: The Case of Head Start," *Annals of the*

American Academy of Political and Social Sciences, CCCLXXXV (September, 1969), pp. 118–132.

29. *Ibid.*
30. See Department of Health and Human Services, *The Impact of Head Start on Children, Families, and Communities: Head Start Synthesis Project* (Washington, D.C.: 1985).
31. Allen V. Kneese and Charles L. Schultz, *Pollution, Prices, and Public Policy* (Washington, D.C.: Brookings Institution, 1975), p. 21.
32. Thomas E. Cronin, Tania Z. Cronin, and Michael E. Milakovich, *U.S. v. Crime in the Streets* (Bloomington: Indiana University Press, 1981).
33. Ralph K. Huitt, "Political Feasibility," in Austin Ranney (ed.), *Political Science and Public Policy* (Chicago: Markham, 1968), p. 266.
34. This discussion leans heavily upon James Q. Wilson, *Political Organizations* (New York: Basic Books, 1973), chap. 16. The student of policy formation cannot afford to ignore this book.
35. In some instances, the regulated group may succeed, at least for a time, in "capturing" the administering agency. A classic case study is Samuel P. Huntington, "The Marasmus of the ICC: The Commission, the Railroads, and the Public Interest," *Yale Law Journal*, LXII (December, 1952), pp. 171–225. Agency "capture," however, is more frequently alleged than proved in the literature of political science.
36. Wilson, *op. cit.*, chap. 16.
37. Cf. Seymour Scher, "Regulatory Agency Control Through Appointment: The Case of the Eisenhower Administration and the NLRB," *Journal of Politics*, XXIII (November, 1961), pp. 667–688; and Terry M. Moe, "Control and Feedback in Economic Regulation: The Case of the NLRB," *American Political Science Review*, LXXIX (December, 1985), pp. 1044–1116.
38. Edward L. Katzenbach, Jr., "The Horse Cavalry in the Twentieth Century: A Study in Policy Response," in Carl J. Friedrich and Seymour E. Harris (eds.), *Public Policy*, Vol. 8 (Cambridge, Mass.: Harvard University Press, 1958), pp. 120–149.
39. Garry D. Brewer and Peter deLeon, *The Foundations of Policy Analysis* (Homewood, Ill.: Dorsey Press, 1983), chap. 13.

EPILOGUE

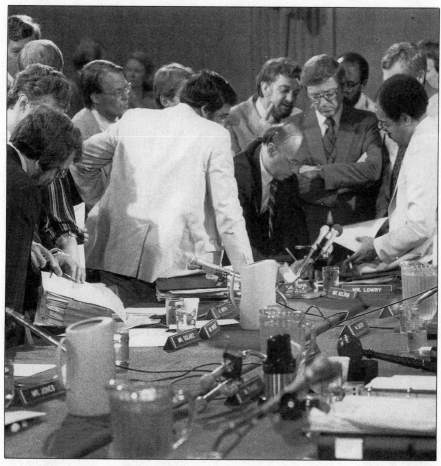

Negotiation and compromise are essential to effective public policymaking.

I n the preceding chapters I have sought to present a general framework as well as a variety of concepts and ideas for the study and analysis of public policymaking. The framework, which treats policymaking as a sequence of functional activities, is not a general theory of the policy process. Rather, it is a means for organizing and directing inquiry into that process. Various theories, such as those discussed in the first chapter, can be accommodated to this model.

My guess is that we will have to wait a long time for the emergence of a viable general theory of policymaking. Not too long ago, political scientists spoke and wrote about the need to develop a general theory of politics.[1] Research projects of more limited scope were often justified in part as contributing to the development of a general theory. Politics (and policy making), however, are too complex to be satisfactorily explained by a single grand theory, and the quest for a general theory has been consigned to the disciplinary dustbin. These remarks are not intended to denigrate or discourage theory development in favor of descriptive or "factual" studies. In developing theories, however, we should focus on more manageable tasks, such as considering why some policies are more successfully implemented than others, or why some distressful conditions in society do not become defined as public problems and achieve agenda status. These are worthy tasks, and manageable tasks.

In these concluding remarks, however, I will deal mostly with two other matters. First, some general conclusions on the nature of the policy-making process will be stated, and some changes in the process since the first edition of this book was published in the early 1970s will be noted. Second, some methodological problems in the study of public policymaking will be treated. In doing these things I will be less dispassionate than I have endeavored to be in the earlier chapters.

SOME CONCLUSIONS ON THE POLICY PROCESS

Once the process of policymaking on most problems—certainly those of any magnitude—gets underway, it tends to be continuous, albeit with variations in the scope and intensity of activity. It has been said that policy-making has "no beginning and no end."[2] This is an overstatement. Clearly there is a point at which one can effectively mark the beginning of the policy-making process on a problem and another, at least when a policy is terminated, that constitutes its end. It is within these bounds that the process is continuous.

As the policy process operates, a problem is recognized, defined, and placed on governmental agendas; alternatives are developed and presented; one alternative (the policy) is officially adapted; implementation begins; some sort of evaluation and feedback occurs; legislative or administrative changes or adjustments may be made; more implementation follows; additional evaluation and feedback occur; legislative or administrative changes or adjustments may be made; more implementation follows; evaluation and feedback again take place; in infrequent instances a policy may be terminated; and so on. Somewhere along the way, because of changes in the policy environment, the problem at which a policy is aimed may be redefined, as when the "farm problem" shifted from one of too little production to surplus production. A problem may also seem to disappear, at least for a time, as when the Reagan administration denied the existence of an energy shortage. When actions like these occur, the consequence may be a substantial change in the direction and content of given policies. Whereas the energy policy of the Carter administration put considerable emphasis on the need for governmental action, the policy of the Reagan administration stressed reliance on the market.

Policies in many areas often become settled and handled by routine administrative processes only to be sometimes disturbed by some action that restarts the policy process. It may be change in the socioeconomic environment, as when the aging of the population creates a crisis in Social Security financing. The AIDS crisis similarly created demands for change in medical research policy, and the animal rights movement threatens to do the same. In all, the policy process is best thought of as cyclical rather than linear, and continuous rather than finite in duration.

Second, in a large, modern, pluralistic society and political system, public policymaking is usually but not always a complex and untidy process. Many players, official and unofficial, may regularly and occasionally participate, and many factors may help shape the content of policy on particular topics. The boundaries of the policy process are thus uncertain. Political authority and power are fragmented and dispersed by governmental structure, and by the social, economic, and ideological diversity of American society. Since the early 1970s power in Congress has been further dispersed by being shifted from committees to subcommittees. Also, interest groups have proliferated in number and variety. The consequence is an increase in *factionalism* in policymaking. Factionalism, as Professor Hugh Heclo says, is an old term but one that serves well to describe the current situation. The primary difference between the factionalism that James Madison wrote about in *The Federalist*, No. 10, and the present factionalism is that "our factionalism has shaped itself around a governmental presence that is doing so much more in so many different areas of life."[3] As a consequence government often seems too responsive to narrow group, sectoral, or regional interests and insufficiently concerned with searching out and caring for the public interest.

Decision making in the policy-making process, because of the fragmentation of power, is characterized by logrolling and alliance building, negotiation and bargaining, and compromise. Delay in decision making and moderation in action flow from these aspects of its style. Action may not be taken on pressing problems, such as child care and the "greenhouse effect," because the necessary consensus cannot be achieved. On the other hand, sometimes the system acts quickly, as in the summer of 1988, when legislation providing financial aid to drought-stricken farmers was quickly approved by Congress. Problems for which solutions are apparent and more readily agreed to are likely to be acted on more quickly.

In all, the policy-making process in the United States is not easy to comprehend, describe, or explain. Those who offer quick, certain, or "pat" explanations as to why given policies were rejected or adopted, or later proved unsuccessful, often oversimplify and at best provide partial explanations. Some historians have asserted that the Sherman Act of 1890 was adopted as a "sop to public opinion," an attempt to quell the public clamor for legislation against the trusts. Such explanations usually have within them a kernel of accuracy. A careful examination of the history of the Sherman Act, however, indicates that far more than the "sop factor" was operative. There were real concerns about the effects of the trusts on the economy, society, and polity, and real differences in view over whether government should act and in what manner.

Journalists and others (political scientists are not fully exempted here) sometimes explain legislative enactments in idiosyncratic fashion, as primarily the result of the machinations of this senator or that representative, or the actions of a particular interest group.[4] Important executive decisions may be attributed to particular officials, acting almost alone and unaided it would seem. People are important, they do make a difference, but they act within an institutional and social context that also works to shape, direct, and constrain action. This also adds to the complexity of the policy process. If studies of policymaking are complex in their substance and uncertain or tentative in their findings and conclusions, it is not because political scientists and other policy analysts are at once obtuse and timid. Rather, it is more likely that the subject is complex, conclusive data are scarce, motives are unclear, influence is subtle, and policy impacts uncertain. Explaining human behavior is a tenuous and complicated task.

Third, the policy-making process in the United States tends to be an adversarial process, featuring the clash of competing and conflicting viewpoints and interests rather than either an impartial, disinterested, objective search for solutions to problems or a cooperative endeavor by interested parties to handle matters. Nowhere is this better illustrated than in the conduct of judicial proceedings, whether trial or appellate, and in the extensive involvement of the judiciary in the policy process, which are brought about by those unhappy with decisions made by other governmental actors. Government-business relationships are also notable for their adversarial quality. Although it is occasionally urged that such relationships should be more cooperative, as they are in Japan, so that the United States can compete more effectively in the world economy, not much changes. The adversarial pattern is more congruent with American culture and its self-assertive values.[5] Most Americans prefer a more independent role of government as a guardian of public interest. Also there is the notion that "Government is not the solution to our problem. Government is the problem." Uttered by Ronald Reagan in his 1981 Inaugural Address, it is a viewpoint undoubtedly shared by many Americans. It is not the stuff from which flows extensive cooperative relationships between government and others. Important interests, including that of the public, may be lost sight of in the clash of adversaries, however.

Fourth, policy analysis has become more widely practiced and its products more heavily drawn upon in the development of policies in the legislative and administrative arenas. Policy evaluation, in its systematic variant, is also much more prevalent. Together these developments have contributed to making the policy process more technocratic. The opposing sides in policy struggles trot out their experts and "objective" policy analyses to support their positions. More and more, policymaking seems to be the domain of experts into which ordinary persons ought not to intrude. Debates over arms control, for instance, are loaded with technical data about missiles and other weapons systems. Mathematical models are devised to estimate the likely responses of the Soviets or other potential aggressors to possible actions.

Policy analysis, however, is not the only cause of technocracy in policy making. In Congress the subcommittee system, which encourages specialization, and the rise of the careerist legislators, who have been incentives and opportunity to specialize, have also been contributory.[6] Of course one must also recognize that some policy matters are by their very nature technical and complex. On the other hand, issues may be deliberately made to seem more technical than they really are in an effort to exclude nonexperts from their consideration. Still worth remembering is the old public administration adage that "the expert should be on tap rather than on top."

Policy decisions remain ultimately political in nature, however, if for no other reason than that they distribute advantages and disadvantages. Sometimes it seems to be assumed that if enough research and analysis are conducted, and enough facts and data are gathered, answers to policy problems will emerge upon which all people, or at least all reasonable people, can agree. If policy problems were only scientific or technical this might happen, as when vaccines are developed and generally administered to eradicate childhood diseases. There was no "propoliomyelitis" lobby that campaigned against the Salk vaccine, for instance.

Most policy problems, and certainly those of any magnitude, generate significant differences of view as to what is socially acceptable, economically feasible, and politically possible. Bargaining, negotiation, and compromise, not simply reliance upon the "facts," are then required to produce decisions. Policy analysis can inform, enlighten, develop alternatives, and even persuade to an extent, but by itself it is unlikely to yield policy decisions. Room still remains in the policy process for generalists, who should be on top, according to the old adage.

Fifth, the notion that policymaking in the United States is essentially incremental is conventional wisdom among political scientists. Incrementalism can mean either that a new policy differs only marginally from existing policies, or that it resulted from a decision-making process involving limited analysis of goals, alternatives, and consequences. Some decisions are characterized by more analysis, others by less analysis, and none by complete (i.e., rational-comprehensive) analysis. To say that a policy was based on limited analysis is to say nothing that really differentiates it from other policies.

If our attention turns to the amount of change embodied in a policy, we find that many new policies indeed make limited or marginal changes (whether additions or deletions, although, accurately speaking, an increment is actually an increase) in existing policies. Some new policies, however, are of sufficient magnitude, impact, or variation from the status quo as to be classifiable as basic or fundamental. Examples include the Social Security Act of 1935, the Marshall Plan (which provided extensive economic aid to post–World War II Europe), the interstate highway program, airline deregulation, and the 1986 tax reform legislation. Although greatly exceeded in number by incremental policies, such basic policies significantly change and shape the content and direction of governmental action. Excessive emphasis on incrementalism therefore obscures the importance of basic policies in the evolution and direction of American public policy.

Over time, it is true that significant changes in policies can occur incrementally. The progressive quality of the graduated income tax, for example, was gradually reduced by a plethora of laws creating deductions, credits, exclusions, and exemptions, mostly for the benefit of higher-income persons. By 1980 its progressive and redistributive effect were as much symbolic as material in nature. In an incremental manner, a basic change was made in public policy without ever directly being considered on its merit. Incremental action tends to mitigate conflict, but the avoidance of conflict, if conflict helps to clarify issues and focus attention, is not wholly desirable.

Sixth, in the study of public policymaking and in the day-to-day observation of the governmental process, our attention is usually focused on conflict. Conflict attracts attention. Major public policies generate conflict and make news. They also receive scholarly attention. Consequently, one may come to believe that policymaking, as a matter of course, is always sharply conflictive in nature. One can find support in this book for such a conclusion, although I have tried to provide a variety of references to less conflictive matters. Environmental protection, tax reform, the War on Poverty, and Social Security reform, for example, have produced much conflict.

At the same time, however, there is ongoing what Professor Herbert Jacob calls the "routine policy process."[7] Although not devoid of conflict, it is characterized by such features as a narrow definition of the problem involved, low visibility, limited participation, low policy costs, and general compatibility between proposed and existing policies. The policies involved may be either regulatory or distributive, and they may be of considerable importance. Examples include the Watermelon Research and Promotion Act of 1985 and laws passed in 1988 regulating the ocean dumping of sewage sludge and medical wastes. At the state level, divorce law reform is a case in point. Since 1966 all of the states, without stirring much controversy, have revised their divorce laws. Now, along with other things, no-fault divorce can be obtained in every state.

In all, the routine policy process differs from the conflictive process more in degree than in genre. There is, for instance, public participation, but less of it. Disagreement occurs over what should be done on a matter, but efforts are made to muffle it. Much of the action takes place at the subsystem level, which contributes to lower public awareness.

Finally, change is a constant companion of the policy process. Changes in the policy process take a variety of forms, including alterations in the number and variety of participants or in their roles and relationships, in the matter in which some issues are handled, and in the procedures for techniques used to deal with problems. When change is deliberately designed and sought, when it takes the form of a deliberate effort to improve the operation of the policy process from some perspective, we often call it reform. When, however, it emerges undesigned and unintended from other events, we do not have a distinctive name for it.

Change in the policy process is more likely to be limited or incremental than sudden and sweeping in scope. The efforts of the Reagan administration to redirect the policy processes, both in style and output, were early on referred to as the "Reagan Revolution." Changes did occur, but not to an extent sufficient to warrant the label "revolution." More executive control of the administrative rule-making process, authorized by executive orders and implemented by the Office of Management and Budget, was put in place. The budget deficit, as a consequence of the large budget deficits incurred during the Reagan years, was put at the top of the national policy agenda and complicated action on other policy matters. Some have argued that large budget deficits were incurred deliberately by the president in order to make difficult the adoption of new spending programs. Not without a touch of plausibility, this line of argument attributes too much guile and strategic thinking to President Reagan. What actually occurred is better thought of as the unintended consequence of other actions.

Using causation as the differentiating criterion, changes in the policy process can be placed into three groupings: First, there are changes that are designed and that operate generally as intended. The establishment of the Environmental Protection Agency in 1970 to consolidate many environmental programs and enhance environmental protection is a case in point. Second, changes in the policy process sometimes are the consequence of changes made for other purposes. The 1974 congressional budget legislation, which set up budget committees in each house of Congress and created a congressional budget process, did bring about some improvement in the rationality of congressional budget action. It has also unintentionally helped shift the role of the House Appropriations Committee from that of "defender of the treasury" to protector of favored programs. Third, other changes, because of broad or multiple sources of causation, can best be thought of as responses to changes in the policy environment. As an example, consider the growing "technocratization" of the policy process. This stems from, among other factors, the shift in power from congressional committees to subcommittees, the increased staff assistance for members of Congress, *and* the fact that policy problems and issues are becoming more complex and technical. This "technocratization" of the policy process in turn makes the meaningful participation by ordinary persons or average citizens more difficult. One cannot point to a particular decision that intentionally or inadvertently has had this consequence.

The conclusion to be drawn from this discussion is not that change is pernicious but rather that successfully and intentionally changing the policy process is not easily achieved. Those, for instance, who suggest that members of Congress should serve for only six years in order to reduce "careerism" and supposed unresponsiveness by members to the electorate, have probably not thought deeply about all the consequences such a change would produce, both in the operation of Congress as an institution and in its participation in the policy process. The political system, as systems theory informs us, is composed of *interdependent* parts. A change in one part will have consequences for the other parts—and their roles and activities. Successful reform of the policy process requires adequate knowledge of the process and its operation. Such knowledge is not easy to acquire, as the next section indicates.

METHODOLOGICAL CONCERNS

Methodological problems exist for all research, although social scientists appear both more self-conscious about their methodology and more inclined to batter themselves for methodological infirmities, than natural and physical scientists. Policy research, especially given the complexity of its subject matter, has its full share of methodological problems. Such problems may impede or limit policy research, and may make it more than a little frustrating at times, but they neither prevent it nor negate the need for it. An awareness of some of these problems, however, will help prevent wasted efforts, needless errors, unsound conclusions, and insomnia.

Solid, conclusive evidence, facts, or data, as one prefers, on the motives, values, and behavior of policy makers, the nature and scope of public problems, the impact of policies, and other facets of the policy process are often difficult to acquire or simply not available. The urge to convert assumptions or speculations about what happened into facts must be resisted, as must the uncritical acceptance of the often self-serving statements or incomplete explanations emanating from public officials and other participants in the policy process. Sometimes numerical measures of political phenomena such as policy impacts are used without sufficient care in determining their validity. Is, for instance, the number of infant deaths (in their first year) per 1,000 live births a good indicator of the general level of health care in a society? Do salary levels and similar data really measure the professionalism of civil servants? The acquisition of hard facts regarding who did what, why, and with what effect should be the goal of research. For example, we need to be able to say with some certainty why members of Congress respond to constituency interests on some issues and not others, or what role the media plays in agenda setting.

In the explanation of behavior in the policy process, empirical data are needed that will permit the demonstration or sound inference of cause-effect relationships. Once a person gets involved in quantitative data-based analysis, it is important to resist the notion that the collection of empirical data is of prime importance and that the more data one has, the more one can explain. One can drown in a sea of data as well as thirst for a lack thereof. To account for or explain behavior, theory is needed that will guide analysis in potentially fruitful directions. To the extent possible, hypotheses about cause-effect relationships need to be developed and tested on the basis of the best available evidence.

The notion that policy analysis is worthwhile only when it involves the examination of quantitative data through the use of statistical techniques, the more high-powered the better, should also be resisted. At this juncture, some policy areas and problems have not been amenable to rigorous quantitative measurement and analysis, although this may not always continue to be the case. Many aspects of social welfare and economic regulatory policies currently fit into this category. How, for example, does one measure the comparative impact of pressure groups, agency values, and economic analysis on public-utility rate making? The prosecution of insider traders by the Securities and Exchange Commission? The total benefits of a public housing program? And how does one measure the power of ideas, as distinct from interests, in the development of programs for the handicapped? Such questions present real puzzles.

Yet it should be stressed that explicit theory, quantitative data, and careful rigorous analysis have not been as frequently utilized in policy study as would be either possible or desirable. Thus political scientist Marver H. Bernstein's hoary contention that regulatory agencies pass through a four-stage life cycle (gestation and birth, youth, maturity, and old age), frequently culminating in their "capture" (which is not well-specified) by the regulated groups, is often cited as though it were a clearly supported phenomenon.[8] Bernstein provided some impressionistic support but by no means strong proof for his theory. It still lacks systematic empirical support. Conventional wisdom of this sort frequently rests on a rather frail intellectual foundation. Another example, also in the regulatory area, is economist George Stigler's theory of economic regulation. It holds that, as a rule, regulation is sought by the affected industry and operated for its benefit.[9] This will not do much to explain a raft of consumer protection, industrial health and safety, and environmental programs.

Many perceptive and informative studies of policy formation exist that employed little or no statistical analysis. As examples I cite Charles O. Jones's *Clean Air*; Alan Stone's *Economic Regulation and the Public Interest*; Barbara J. Nelson's *Making an Issue of Child Abuse*; and I. M. Destler's *American Trade Politics*.[10] The quality of analysis and the careful use of sound data (or information) are more important than whether and to what extent quantitative analysis is employed when it comes to determining the worth of a study. To be rigorous analysis does not have to be quantitative, and not all quantitative analysis is rigorous. Those who use quantitative techniques have been known to quarrel with enthusiasm and even a touch of rancor over the reliability or appropriateness of their techniques and the validity of their findings. (Here one can recall the discussion in Chapter 2 on whether socioeconomic or political variables better explain policy.) Also, to be fairminded, one should avoid developing a phobia for quantitative or statistic analysis, as some did in reaction to the behavioral movement in political science.

Data gained through interviews and questionnaires administered to public officials and other players in the policy process are often invaluable and may not otherwise be available to researchers. Care, however, is required in the use of both such techniques and the data acquired. Questions must be properly framed to elicit the needed information. Questions that are "loaded" and therefore bias responses, or that are so general as to create strong doubt concerning their intent, need to be avoided. Officials and others may not always respond fully or candidly to questions, their memories may be hazy, and they may overstate their own roles in events. Data gained from these sources obviously should not be viewed as "gospel."

Rather, they should be checked against other sources, used with care, and regarded as representing particular viewpoints on some event.

Many studies of policy making take the form of case studies; that is, they focus on particular programs, statutes, or areas of public policy. Case studies have been the butt of much criticism because, being narrowly based, they do not permit generalization. "What is a case study a case of?" is a common jibe. Preferred are studies that deal with all of the cases in a universe, such as all regulatory commissions or sunset laws, or a meaningful sample thereof, such as Supreme Court decisions on the rights of the accused or the benefit decisions made by a welfare agency. These afford a better basis for generalizations. Case studies, however, do have a variety of uses.[11] They can be used to test existing theories, to develop new theories, to provide detailed, contextual analysis of particular events, to analyze deviant cases that run counter to our generalizations, and to help provide an "intuitive feel" for the subtleties and nuances of the policy process and the practice of politics. There is plenty of room in the policy study area for both case studies and more general and comparative studies.

THE VALUE OF A POLICY APPROACH

In conclusion, I want to comment briefly on the value of a policy approach to the study of politics. A policy approach yields more than information about the causes, content, and consequences of public policies. It can also provide much information on and insight into the nature and operation of the political system and political processes generally. It helps shift our attention from a narrow concern with micropolitical phenonema (such as voting behavior, political socialization, and political attitudes) to their role in the broad political process. The argument here is not that we should be unconcerned with such matters as how individuals acquire political attitudes. An interesting activity, this can produce a lot of information on learning behavior, the process of socialization, and related matters. However, we should also be concerned with the "so what?" question. What difference does it make, for instance, so far as governance and public policy are involved, why people acquire certain political values and beliefs, and how they do so? The answer of course is that it can make a lot of difference as to what government does and how it operates. Whether people generally believe that "a public office is a public trust" rather than an appropriate means for private benefit helps to determine what is expected of office-holders and in turn how they behave.

A focus on policymaking performs an integrating and unifying function for political inquiry and provides a criterion of relevance to use in deciding which political phenomena or events should be examined. Diverse actions are pulled together to explain the adoption and implementation of policies and the public's reactions thereto. Moreover, a policy approach is a highly useful approach to the study of politics because it can generate knowledge that has both social scientific and practical value, and that helps explain how the governing process works and what can be done to shape its course. As has often been said, there is nothing so practical as a good theory, a theory that satisfactorily explains some aspect of the political process.

Notes

1. David Easton, *The Political System* (New York: Knopf, 1953).
2. Charles E. Lindblom, *The Policymaking Process*, 2d ed. (Englewood Cliffs, N.J.: Prentice-Hall, 1980), p. 5.
3. Hugh Heclo, "The Emerging Regime," in Richard A. Harris and Sidney M. Milkis (eds.), *Remaking American Politics* (Boulder, Colo.: Westview Press, 1989), p. 310.
4. As an example, consider Hedrick Smith's informative work on Washington politics and policy making, *The Power Game* (New York: Random House, 1988). The power players discussed therein often seem to be acting within an institution-free context.
5. See Steven Kelman, *Regulating America, Regulating Sweden* (Boston: MIT Press, 1981), pp. 133–141, 229–236.
6. Lawrence C. Dodd, "The Rise of Technocratic Congress: Congressional Reform in the 1970s," in Harris and Milkis, *op. cit.*, chap. 4.
7. Herbert Jacob, *Silent Revolution: The Transformation of Divorce Law in the United States* (Chicago: University of Chicago Press, 1988).
8. Marver H. Bernstein, *Regulatory Business by Independent Commission* (Princeton: Princeton University Press, 1955), pp. 74–95.
9. George Stigler, "The Theory of Economic Regulation," *Bell Journal of Economic and Management Science* (Spring, 1971), pp. 3–21.
10. Charles O. Jones, *Clean Air* (Pittsburgh: University of Pittsburgh Press, 1975); Alan Stone, *Economic Regulation and the Public Interest* (Ithaca, N.Y.: Cornell University Press, 1977); Barbara J. Nelson, *Making an Issue of Child Abuse* (Chicago: University of Chicago Press, 1984); and I. M. Destler, *American Trade Politics* (Washington, D.C.: Institute of International Economics, 1986). All are political scientists.
11. See Harry Eckstein, "Case Study and Theory in Political Science," in Fred I. Greenstein and Nelson W. Polsby (eds.), *The Handbook of Political Science*, Vol. 7, *Strategies of Inquiry* (Reading, Mass.: Addison-Wesley, 1975), pp. 79–137.

ANNOTATED
BIBLIOGRAPHY

Ackerman, Bruce A., and William T. Hassler, *Clean Coal Dirty Air* (New Haven: Yale University Press, 1981). A case study of the Environmental Protection Agency's requirement that new plants use smokestack scrubbers. Good on the decision-making process.

Allison, Graham T., *Essence of Decision: Explaining the Cuban Missile Crisis* (Boston: Little, Brown, 1971). Decision making during the Cuban missile crisis from the rational actor, organizational process, and governmental politics perspectives.

Art, Robert J., *The TFX Decision: McNamara and the Military* (Boston: Little, Brown, 1968). A case study of the controversy over the decision to select a multipurpose aircraft for the military, contrary to its wishes. Insightful on the decision process in the bureaucracy.

Bailey, Stephen K., *Congress Makes a Law* (New York: Columbia University Press, 1950). A classic case study of the legislative process, showing how ideas, interests, individuals, and institutions contributed to the adoption of the Employment Act of 1946.

Barke, Richard, *Science, Technology, and Public Policy* (Washington, D.C.: CQ Press, 1986). An insightful, informative introduction to science and technology policies and to their impact on policy formation.

Bauer, Raymond A., and Kenneth J. Gergen (eds.), *The Study of Policy Formation* (New York: Free Press, 1968). A series of original essays dealing with theoretical and methodological concerns in the study of public policy.

Berman, Larry, *Planning a Tragedy: The Americanization of the War in Vietnam* (New York: Norton, 1982). An outstanding case study of the Johnson Administration's decision in mid-1965 to escalate U.S. involvement in Vietnam.

Bernstein, Marver H., *Regulating Business by Independent Commission* (Princeton: Princeton University Press, 1955). A dated but still useful treatment of independent regulatory commissions as policy formulators and implementors.

Bosso, Christopher J., *Pesticides and Politics: The Life Cycle of a Public Issue* (Pittsburgh: University of Pittsburgh Press, 1987). A historical and analytical treatment of the pesticides issue and the relevant political institutions and processes.

Brown, Anthony E., *The Politics of Airline Deregulation* (Knoxville: University of Tennessee Press, 1987). An analytical study of the development, operation, and abolition of commercial airline regulation. Several deregulation strategies are discussed.

Browne, William P., *Private Interests, Public Policy, and American Agriculture* (Lawrence: University Press of Kansas, 1988). A thorough and insightful examination

273

of the large number and variety of groups involved in agricultural policy formation.

Cigler, Allan J., and Burdett A. Loomis, *Interest Group Politics*, 2d ed. (Washington, D.C.: CQ Press, 1986). A collection of original essays that emphasizes the role of groups in the policy-making process.

Cobb, Roger W., and Charles D. Elder, *Participation in American Politics: The Dynamics of Agenda-Building*, 2d ed. (Baltimore: Johns Hopkins University Press, 1983). A leading study of how problems are placed on the systemic and policy agendas in American society.

Dahl, Robert A., and Charles E. Lindblom, *Politics, Economics, and Welfare* (New York: Harper & Row, 1953). A comparison of policy making by polyarchy, hierarchy, bargaining, and the market system. A classic work.

Davies, J. Clarence, *The Politics of Pollution*, 2d ed. (Indianapolis: Bobbs-Merrill, 1975). A discussion of the formation and implementation of pollution control legislation. Especially good on the administrative aspects thereof.

Derthick, Martha, *Policymaking for Social Security* (Washington, D.C.: Brookings Institution, 1979). A superb analysis of the Social Security program and policymaking process. Views the current program as the product of an incremental, vertical process.

———, and Paul J. Quirk, *The Politics of Deregulation* (Washington, D.C.: Brookings Institution, 1985). A study that focuses on the airline, trucking, and telecommunications industries to make the case that ideas and economic analysis were important contributors to deregulation.

Dror, Yehezkel, *Public Policymaking Reexamined* (Scranton, Pa.: Chandler, 1968). A comparative treatment of policy making procedures with suggestions for reform. Tough reading and general in approach but useful.

Dye, Thomas R., *Politics, Economics, and the Public: Policy Outcomes in the American States* (Chicago: Rand-McNally, 1966). A leading study that compares the effects of political and socioeconomic variables on state policies, and concludes that socioeconomic variables are more important.

———, *Policy Analysis* (University: University of Alabama Press, 1976). A series of lectures setting forth Dye's ideas on public-policy research.

———, *Understanding Public Policy*, 6th ed. (Englewood Cliffs, N.J.: Prentice-Hall, 1987). A study that discusses a number of models of policy analysis, illustrates them with case studies, and compares their utility for policy analysis.

Edwards, George C., III, *Implementing Public Policy* (Washington, D.C.: CQ Press, 1980). A discussion of communication, dispositions or attitudes, resources, and bureaucratic structure as major forces shaping future policy implementation. Draws on a wide variety of illustrative materials.

———, and Ira Sharkansky, *The Policy Predicament* (San Francisco: Freeman, 1978). Another introduction to the study of public-policy formation, covering such matters as problems in rational decision making and economic and political constraints on decisions.

Elder, Charles D., and Roger W. Cobb, *The Political Uses of Symbols* (New York: Longman, 1983). A solid, perceptive study of this topic, which has much utility for the study of policy formation as well as politics generally.

Engler, Robert, *The Politics of Oil* (New York: Macmillan, 1961). An analysis of the impact of the petroleum industry on pertinent public policies. Good background reading for the "energy crisis."

———, *The Brotherhood of Oil* (Chicago: University of Chicago Press, 1977). A sequel to *The Politics of Oil* in which Engler remains critical of the industry.

Foreman, Christopher H., Jr., *Signals from the Hill* (New Haven: Yale University Press, 1988). A study focusing on congressional efforts to oversee and evaluate social regulatory agencies. Of much value to students of both Congress and the policy process.

Freeman, J. Leiper, *The Political Process*, 2d ed. (New York: Random House, 1965). A brief analysis of the role of executive bureau, congressional committee, and interest-group subsystems in policy formation.

Fritschler, A. Lee, *Smoking and Politics*, 4th ed. (Englewood Cliffs, N.J.: Prentice-Hall, 1989). A case study of the cigarette controversy that focuses on the role of the bureaucracy in the tobacco subsystem.

Frohock, Fred M., *Public Policy: Scope and Logic* (Englewood Cliffs, N.J.: Prentice-Hall, 1979). A political philosopher combines theory and practice in treating both normative and empirical policy issues and the policy process.

Goggin, Malcolm L., *Policy Design and the Politics of Implementation* (Knoxville: University of Tennessee Press, 1988). An important study of policy implementation, substantively focused on child health care at the state level.

Halperin, Morton H., *Bureaucratic Politics and Foreign Policy* (Washington, D.C.: Brookings Institution, 1974). An analysis of bureaucratic participation and decision making in American foreign policy in the post–World War II era.

Harris, Richard A., and Sidney M. Milkis, *The Politics of Regulatory Change* (New York: Oxford University Press, 1989). A study of deregulation politics during the Reagan administration that focuses on the Federal Trade Commission and the Environmental Protection Agency.

Heidenheimer, Arnold, Hugh Heclo, and Carolyn Teich Adams, *Comparative Public Policy*, 2d ed. (New York: St. Martin's Press, 1983). A well-done comparative treatment of public policies on health care, housing, education, taxation, and other topics in the United States and Western Europe.

Jacob, Herbert, *Silent Revolution: The Transformation of Divorce Law in the United States* (Chicago: University of Chicago Press, 1988). A discussion that develops a theory of routine policy making to explain action in divorce law.

Jones, Charles O., *Clean Air* (Pittsburgh: University of Pittsburgh Press, 1975). A study of the formation and implementation of air pollution control policy. Intergovernmental relations are well-treated.

———, *An Introduction to the Study of Public Policy* (Monterey, Calif.: Brooks/Cole, 1984). A highly useful volume that presents the sequential, functional approach to policy-formation study illustrated with case studies and other materials.

Katz, Michael B., *In the Shadow of the Poorhouse* (New York: Basic Books, 1986). A history of American welfare policy in which Katz argues that there will always be a need for governmental action in this area.

Katzman, Robert A., *Institutional Disability* (Washington, D.C.: Brookings Institution, 1986). A study of the development of national policy on transportation for the handicapped.

Kettl, Donald F., *Leadership at the Fed* (New Haven: Yale University Press, 1986). A discussion of policy making by the Federal Reserve Board that focuses on the role of its chairmen.

Kingdon, John W., *Congressmen's Voting Decisions*, 2d ed. (New York: Harper & Row, 1981). A very valuable empirical study of how members of the House of Representatives make decisions and the factors influencing them.

Krasnow, Erwin G., and Lawrence D. Langley, *The Politics of Broadcast Regulation*, 2d ed. (New York: St. Martin's Press, 1978). An analysis, with case studies, of the development of broadcast regulation policy by the Federal Communication Commission.

Light, Paul, *Artful Work: The Politics of Social Security Reform* (New York: Random House, 1985). An excellent case study of the 1983 Social Security reform legislation that conveys much insight into the operation of the policy process.

Lindblom, Charles E., *The Intelligence of Democracy* (New York: Free Press, 1965). An examination of bargaining and other forms of mutual adjustment in policy formation.

Lineberry, Robert L., *American Public Policy: What Government Does and What Difference It Makes* (New York: Harper & Row, 1977). A study that is equally divided between a discussion of how to analyze policy formation and a readable and chatty consideration of four domestic policy problems (e.g., inequality).

Lowi, Theodore J., "American Business, Public Policy, Case Studies, and Political Theory," *World Politics*, XVI (July, 1964), pp. 667–715. An influential essay that seeks to develop a new framework for policy study. Lowi suggests that the kind of policy (distributive, regulatory, or redistributive) involved in a situation shapes the nature of the policy-making process.

———, *The End of Liberalism: The Second Republic of the United States*, 2d ed. (New York: Norton, 1979). A study that argues that juridical democracy is needed because American public policies no longer are responsive to public needs because of the impact of interest-group liberalism and that legislation delegates too much discretion.

Lunch, William M., *The Nationalization of American Politics* (Berkeley: University of California Press, 1987). A discussion that asserts that during the last three decades the American political system has become "nationalized" and is now dominated by political ideas rather than material interests.

McConnell, Grant, *Private Power and American Democracy* (New York: Knopf, 1966). A highly insightful examination of the role of private groups in policy formation and how pluralism and decentralization have often made them the dominant force.

Meier, Kenneth J., *The Political Economy of Regulation: The Case of Insurance* (Albany: State University of New York Press, 1988). A major analysis of insurance company regulation that combines history, politics, and economics.

Melnick, R. Shep, *Regulation and the Courts* (Washington, D.C.: Brookings Institution, 1983). An analysis of the impact of judicial decisions on clean air policy and of the interaction between the courts and other political institutions.

Nachmias, David, *Public Policy Evaluation: Approaches and Methods* (New York: St. Martin's Press, 1979). An analysis and comparison of various conceptual models for evaluatory policies and statistical techniques useful in evaluation research.

Nadel, Mark V., *The Politics of Consumer Protection* (Indianapolis: Bobbs-Merrill,

1971). A good analysis of the formation and adoption of consumer protection legislation.

Nathan, James A., and James K. Oliver, *Foreign Policy Making and the American Political System*, 2d ed. (Boston: Little, Brown, 1987). A survey of American foreign policy since World War II and analysis of its formation.

Nathan, Richard P., *Social Science in Government: Uses and Misuses* (New York: Basic Books, 1989). A discussion of the roles and uses of applied social science research in the development and evaluation of public policies.

Nelson, Barbara J., *Making an Issue of Child Abuse* (Chicago: University of Chicago Press, 1984). A perceptive and absorbing analysis of how child abuse became an important social welfare issue in the United States.

Neustadt, Richard E., *Presidential Power: The Politics of Leadership from FDR to Carter* (New York: Wiley, 1980). A classic study of presidential power and leadership in the policy process that finds that the effective influence of the president is limited.

————, and Harvey v. Fineberg, *The Swine Flu Affair* (Washington, D.C.: U.S. Department of Health, Education, and Welfare, 1978). An examination of the abortive effort of the Ford administration to combat an expected swine flu epidemic.

Olezak, Walter J., *Congressional Procedures and the Policy Process*, 3d ed. (Washington, D.C.: CQ Press, 1988). A thorough treatment of congressional legislative procedures and how they can affect the course and content of legislation.

Pertschuk, Michael, *Revolt Against Regulation: The Rise and Pause of the Consumer Movement* (Berkeley: University of California Press, 1982). A spirited analysis of consumer policy and politics by a Federal Trade Commissioner.

Peters, B. Guy, *American Public Policy*, 2d ed. (Chatham, N.J.: Chatham House, 1986). A readable introduction to the policy process that examines several areas of substantive policy.

Pierce, Lawrence C., *The Politics of Fiscal Policy Formation* (Pacific Palisades, Calif.: Goodyear, 1971). A political scientist's analysis of the process and politics of fiscal policy formation. Especially strong in its treatment of the development of policy proposals by fiscal agencies.

Piven, Frances Fox, and Richard A. Cloward, *Regulating the Poor* (New York: Pantheon Books, 1971). A normative evaluation of welfare policies that finds them to be a means more for controlling the poor than for meeting their substantive needs.

Pleck, Elizabeth, *Domestic Tyranny* (New York: Oxford University Press, 1987). A historical treatment of the problem of family violence and American social policy thereon since colonial times.

Pressman, Jeffrey L., and Aaron B. Wildavsky, *Implementation* (Berkeley: University of California Press, 1973). An account of the problems of implementing the public-works program of the Economic Development Act of 1965 in the Oakland area.

Quirk, Paul J., *Industry Influence in Federal Regulatory Agencies* (Princeton: Princeton University Press, 1981). An empirical examination of some theories on the influence of industry on regulatory agencies' policy incentives. A very valuable study.

Ranney, Austin (ed.), *Political Science and Public Policy* (Chicago: Markham, 1968).

An uneven collection of essays on issues, problems, and theoretical concerns in the analysis of policy and policy outcomes.

Reagan, Michael, *Regulation: The Politics of Policy* (Boston: Little, Brown, 1987). An excellent, succinct treatment of governmental regulation of private economic policy from a political perspective.

Redford, Emmette S., *Democracy in the Administrative State* (New York: Oxford University Press, 1969). An insightful examination of the role of administration in the policy process together with concern for democratic control of administration.

————, *The Regulatory Process* (Austin: University of Texas Press, 1969). An analysis of the economic regulatory process with emphasis on administrative agencies and commercial aviation regulation.

Regens, James L., and Robert W. Rycroft, *The Acid Rain Controversy* (Pittsburgh: University of Pittsburgh Press, 1988). A discussion of the acid rain problem; its scientific, economic, and political dimensions; and the policy-making process as it centers on the issue.

Reich, Robert B. (ed.), *The Power of Public Ideas* (Cambridge, Mass.: Ballinger, 1988). An anthology of integrated essays that collectively argue that ideas about the public good are important in shaping public policy.

Ripley, Randall B., and Grace A. Franklin, *Bureaucracy and Policy Implementation*, 2d ed. (Homewood, Ill.: Dorsey Press, 1986). An empirical discussion of distributive, competitive regulatory, protective regulatory, and redistributive programs.

Robyn, Dorothy, *Breaking the Special Interests* (Chicago: University of Chicago Press, 1987). An analysis of the deregulation of the motor carrier industry that covers topics such as coalition building, economic analysis, and presidential bargaining.

Rogers, Harrell R., Jr., and Charles S. Bullock III, *Law and Social Change* (New York: McGraw-Hill, 1972). An evaluation of the impact of the civil rights legislation of the 1960s.

Rosenbaum, Walter A., *Environmental Politics and Policy* (Washington, D.C.: CQ Press, 1985). A comprehensive survey of environmental policies and politics, that includes solid chapters on science and energy and their relationship to environmental policy.

————, *Energy, Politics, and Public Policies*, 2d ed. (Washington, D.C.: CQ Press, 1987). A survey of energy policies and the policy-making processes that explores major shifts in energy policy.

Rourke, Francis E., *Bureaucracy, Politics, and Public Policy*, 3d ed. (Boston: Little, Brown, 1983). A discussion of administrative agencies and their role in the formation of public policy.

Schattschneider, E. E., *The Semi-Sovereign People* (New York: Holt, Rinehart and Winston, 1960). A critique of group theory and an influential discussion of the impact of conflict on political decision making.

Schneier, Edward V. (ed.), *Policy-Making in American Government* (New York: Basic Books, 1969). An anthology organized under the headings of policy formulation, articulation, mobilization, codification, application, and redefinition.

Schultze, Charles L., *The Public Use of Private Interest* (Washington, D.C.: Brookings

Institution, 1977). An analysis of how market incentives can be used to improve governmental intervention in the economy.

Smith, T. Alexander, *The Comparative Policy Process* (Santa Barbara, Calif.: Clio Books, 1975). A distinctly comparative treatment of policy formation employing case studies from Western democracies and organized around the categories of distribution, sectoral fragmentation, emotive symbolism, and redistribution.

————, *Time and Public Policy* (Knoxville: University of Tennessee Press, 1989). A carefully reasoned, profound study that focuses on the effect of time and time horizons on politics and public policy.

Sorensen, Theodore C., *Decision-Making in the White House* (New York: Columbia University Press, 1963). A short analysis of presidential decision making by the former counsel to President John Kennedy.

Spanier, John, and Eric M. Uslaner, *How American Foreign Policy Is Made*, 4th ed. (New York: Holt, Rinehart and Winston, 1985). An introduction to foreign policy formation that deals with the interaction of president and Congress, and with foreign and domestic policy.

Steiner, Gilbert Y., *Social Insecurity: The Politics of Welfare* (Washington, D.C.: Brookings Institution, 1966). An analysis of welfare policy making that illustrates the relationship between the nature of the policy process and the substance of policy.

Stevenson, Gordon McKay, Jr., *The Politics of Airport Noise* (North Scituate, Mass.: Duxbury, 1972). A systematic analysis of the participants in and process of the development of noise abatement policies. Good on the details of policy action.

Stokey, Edith, and Richard Zeckhauser, *A Primer for Policy Analysis* (New York: Norton, 1978). A useful and comprehensive treatment of quantitative approaches to policy analysis and decision making.

Stone, Alan, *Economic Regulation and the Public Interest* (Ithaca: Cornell University Press, 1977). A thorough, insightful, and critical examination of the Federal Trade Commission and trade regulation policies.

————, *Regulation and Its Alternatives* (Washington: CQ Press, 1982). A wide-ranging, insightful analysis of the nature, justifications, and politics of economic regulation.

————, and Edward J. Harpham, *The Political Economy of Public Policy* (Beverly Hills: Sage, 1982). A critical and challenging collection of essays dealing with various major issues in policy formation and public policy.

Stone, Debra, *Policy Paradox and Political Reason* (Boston: Little, Brown, 1988). An insightful, engaging, theoretical, and somewhat unconventional look at goals, problems, and solutions in the policy process, which is portrayed as full of paradoxes.

Sundquist, James L., *Politics and Policy: The Eisenhower, Kennedy and Johnson Years* (Washington, D.C.: Brookings Institution, 1968). Highly informative case studies of several major areas of domestic policy are combined with a general explanatory analysis.

Tatalovich, Raymond, and Byron W. Daynes (eds.), *Social Regulatory Policy* (Boulder, Colo.: Westview Press, 1988). A collection of case studies of policies on school prayer, pornography, crime, gun control, affirmative action, and abortion, plus theoretical chapters on social regulatory policy.

Truman, David B., *The Governmental Process* (New York: Knopf, 1951). A classic treatment of the role of interest groups in the American political process. Indispensable for an understanding of group theory.

Tufte, Edward R., *Political Control of the Economy* (Princeton: Princeton University Press, 1978). A carefully prepared comparative study that contends that economic policy is substantially shaped by the quest for partisan political advantages.

Van Horn, Carl E., Donald C. Baumer, and William T. Gormley, Jr., *Politics and Public Policy* (Washington, D.C.: CQ Press, 1988). A view of public-policy making as it occurs in six arenas: the board room, the bureaucracy, the cloakroom, the chief executive, the courtroom, and the living room.

Vig, Norman J., and Michael E. Kraft, *Environmental Policy in the 1980s* (Washington, D.C.: CQ Press, 1984). Seventeen original essays that yield much information on environmental policies generally while providing critical appraisals of Reagan administration environmental actions.

Vogel, David, *National Styles of Regulation* (Ithaca: Cornell University Press, 1986). A comparative treatment of environmental regulation in the United States and Great Britain that finds that differences reflect each nation's "regulatory style."

Wade, Larry L., *The Elements of Public Policy* (Columbus: Merrill, 1972). An introduction to policy analysis that focuses on decision making and policy costs and benefits.

———, and R. L. Curry, Jr., *A Logic of Public Policy* (Belmont, Calif.: Wadsworth, 1970). An examination of American public policy from the "new political economy," or public-choice, perspective.

Wasby, Stephen L., *The Impact of the United States Supreme Court* (Homewood, Ill.: Dorsey, 1970). A nonquantitative analysis of the Court's impact on public policy that attempts to develop a theory of impact.

Waste, Robert J., *The Ecology of City Policymaking* (New York: Oxford University Press, 1989). A complex theoretical framework for analyzing urban policy making.

Weiss, Carol H., *Evaluation Research* (Englewood Cliffs, N.J.: Prentice-Hall, 1972). A short but valuable treatment of the methodology of evaluation research.

Welborn, David M., *Governance of Federal Regulatory Agencies* (Knoxville: University of Tennessee Press, 1977). A perceptive study of the organization, operation, and decision making of the "big seven" independent regulatory commissions.

Wholey, Joseph S., *et al.*, *Federal Evaluation Policy* (Washington, D.C.: Urban Institute, 1970). A survey and assessment of the extent and quality of social policy evaluation by federal administrative agencies.

William, Walter L., *Social Policy Analysis and Research* (New York: American Elsevier, 1971). A solid introduction to the systematic evaluation of social policies.

Wolman, Harold, *Politics of Federal Housing* (New York: Dodd, Mead, 1971). A succinct analysis of the formation and implementation of public housing policies.

INDEX